The Kaleidoscopic Lens

THE KALEIDOSCOPIC LENS

How Hollywood Views
Ethnic Groups

edited by

Randall M. Miller

Jerome S. Ozer, Publisher

The authors gratefully acknowledge the cooperation of the following in providing many of the illustrations used in this book: New York Public Library Picture Collection; Movie Star News; Englewood Public Library.

The publisher and editor disclaim responsibility for statements, either of fact or opinion, made by contributors to this book.

Library of Congress Cataloging in Publication Data
The Kaleidoscopic Lens.

Bibliography: p.
Includes index.
1. Minorities in motion pictures—United States.
2. Moving-pictures—United States—History. I. Miller, Randall M.
PN1995.9.M56K3   791.43′09′09535203   80-16797
ISBN 0-89198-120-9
ISBN 0-89198-121-7 (pbk.)

Manufactured in the United States of America

For Nathaniel, truly a gift from God

CONTENTS

The Kaleidoscopic Lens

PREFACE

This is not a movie book. It is not about movie stars, studio politics, directorial triumphs, innovative film techniques, or even the "art" of film, although all these elements appear in this book to some degree. Rather, this is a book about the social substance and meaning of American movies, particularly Hollywood feature films. Insofar as American movies as mass entertainment mirror the values and dreams of the American public, it is, then, a book about America.

American movies have always had a special relationship to American ethnicity. In its early years, the motion picture industry in America found its largest audiences among urban immigrants and blacks for whom the movies offered cheap entertainment and escape from the frustrations and disappointments of daily life. The motion picture industry also drew much of its creative energy and economic sustenance from the immigrant masses. Immigrant entrepreneurs, who were very close to the market and quickly saw the enormous potential of moving pictures, came to dominate the industry. Immigrant and black performers were drawn to the new medium. Thus, from a variety of angles, the history of motion pictures in America is one of the more graphic chapters in the history of American ethnicity.

The authors of this book examine the origins, development, and significance of ethnic representations in American feature films. They explore the various ways movies helped to shape people's perceptions of themselves and the world about them. Movies served many functions—as a form of art, as entertainment, as an instrument of propaganda, as a medium of social change, and as a transmitter of cultural values. The latter function particularly affected ethnic groups in America. Hollywood movies became a major transmitter of "assimilationist" values and helped to reinforce a narrow conception of American life to which all groups were expected to conform.

The authors relate the history of nine different ethnic groups in American life—blacks, Asians, American Indians, Hispanics, Germans, Irish, Italians, Jews, and Slavs—to their portrayal in American movies. In their essays, the authors tie each group's experiences to the

xi

changing cultural, social, intellectual, and political environments in America. They show how Hollywood movies gave immigrants and non-white peoples a view of what they had to do to become "Americans" and, in turn, how other Americans came to view these ethnic groups.

Several themes run through these essays, but two themes predominate. One is that Hollywood movies were eclectic. Filmmakers borrowed images and stereotypes that had been knocking around in literature, drama, and vaudeville. They refined them, nationalized them, and in a sense even "confirmed" them, but they did not invent them. Films are products of collective effort—a merger of commerce and art—and so reveal collective, popular attitudes more than do individually created novels, art, and plays. Thus, the authors are not overly concerned with individual actors, directors, producers, or writers so much as they are concerned with Hollywood's collective attitudes and practices regarding ethnic groups and images. In discussing the meaning of Hollywood's images, the authors know the images were not comprehensive. Filmmakers chose one social reality and ignored others in depicting groups. By selecting fragments, or frames, of life, they necessarily missed the fullness and complexity of any group's experience. Popular movie stereotypes of American Indians, blacks, Asians, Jews, and European immigrants suggest mass prejudices and beliefs about those people as groups, for stereotypes refer to mental pictures of groups not individuals. For the authors, American feature films become social documents of American cultural history.

The second major theme in this book is that ethnic images are not static. As groups improved their position in American society and in the film industry, they helped to effect changes in their public images. Likewise, if a group's public status deteriorated, its images suffered accordingly in film. The degree and pace of change for each group varied enormously. According to the authors, war, international diplomacy, ethnic politics in America, economic hard times or flush times, changing racial attitudes, the rise and fall of Old Hollywood, and a host of other factors explain why some groups prospered and other groups languished in American film.

The authors do not agree on everything, of course, but they do agree that American feature films played an important role in fixing images of ethnic groups in the American mind. They agree that the ethnic dimension in American movies reveals much about American values and growth in the twentieth century.

* * *

This book owes much to the encouragement and guiding hand of its editor and publisher, Dr. Jerome S. Ozer, who handled the publishing process with unfailing good humor, patience, and skill. The Annenberg School of Communications Library of the University of Pennsylvania, the Balch Institute, the Drexel Library of Saint Joseph's College, the Free Library of Philadelphia, Haverford College Library, the Library of Congress, the Museum of Modern Art, the New York Public Library, and Temple University Library all provided valuable services and materials. Dr. Linda Patterson Miller of Temple University read portions of the manuscript and made useful suggestions for improvement. Several sentences in my introduction first appeared in my introduction to Randall M. Miller, ed., *Ethnic Images in American Film and Television* (The Balch Institute, 1978), and are used with the kind permission of the Balch Institute. Saint Joseph's College, Philadelphia, provided space and financial support for preparing this book. To all of the people and institutions who helped bring this book out, I offer my thanks.

R. M. M.

INTRODUCTION

Randall M. Miller

In the twentieth century, mass communications gave urban forces the power to break down rural and small-town isolation and so to forge a national culture. For almost half a century millions of Americans regularly attended the movies to watch the feature-length productions of the Hollywood dream factory, which worked to create a national consciousness. Even today, after the rise of television and the breakup of Old Hollywood, the movies hold a firm grip on the American consciousness. The proliferation of movie magazines, the public's almost pathological fascination with movie "personalities," and the intimate ties between television and Hollywood all testify to that fact.

The myths and stereotypes simultaneously paraded across silver screens in small towns and big cities in America gave the nation a common fund of references, and still do. Not everyone accepted, or accepts, these myths and stereotypes, and indeed, Hollywood itself sometimes questioned and discarded them. But the signal fact of American movies has been the tenacity of Hollywood's images, genres, and myths. This persistence in an industry geared to mass appeal suggests that Hollywood screen creations mirrored public attitudes, and reinforced them. Movies have also challenged public beliefs. In subtle ways, American movies have offered alternative lifestyles and patterns of social behavior which have undermined some of the very stereotypes Hollywood helped to perpetuate. Hollywood was a world founded by immigrant producers and filmmakers ambivalent about their own identities. Their ambivalence crept into their products, for despite commerical pressures and the mechanics of cooperative production, Hollywood could not wholly suppress the individual producer, director, writer, editor, or actor. Nor did it necessarily want to do so. But as long as the studio system ruled in

1

Hollywood and Hollywood was synonymous with movies, the recurring theme of American movies was the belief in the melting pot and the American Dream. Only in the last decade did that theme suffer serious erosion in the American moviemaking world, but it persists still as the legacy of Hollywood to television in the form of old movies leased to television and television's assumed role of purveyor of American values.

American movies began as democratic entertainment. Early movies provided access to American culture for immigrant and working-class city dwellers. Film also offered them a new medium of communication—one that was their own. Indeed, they did not need to master English to derive meaning and amusement from film. The early movies were often short, bawdy, unedited presentations of beguiling women or comedy routines. They were not self-consciously subversive of the dominant American culture, but the early filmmakers' emphasis on titilation, fantasy, and thrills—then, as now, the staples of mass entertainment in America—challenged the conservative values that the dominant class wanted the immigrants and working classes to accept. In time, the movies moved from seedy storefront theaters and penny arcades to movie palaces, but they could never wholly slough off their identification with their lower-class roots.

By the 1970s American films reached a wider audience via drive-in theaters, suburban-mall theaters, and television sets in American homes. Although the content of movies changed to include more complex subject matter and elaborate productions, and although control over the industry shifted from independent immigrant filmmakers to the executive boards of major corporations, the movies thrived in America because they functioned unabashedly as mass entertainment. More than that, they also helped to shape American culture. In that way, movies became something more than mere entertainment.

The popularity of early movies among the working classes and immigrants worried the guardians of the dominant American culture. They feared the potential of the new medium in the hands of immigrant filmmakers, for they knew that unless "responsible" citizens controlled the content of the movies by emphasizing middle-class "American" values, the movies might divide the nation further along the ethnic and class lines developing in the late nineteenth and early twentieth century. Reformers, then, wanted to make the new technology of film into an instrument of consensus, to use film to close the gap separating the poor and the immigrants from the dominant American culture.

For reasons of economy, the film industry began to move in the direction of consensus charted by the middle-class reformers. By the

1920s the sophistication of film technology and production had driven up the cost of making movies. Increased capitalization in the film business led to consolidation. By the end of the 1920s vertical economic integration had occurred in the movie industry as a few companies controlled all lines of activity, from production to exhibition. The heads of these companies believed that expansion into the middle-class market was the only way to recover the increased costs of production. They courted the middle class by cutting their production of shorts, the original fare of immigrant and working-class audiences, and making longer, more elaborately staged features attuned to the tastes of the middle class.

To avoid outside interference, while seeking an expanded audience, the movie moguls proposed self-regulation of their industry. When several scandals involving screen personalities threatened the image of respectability which the producers were trying to establish, the major producers expelled a few individuals to show that the industry could govern itself. As early as the 1910s, the film industry offered up "Fatty" Arbuckle, a popular comedian but notorious womanizer wrongfully accused of rape and murder, as a sacrifice to middle-class moralists. Others would follow. Hollywood, however, relied on something more sustaining and powerful than an occasional blood offering to prove its claims of respectability. It enlisted the aid of Will H. Hays, onetime Postmaster General of the United States under Warren G. Harding and a Presbyterian elder, to protect the industry's good name. He intervened on behalf of Hollywood in Washington, and he negotiated agreements with the major church and civic organizations critical of the movie business.

Under Hays's guidance through the 1930s, the major studios set basic rules which guided the industry thereafter. The principal guidelines were embodied in the so-called Production Code, drafted by a Catholic priest and a Catholic publisher. Sex and crime—the necessary ingredients for box office success—were permissible provided that the film had a recognized compensating moral value. The Code insisted that "Evil and good are never to be confused throughout the presentation," and good must prevail in the end. The Code did something else. It prohibited scenes and subjects which, however distantly, suggested miscegenation as desirable, thereby building a color barrier in Hollywood's dream worlds as rigid as the color line in America's real world. By casting the issue of racial mixing in black and white terms, the Code proclaimed an assimilationist ideal for European ethnic groups and a segregationist ideal for the "colored folks." Long after the Code's demise, this principle continued to influence the content of some major films.

In the 1950s the public's interest in movie content expanded. World War II had taught many Americans much about the propaganda power of films, from Hitler's carefully staged "documentaries" to Frank Capra's "Why We Fight" series for the United States. The rampant anti-Communism of the McCarthy era invaded the film industry. Films came under fire for their "political" as well as their social and moral implications. Red hunters on the House Un-American Activities Committee sniffed out any trace of Communist "influence" in the movie business; their efforts illustrated the popular belief that movies were an important source of cultural values. The Committee insisted that everyone in the film industry must be politically orthodox. Many film companies caved in under the Committee's pressure. To satisfy powerful critics and to regain public confidence during a period of declining attendance and vigorous anti-trust activity directed at Hollywood, they offered new sacrificial lambs—persons whose alleged sins were of the mind rather than of the flesh. It was an ugly business, and the film industry lost much of its moral authority among intellectuals and working-class people because of its cowardice.

Losing audiences to television and undergoing dramatic internal reorganization in the 1950s, the film industry lacked the confidence and cohesion to fight a concerted defense on film content. Filmmakers became increasingly sensitive to their public obligations, and so potentially they were more responsive to public-interest pressure groups. But nobody was pressing very hard after the fall of McCarthy—at least nobody until the rise of the civil rights movement and the new ethnicity of the 1960s. To be sure, church and civic groups were angry about Hollywood's growing tendency to display unbridled violence and sex, but Hollywood knew those critics well. The industry adopted a new coding system and assured the critics that their children would not learn everything they wanted to know about sex from commercial movies. Besides, parents and reform groups were shifting their criticism to television; movies did not seem to matter so much anymore. The movies continued the old formulas of sex and crime, and at the production level, anyway, self-regulation remained the standard industry response to calls for censorship. The Supreme Court later helped by placing film inside the First Amendment protection.

Self-regulation succeeded for so long because the immigrant moviemakers who settled and prospered in Hollywood in the 1920s celebrated and imparted middle-class values in their films. Their physical and social isolation in Hollywood, apart from the great mass of Americans living in the industrialized East, affected their social vision and helped to breed among them a consensus about values and purpose as they courted the middle-class audience. By the end of the 1920s they were expressing ambivalence about ethnic groups and lower-class culture; indeed, Hollywood had become the mecca of assimilation, of consensus, except for "colored" peoples. Hollywood denizens accepted the myth of the melting pot, adapted and reworked it in countless ways on the screen, and came to live it themselves. Ethnic differences blurred on the screen as the Cohens embraced the Kellys; they blurred in Hollywood as the Jewish movie moguls married Protestant, middle-class women and assumed WASP America's tastes and habits. The moviemakers and moguls anglicized their own names and those of their stars. In one sense, their visible adoption of "American" standards and the celebration of "American" values in their movies facilitated the assimilation of many immigrants who viewed Hollywood's activities.

Ethnic pluralism in America had limited the range of the moviemakers. They were primarily capitalists, not social activists or apologists for special groups. Organized groups opposed certain subjects, middle-class reformers demanded at least an outward conformity to American customs and values, rising costs of production prevented too much risk-taking by the major studios, and the filmmakers were devoted to the American Dream anyway. Producers followed the line of least resistance; they produced movies that offended the fewest and the weakest people. They employed old formulas and revised them to play to shifting public tastes. With a few notable exceptions, from the 1920s through the 1960s, they shied away from the exploration of ethnic and religious issues, preferring instead the universal themes of romance and crime.

Movies never fairly represented the full range of American institutions, people, or values. The problems of the young, for example, received more attention than the problems of the elderly. In its heyday, Hollywood generally ignored the lives of industrial and agricultural workers in depictions of "contemporary" life and doted on the lives and loves of the leisure class. The content was not dull, and it was not necessarily conservative in social outlook. Moviemakers dressed up their films in middle-class cliches about honesty and thrift, but they relied on the old appeal of thrills and sexual titilation to gain and hold audiences. In the process they took some jabs at many social conventions, but never at the fundamental institutions of the nation. Charlie Chaplin and a long line of comedians revealed the arrogance, pomposity, and stupidity of the wealthy and powerful, but they never suggested that they did not want to share that wealth and power on an American model. Lower-class audiences and middle-class audiences could laugh together at parodies of American life. The moguls did not forget their original audience so much as they broadened it.

The Depression threatened to change all that. Hollywood began poking into the dark corners of urban life and offered movies which expressed misgivings about some sacred American institutions. Warner Brothers especially focused on the problems of class and ethnic conflict in America and tolerated serious doubts about the regenerative powers of American capitalism and democracy in such movies as *Little Caesar* (1931), about gangsters and Italians; *The Public Enemy* (1931), about gangsters and the Irish; *Lawyer Man* (1932), about political bosses and urban blight; *I Am a Fugitive from a Chain Gang* (1932), about the corruption of the justice system and black-white relations; *Massacre* (1934), about governmental corruption in managing Indian reservations; *Black Fury* (1935), about labor unrest in the coal fields; and *Black Legion* (1936), about vigilante nativism.

The gangster movie came into its own in the 1930s and embodied the film industry's changing social consciousness. Although many of the "old" values persisted in them, gangster movies exposed the duplicity of American society. Ethnic distinctiveness reappeared in the gangster movies of the 1930s. *Little Caesar,* of course, was *the* gangster film which provided a model for the genre thereafter. The central character in the movie was an outlaw, but he was not rootless. He was an immigrant who had a clear ethnic identity, as did the other characters in the film. He entered crime in order to survive because traditional avenues of economic mobility were closed to him. He was not isolated, however, for respectable people entered his world to drink illicit whiskey or to gamble. The whole society was corrupt: policemen and public officials were dishonest, "respectable" persons were hypocritical. At least the gangster had a code of honor and stood by it. The movie suggested to lower-class viewers that their situation in life was not their fault and that "joining" America did not mean virtue.

But as Andrew Bergman shows in his book, *We're in the Money: Depression America and Its Films,* Hollywood was uncomfortable with such themes; it clung to the belief in upward mobility. By the end of the 1930s Hollywood reaffirmed its trust in America as a classless society. Gangsters became G-Men, rich girls wed gumshoes and reporters, angels had dirty faces, and Mr. Smith went to Washington. In the end, Hollywood blamed individuals for America's misery. Bad men in politics, business, law, and the press were the real sources of society's ills, for they bred crime and slums, cynicism and conflict. In its late 1930s movies Hollywood assured the nation that good men were ready to unmask the corrupt, to heal society's divisions, and to rebuild neighborhoods on communal trust. The message was clear. To survive evil and hard times, good people must stand together. Again, consensus became the matrix of the nation's strength. The surface differences of the Jewish tailor, Irish cop, Italian grocer, German hausfrau, and Polish butcher of the typical Hollywood big city block could not hide these people's consanguinity and their common commitment to the American Dream—or so numerous movies suggested. By ignoring racial minorities, or, as in westerns, casting them outside "modern" civilization, the movies kept alive such wishful thinking. In this, it is significant that an immigrant filmmaker, Frank Capra, more than anyone else, championed the theme of a classless, assimilated society.

During World War II Capra developed this theme further in the "Why We Fight Series" of propaganda films produced for the United States government and widely shown in the armed services' orientation programs. The theme of "One America" reached its apotheosis in *The Negro Soldier,* a Capra production for the War Department. In this film a black congregation sings hymns to the American Dream; there is no hint that slavery or racism ever prevented blacks from sharing in that dream. Throughout the war, Hollywood echoed this theme of the cooperative people, untrammeled by class or ethnic differences. In Hollywood's war movies representatives of various ethnic and racial groups fought together to defend their common American values. The European groups were so fused by common purpose they had only their names, and sometimes their accents, to distinguish them from their comrades.

After World War II the theme of assimilation loosened its grip on the movie business. With television cutting deeply into the film industry's national audience, the movies had to change. Studies of movie audiences revealed that in the postwar era moviegoers tended to be educated, young, and committed to film as both an art form and an entertainment medium. These facts invited innovations in themes and the end to tired formulas and stereotypes in movies. Hollywood had the chance to address contemporary social problems and to direct films to well-defined audiences. New directions in social consciousness did emerge in the late 1940s in Hollywood. Flushed with its success as a propaganda device during the war and sensitive to changing social values, the film industry offered a series of "message" movies on race (*Intruder in the Dust* in 1948 and *Pinky* in 1949), prejudice (*Crossfire* in 1947 and *Gentleman's Agreement* in 1947), and crime (*I Walk Alone* in 1947 and *Key Largo* in 1948). Hollywood seemed to be more willing to deal with contemporary problems. But the confusion of the rapidly disintegrating "Old Hollywood" system and the repressive atmosphere of McCarthyism retarded these developments. Many producers played it "safe" in the 1950s by offering the usual fare of entertainment movies, laced with old stereotypes and the old bromides on the American way.

Perhaps the most significant factor changing the direction of the movie industry in the postwar era was the breakdown of the studio system. Partly for tax reasons and partly to gain control over films and careers, many directors and performers sought to establish themselves as independents. The Supreme Court opened the way for them by ordering the studios to divest themselves of their theaters. Old Hollywood unraveled. The studios' loss of control over theaters meant the loss of guaranteed income that came from blind- and block-booking. Studios could no longer afford to keep many artists on their payrolls. Filmmakers began to direct their work to smaller, more select audiences. Some independents prospered by doing what Hollywood's major studios could not do: bringing empathy to their subjects. That very empathy, of course, limited the size of the audience. Independents struggled to establish their identities and influence, and some scored remarkable successes commercially and artistically with their films. Whatever their success, they often tried to approach film themes in a realistic manner. The gritty texture of working-class and ethnic life began to reappear on the screen.

Still, the independents have never gained control over Hollywood or the American film industry. Without blind- or block-booking, producers must persuade exhibitors to take their films. Distributors handle each film individually. They apply pressure on producers to insure proper content and casting for any films they agree to handle. Distributors want formulas and stars that are "sure fire" because they cannot afford to handle marginal films, and they refuse to take on films which do not have a significant potential audience. Consequently, as Robert Sklar has pointed out in his *Movie-Made America,* the independents have discovered that banks will not advance them capital for a film until they have lined up a major distributor to market the film. The independents must bow before the will of the distributors, who insist on following successful formulas. And the major distributors in Hollywood enjoy overwhelming dominance. In 1974, for example, five companies (Warner Brothers, Universal, Twentieth Century-Fox, Paramount, and United Artists) controlled seventy-one percent of the film market for first-run theaters. Independents remain the poor stepchildren of Hollywood.

The major distributors, of course, do not control all productions. Beginning in the 1960s, for example, small producers, funded by "local" businessmen and investors, began making "on location" "country" movies directed to regional markets. These movies prospered in rural and suburban drive-in theaters. Their success and proliferation, however, bespeak the fragmented nature of the national consciousness, for they celebrate "country" values. Similar to this trend was the rise of black films made by blacks for blacks. But the success of black films awakened major producers to the potential of black audiences to fill empty inner-city theaters. Black actors and themes were recruited for major productions, and black audiences responded favorably. When major producers discovered that blacks would also turn out in large numbers to see blockbusters like *The Godfather,* which had no black presence, or the slick *Lady Sings the Blues,* they knew what they had to do. They might apply a black gloss to films, but they could rely again on the old standbys of sex and violence, accompanied by a good musical score, to attract both black and white audiences. The New Hollywood, like Old Hollywood, absorbed the black audience. And it began to enter the "country" market as well. At least in trying to reach these select audiences, major producers will have to soften old stereotypes which might offend members of these audiences.

The costs of making motion pictures are rising dramatically, and this fact colors the themes of major productions. It also discriminates against the independents. In recent years the moviegoing public has developed a large appetite for big budget, lavishly appointed movies. Major studios, which still produce most major motion pictures in the United States, are making fewer films, but are spending freely on the ones they do produce. They are sticking to formulas and avoiding risks by not treating sensitive, controversial subject matter, except in the most superficial ways. As film critic Pauline Kael argues, the success of "blockbusters" in the 1970s has led the industry to concentrate its promotional resources on the "big grossers," and so to ignore minor movies, however socially or critically important they might be. Since movies rely on media exposure to create a mass audience, this neglect of all but the potential big grossers leaves many films without big box office earnings and therefore without influence on the industry's moviemaking habits.

With corporate managers taking charge of the movie industry in the mid-1970s, the number of productions directed to special audiences dropped. In his recent book, *American Film Now* (p. 20), James Monaco observes that it is more difficult "to make a profitable small picture than a profitable large one," because the "small picture has to be precisely tuned to its minority audience, costs have to be watched carefully, and even if it's a success, the profit margin is narrow." The big budget blockbuster will turn a nice profit because the studio is committed to its promotion. The very size of its budget attracts attention and insures media coverage. For the big budget movie to be successful, indeed even for it to be made, it must, of course, appeal to a national audience, which necessarily implies dilutions of minority viewpoints in production and content.

The restructuring of the film industry in recent years seemingly gives new power to stars, and to filmmakers with independent sources of capital. Filmmakers generally will not produce a film and distributors will not handle a film unless the film has attractive stars with box office power. The stars, through their agents, grow stronger, sometimes even gaining control over scripts. Bankable stars such as Robert DeNiro, John Travolta, Al Pacino, Sylvester Stallone, among Italian-American actors, can pick scripts and force filmmakers to treat subjects which interest them. The current rage for Italian stars, and directors too for that matter, has demonstrated the potential for introducing ethnic themes and images into major film productions. But the stars' power rests on their continued popularity. Unless they are bold and willing to risk reputation and capital on special interest films, which rarely pay off so handsomely as did the independently produced *Rocky,* they remain committed to formulas. And the pull of formulas is strong. Audience surveys reveal that the public prefers genre films—romance, crime, and musicals—to realistic, complex explorations of social themes. The stars know this; so too do the producers and bankers. There will be no revolutions coming from the New Hollywood.

The signs for a vigorous, daring American movie industry, open to minority group influence, in the 1980s are not very heartening. Too many movies are "packaged goods"—the offspring of "bestsellers" generated more by media "hype" than the originality or power of their stories. Serious social commentary is rarely evident in such works. Worse, too many filmmakers today lack confidence in their own stories; they prefer to "revive" and remake old films. The new renditions often include a contemporary perspective or setting, but they are pale imitations of their earlier models. The major filmmakers' timidity in stories and themes reflects their enslavement to the blockbuster mentality that pervades the film industry today. Even independent filmmakers follow this pattern.

As filmmaking becomes more complex and expensive, it can inhibit as well as liberate its practitioners. Filmmakers operating within the structure of the New Hollywood will have limited opportunities to unseat all the old stereotypes and formulas. They will wait for society to do that.

* * *

The power of film is elusive. Despite decades of research, it is impossible to determine the actual effect that movies have on audiences. This is not to say that movies have no effect. The public's adoption of the dress styles, language, and mannerisms of the movies, for example, suggests the awesome potential influence of the medium.

It is unlikely that people regularly pay to see movies that offend their basic values. Also, people do not seek in entertainment an "escape" to a wholly alien, hostile world. They probably attend movies which have meaning to them, movies to which they can relate in some way. Thus, Hollywood's themes and images of race and ethnicity collectively must work to reinforce viewers' conceptions of the world. They also offer what Michael Wood has termed "structures of thought and feeling" by giving order to the loose, disparate fantasies, fears, and feelings of American moviegoers. In that sense, movies help to define and direct American values and behavior. That is why so many groups have wanted to control the content of films.

The victims of Hollywood's stereotyping never doubted the force of movies. In 1915, when D. W. Griffith's monumental and compelling *Birth of a Nation* depicted blacks as lascivious and bestial and when white audiences cheered as the Ku Klux Klan rescued a white girl from a black's clutches in one concluding scene, many blacks understood that they might suffer repercussions in real life as a consequence. Black groups fought to prevent the showing of *Birth of a Nation* in 1915 but succeeded only in raising some public concern about the implications of stereotyping in mass entertainment. For the next six decades other ethnic groups would decry film's denigrations of their people, again with only modest success in arousing interest in the issue of stereotyping. Ironically, such protests often worked to generate public interest in the films under attack, and sometimes promoters manipulated such interest to increase attendance.

Generally, the film industry has responded to criticism of its ethnic stereotypes by hiring technical advisors to insure "fair" portrayals of groups or, as Allen Woll points out in his discussion of Latin images, by denationalizing the group. But technical advisors can be wrong. Griffith's interpretation of blacks during Reconstruction was based on the "best" historical scholarship of his day. Participation of ethnic minorities in the movie industry did not and does not guarantee fair treatment of ethnic groups in movies. It raises the obvious, if unanswerable, question of who speaks for the group. The lack of consensus within each ethnic group about its own "real" nature diluted the strength of technical advisors, who, partly because of this confusion, lacked veto power over scripts anyway. Worse, the participation of ethnic groups in the creation of screen images about themselves lent an aura of authenticity to many productions which they did not deserve. The visibility of Italians in the production of *The Godfather,* for example, greatly confused the problem of authenticity and accountability.

Hollywood has always been good at adapting and reworking popular mythology, and, as the authors of this book show, Hollywood readily borrowed many popular ethnic stereotypes and encased them in film footage. Hollywood movies repeat almost endlessly similar themes and characters, and as Michael Wood argues in his book, *America in the Movies,* Hollywood remade its successful formulas so often that plots and people became interchangeable, being "transferred from India or the African desert to the American West; from Ireland to the American ghetto." (p. 10) The stereotypes became self-perpetuating, and therefore dangerous. The danger lay in film's real power, which is often indirect. Movies serve as handbooks of social behavior. They introduce many people to people and places that they would otherwise never meet or know, and so establish the basic identity of those people and places. The very persistence and ubiquity of ethnic stereotypes in movies created an aura of "truth" about them. More than that, their interchangeability, with whites in blackface or donning American Indian garb in many movies, for example, obscured any real ethnic distinctiveness. Non-WASP groups blurred together and "colored" people blurred together in the shadowy world of "other peoples"—quaint perhaps, but odd, different, and somehow disreputable.

Popular myths and stereotypes, however, are not static. As several authors in this book show, international political considerations altered screen images of some groups; indeed Asian and German images experienced some striking transfigurations in American movies. Domestic political and social pressures and the liberalization of American racial attitudes after World War II also undermined some stereotypes. As society allowed, and even encouraged, wider minority participation in its political and economic life, and as society in the 1960s and 1970s recognized the "New Ethnicity," movies began to reflect such changes. It is no surprise that Sidney Poitier came to dinner during the height of the civil rights movement, for national sympathy and support for blacks was widespread then. Of course, changing public perceptions and attitudes do not mean greater public acuity. New stereotypes often replace older ones.

Of themselves, movies have changed few people's minds about the American social structure and ethnic life. Moviemakers did not, and do not, often run far ahead of public opinion and beliefs. Filmmaking is too expensive for that. But for all its conservatism about the American Dream and the melting pot, even Old Hollywood retained a residue of liberalism. This liberalism surfaced hesitantly, and sometimes gracelessly, but it was there. More often than not, Hollywood movies portrayed blacks as buffoons, but they could also suggest, as in *Casablanca* (1942), that a black person could be intelligent, sensitive, and capable of a meaningful relationship with white people. Even in its heydey Hollywood took on some serious subjects. It dealt with miscegenation, despite Production Code strictures, in several films—with Asians in *The Bitter Tea of General Yen* (1933), with blacks in *Pinky,* with Indians in *Broken Arrow* (1950), and with Chicanos in *My Man and I* (1952), to cite several cases. The outcome in such movies was often unhappy for the "colored" people, who died for their efforts; this was in striking contrast to the wedding madness of Hollywood's mixing of European ethnic groups in movies. Still, the films on miscegenation conveyed feelings of sympathy and respect for the "darker" people, who appeared as complex, interesting individuals. Old Hollywood also assailed anti-Semitism in movies such as *Crossfire* and *Gentleman's Agreement,* and it tackled the evils of lynching, racism, delinquency, drugs, and poverty in movies made in the 1940s and early 1950s. These occasional forays into issues related to race, class, or ethnic identity were hardly revolutionary, but they did offer a "liberal" stock of images, ideas, and memories to the viewing public.

One should not make too much of any single film, or even whole groups of films. For all its attention to market tastes, Hollywood produced a surprising number of slapdash movies of no meaning at all. Some movies were vehicles for stars to work off contracts, some were "lost" on the cutting room floor, some were contorted into grotesque shapes to satisfy the whims of a producer, director, or actor, and many were simply grist for the production mill. Every film has its idiosyncracies. To analyze any movie as a social text it is necessary, of course, to appreciate the social, economic, cultural, intellectual, and political context in which it was created, but it is also important to consider mundane factors such as the availability of a director or actor, the size of the film's budget, and shooting arrangements.

Nor should one exaggerate any individual's particular imprint on the run of Hollywood movies. Moviemaking in Hollywood was, and is, a collective enterprise. Scripts are written and rewritten, often by teams of writers. Directors and actors improvise further. The editors cut and splice narratives into new configurations. The rise of the writer/director/producer in recent years has given greater cohesion to many movies, so that individual filmmakers again do create distinctive film styles and identities. But even here commercial necessity intrudes. Few individuals have the financial resources to operate outside the network of major producers and distributors anyway. Commercial factors will dictate compromises with art and "message" as long as filmmakers want their movies to reach a national audience.

And that is just the point. Mass entertainment cannot depart too far from the tastes and beliefs of the masses. However much it might lead society to new values, its very survival depends on following society's fundamental values. As America's ethnic and class configurations take new forms, the silver screen will reflect their variegated new shapes and patterns. But showing is not always telling. Movies identify problems and chart social change, but they do not solve social problems. The leitmotif of the New Hollywood, like that of the Old, is entertainment, not the construction of a brave new world.

1

THE DARK SPOT IN THE KALEIDOSCOPE: BLACK IMAGES IN AMERICAN FILM

Thomas Cripps

Stereotyping, as it applies to Afro-Americans, must be approached with the expectation of finding ambiguity and flux rather than persistency of image. Our anticipation grows from two truisms. First, as the place of blacks in American life changes—not necessarily always for the better—the broad outlines of black imagery change to accommodate to new conditions. That is, stereotypes alter form or style in order to maintain their "cognitive consistency" with observed social data or risk losing their aesthetic or social credibility. Some stereotypes erode as the social conditions that inspired them disappear.[1] Second, blacks themselves often choose counter-stereotypes as aesthetic and political strategies that heighten consciousness or call attention to gains or goals. Recent cases include photographic images of Huey Newton of the Black Panthers, armed and seated in a wicker throne; Angela Davis shot from below, framed by a high contrast aura of her own hair; and John Shaft "giving the finger" to an irate driver in the title sequence of MGM's *Shaft* (1971).

Most stereotypes emerge from a popular culture that depends upon imaginative use of familiar formulas for its audience appeal.

15

Deriving as they do from the familiar, they tend to assert a conservative point of view that speaks for a changeless status quo in which blacks take up a well-known place. Conversely, black political usage of stereotypes requires images that disturb things as they are. Though many of the creators of these formulaic figures appear politically naive or thoughtless, the results of their work reflect current political ideologies, if for no other reason than they are intended to attract a large and profitable audience.[2]

Some of these political statements come to rest in the popular consciousness as stereotypes. These stereotypes frequently become the intellectual currency of barrooms or barbershops. Thus, unconsciously, or at least unintentionally, popular thought may be conservative simply because, year-by-year as the place of blacks in American life changes, each generation is left with the outmoded racial attitudes that may have once been used to explain a reality that has passed.[3]

On the other hand, this inertial force is opposed by such sentiments as empathy for the underdog that provide the scaffolding for the vague, unprogrammed social ideology that we might call "conscience-liberalism." Although centered in the urban wing of the Democratic Party, this white conscience-liberalism in alliance with black activists has enlisted a political coalition across party lines that has resulted in social gains for blacks no matter what party is in power.

In practice this means that we should expect a few stereotypes to fall into disuse as the social conditions that inspired them disappear; like latent images on an old photographic plate, they survive only in muted outline. To take only one example of these washed-out stereotypes, we may turn to Broadway at the beginning of the century when so many racial and ethnic stereotypes of the stage seemed permanently freighted with socio-political meanings. In a time when comedians "at liberty" advertised for gigs in the trade journals as "Two Hebe Comics" or a "Carnival of Celtic Comedy," Biograph released a one-reel comedy called *A Bucket of Cream Ale* (1904) in which the audience sees a brief spat between a white man and a blackfaced maid. A modern sensibility is drawn unfailingly to the coarsely typed maid, and yet a glance at a Biograph catalogue reveals that the man too is a type, not merely white, but a "Dutchman" as well. In the ensuing three quarters of a century we have forgotten his tribal marks because we have had no compelling reason to remember them.[4]

At the opposite extreme from stereotypes that die of disuse are the metaphors that minority groups often dredge up as reminders of the group's progress toward some collective goal. As early as 1904 Benjamin Davis, editor of the black fraternal paper, *Atlanta Independent*, taunted those of his readers who wheedle favors from whites rather than demand social justice. These columns were titled in the country dialect of an Uncle Tom—"K'ase I'se a Nigger." More recently blacks have revived other ancient stereotypes as devices for contrasting the oldtime Negro with "the new Negro," a term used by several black generations to characterize new departures from old customs.[5]

The most frequent use of this rhetorical device is in the invocation of Uncle Tom as a symbol of the regressive opposite of black assertiveness. In this way, Stepin Fetchit, a comic fixture in a cycle of Will Rogers' rural genre films of the 1930s, has become an American black version of an old German stereotype, *Der ewige Jude*—the eternal Jew who was a straw man against whom generations of Germans rallied in the name of national unity and racial purity. Black critics and white conscience-liberals constantly invoke Fetchit's name as a symbol of a dead past against which to compare a more sanguine present. By 1944 Fetchit had fallen from favor because of the unctuousness he had come to symbolize. As one white theatre manager in Ohio complained to an agent: "We are not interested in playing a colored show at any time and particularly not interested in playing any show with Stepin Fetchit." By 1949 he had fallen into cheaply mounted "race movies" made for ghetto audiences not yet won over to Hollywood's postwar social "message movies." Black critic Abram Hill labeled one of Fetchit's race movies "a hustle." In 1952 an interracial club in Toronto complained to the black magazine *Ebony* that "everyone of us was very sorry to see a magazine as great as yours print an article using Stepin Fetchit" whose last movie, *Bend of the River,* they saw as "a backward step." By the decade of the 1970s Oxford University Press advertised my book, *Slow Fade to Black,* as the history of black movies from "stereotypical parts" such as "Stepin Fetchit characters" to World War II. And in a typical journalistic account, Dorothy Gilliam of the *Washington Post* described Fetchit as "an ace coon," "a study in molasses-motion," and a "self-loathing stereotype."[6]

Between these fading stereotypes and strategically invoked types is the broad center, the general case, the stereotypes designed to provide easily recognizable minor characters that casually set off main characters. That is to say, most stereotypes are literary conventions lacking in conscious political intent and surviving only so long as they serve the popular artist's purpose of providing recognizable, convenient images that may be used to flesh out, furnish atmosphere, or counterpoint major figures or otherwise enhance a formula story-line. Unfortunately, the most successful stereotypes grow beyond their original intentions by reinforcing ethnocentricity, by contributing to the persistence of outmoded types, and by winning fans who often confuse theatrical personae and devices with literal social reportage.

Every ethnic group in America has laid claim to and mythologized unique virtues in its life and history, much as nations personify themselves in El Cid, Siegfried, Roland, or Arthur. Indeed, the word "ethnic" as it comes to us from the Greek means something peculiar or pagan, and therefore inferior, as a Chinese might characterize a foreigner as barbarian, or a Jew would use *goy*. Thus, in a society of many groups, stereotypes affirm the values of the dominant group. If these stereotypes become popular, then they easily assure, soothe, and support, thus growing into political spokesmen for the status quo. As social scientist Franklin Fearing in 1947 described this subtle politicizing, the viewer "utilizes the pictured situation in the process of coming to terms with the larger environments." This is not to argue that stereotypes constitute the height of propaganda effectiveness; indeed, investigators have measured a "boomerang effect" that follows from heavy-handed and intellectually insulting stereotyping.[7] Even at its most effective, the stereotype may merely reinforce attitudes rather than convert its audience to new ones. This may be seen in Hollywood's tendency to follow rather than lead trends, thus supporting its audience's convictions rather than leading it by the hand to fresh ideas. Performers themselves can do only so much toward shaping attitudes. To step outside the perimeters of familiar character spoils the cozy relationship between actor and audience, weakens the power of the stereotype, and discredits the burden of its political message. Actors who depend upon fan loyalty of the sort that induces viewers to accost a favorite "soap opera" actor in a supermarket or to paw at a current popular singer can retain credibility only in the narrow range accepted by the audience. Fetchit, for example, shrewdly insisted that all interviews be "translated" into his "dialeck" before they appeared, while Louise Beavers always maintained an orotund corpulence that served as a prop for her calculatedly "lovable" roles.[8]

Here a word must be said about black history as it applies to movies. More than any other group, Afro-Americans have been kept apart from the centers of American culture by means of southern law and custom, isolation from urban centers, and the absence of usable survivals from the "old country" culture. Even after the worst excesses of racial discrimination faded, the "high visibility" of blacks deterred social equality and assimilation. This meant that for many years black political effectiveness depended upon cooperation with conscience-liberals rather than cultivation of indigenous political forms. This political arrangement, as it affected the screen, forced blacks into three often ineffective political postures: they spent energy and money affecting movies at their white sources or by seeking censorship; they made war upon the livelihoods of the black actors who performed stereotypical roles; they made "race movies," often far removed from Hollywood sources of expertise, funds, and distribution chains. Thus, during the quarter of a century between the world wars, blacks confronted Hollywood not in a unified phalanx but in three discrete factions: activists, usually based in the East, in such groups as the National Association for the Advancement of Colored People; Hollywood Negroes, a threatened species and often hostile to organized blacks; and the small independent producers of the "race movies" intended to give ghetto audiences a cheap alternative to Hollywood. With their forces thus divided, Negroes engaged in uncoordinated, sporadic assaults on stereotyping that had little effect until World War II helped release liberal social forces that shared many of the blacks' goals and ambitions.[9]

None of the groups enjoyed a spotless reputation for forthright dealing with stereotypes. The NAACP often seemed too cozy with the Hollywood "moguls" and more at war with the Hollywood Negroes than with the studios. The Hollywood Negroes themselves feared for their jobs if black movie images evolved too abruptly and so confined themselves to exaggerated defenses of their roles as interracial goodwill ambassadors. The makers of "race movies," their white allies, and their backers might have provided ideological alternatives to Hollywood stereotypes but often chose to create only mirror images of Hollywood heroes—black cowboys, cops, and crooks. At their best they dramatized black demands for the rewards accruing to those who practiced the Puritan work-ethic, but rarely did they speak to more radical, collective, Marxist, or racial nationalist points of view.[10]

Throughout the history of blacks in American film that began in 1896 these factions, each in its own way, shaped the images of blacks on the screen. In the primitive era between 1896 and 1909 black images on the screen compared favorably with and perhaps exceeded the range of their roles in real life. In the view of historians the period was a "nadir" in which "progressivism" was for whites only, yet the moviemakers' limited editorial control over their new medium allowed a surprisingly broad range of black figures to populate the brief topical films that characterized the era—a range that included chicken thieves as well as cavalrymen who fought in Cuba in the Spanish-American War.[11]

The seminal period for both the cinema and for black images in it, the years from 1910 to 1915, happened to be the golden anniversary of the Civil War, a coincidence that helped shape black images along lines derived from outmoded rural southern sources. Films had developed both as narrative and symbolic expression just as southern sensibilities returned to the White House in the form of Woodrow Wilson's strongly southern Democratic administration. At the same time the Republican Party drifted from its tradition as "the party of

More than any other film, D. W. Griffith's monumental The Birth of a Nation *fixed the image of the inferior, gullible, and, if unguarded, even dangerous Negro in the public mind. In the racial politics of the early twentieth century the Ku Klux Klan played the part of white knights, and blacks were portrayed as villains or comical Sambos.*

Lincoln" and blacks toward a new image as the party of big business. For blacks this meant an abandonment of the goals of Reconstruction, a policy reflected in the shift of black leadership from the old abolitionist, Frederick Douglass, who died in 1895, to that of Booker T. Washington, an accommodationist who worked within the segregated society rather than press against its limits.

D. W. Griffith's *The Birth of a Nation* (1915) exemplified both the attainments of cinema art and the racial politics of the age. A masterpiece that synthesized all the cinema techniques known into an epic, Griffith's film presented blacks as endearing inferiors duped into rising above their accustomed station by misinformed abolitionists and vindictive Reconstruction congressmen who had betrayed Lincoln's benign plans for the defeated South. *The Birth of a Nation* set in motion the images that marked off the succeeding decades, such as the creation of black comic figures that studios would use to ward off black protest against villains. Blacks responded with the first feature-length "race movie," *The Birth of a Race* (1916), an under-distributed and therefore ineffectual antibody designed to confront *The Birth of a Nation.*[12]

Makers of "race movies" jostled each other trying to fill the void. The Lincoln Company, Oscar Micheaux, the Colored Players, Douglass, Democracy, and white-backed Ebony and Reol, among others, tried the genres that Hollywood had neglected. Contributing to the "race movie" movement were black critics, such as Lester Walton of the New York *Age,* who began to build a black critical sense.

Two of the films, Micheaux's *Body and Soul* (1924) and the Colored Players' *The Scar of Shame* (1927), reveal how "race movies" tried to break with Hollywood images. *Body and Soul* not only gave needed work to singer and football player Paul Robeson, but used the medium to attack corrupt preachers who exploited the spiritual needs of their flocks. *The Scar of Shame* introduced its audiences to complicated black issues of color caste, class rivalry, and the pitfalls of urbanization.[13] Hollywood, because of its geographical and social

Early Hollywood largely ignored black dramatic narratives and favored musicals, set in the rural South. Movies such as Hallelujah! *reduced much of black life to tunes and spirituals.*

isolation from centers of black life, could not match such social concerns.

At the height of the silent-film era Hollywood looked backward for its racial inspiration to Universal's *Uncle Tom's Cabin* (1926) and *Showboat* (1927), two major films that depicted blacks in a nostalgic southern rural past. Except for the residue of abolitionist tone of *Uncle Tom's Cabin* and a brief brush with the theme of miscegenation in *Showboat,* the two movies did little to address "the New Negro" and urban concerns. Inevitably, the black stevedores, deckhands, slaves, and servants, unrelieved by fresh black images, constituted an unconsciously political stereotype that reinforced a sentimental image of southern life.[14]

Near the end of the decade sound film brought with it a high season of stereotyping that lasted until after World War II. Sound film should have been a medium through which to express the richness of ethnic life—cantorial chants, Irish wakes, black musical ecstasy, Gypsy violins, brogues, burls, and accents of every immigrant group that had filed through Ellis Island.

But Hollywood knew little of black culture, and its habit of imitating success in search of sure-fire hits diverted attention from urban black themes in favor of well-worn regional comedy and sentimentality. The high scorers of the decade were Paul Sloane's *Hearts in Dixie* (1929), King Vidor's *Hallelujah!* (1929), and Marc Connelly's *The Green Pastures* (1936), each of them by white men with a soft spot in their souls for Negro music, regional wit, and genre style, and a cinematic sense that earned them praise from black critics, audiences, and even black Congressman Oscar DePriest. The point is not their considerable merits but that in the absence of a variety of black screen images their sameness constituted a stereotype. With unrelieved constancy blacks were either naive, musical, serio-comic primitives, larded with an occasional frock-coated preacher, conjure-woman, or jug band musician, or they were urban blacks shattered by city life and transformed into razor-toting, tippling, cheaply sexual, petty thugs.[15]

Obviously, organized Negroes, the churched, affiliated, lettered "respectables" of city life, objected to these characterizations, but many blacks were of two minds. The work of Stepin Fetchit and his imitators reveals the dilemma that divided them. In Fox's *In Old Kentucky* (1926) Fetchit believed that his comic depiction of black manhood offered white audiences a disarming, unthreatening scamp who would improve deteriorating race relations. Unfortunately, Fetchit's employers encouraged repetition rather than breaking new ground, and his oft-repeated roles helped bar the screen to serious black roles. As late as *Hearts in Dixie* he was allowed a tragic scene, but in the dislocations of the depression era his work grew into a whimsi-

The character created by Stepin Fetchit was reduced almost to caricature by other blacks in a host of B-movies in the 1930s and 1940s. In various Charlie Chan movies, Fetchit's negative black stereotype serves a positive Asian stereotype.

cal, drawling purr. In the middle of the Depression in *David Harum* (1934), *Steamboat Round the Bend* (1935), *Judge Priest* (1934), and *The County Chairman* (1935), Fetchit joined with Will Rogers in presenting audiences with a Jeffersonian liberal way out of economic despair. Rogers, as Yankee banker, southern steamboat captain, or rural judge, used native wit to prevail against adversity as though to hold out such hopes to Americans; Fetchit merely survived through trickery within the shackles of black status.[16]

If only it had stopped there. At least it was an honest political statement in comic terms, depicting both black plight and black hope. But after Rogers died in a plane crash in 1935, Fetchit's career all but ended. The next decade brought a rash of thoughtless, exploitive imitators whose B-movie images glibly repeated Fetchit, thereby perpetuating his work long after it had lost its presumed usefulness as interracial harmonizer. Fred Toones was "Snowflake" in horse operas, Willie Best was "Sleep 'n' Eat" in dozens of servile roles, Nick Stewart became "Nicodemus," and below them talentless clowns followed a yet lower road to Hollywood fame. Black critics were intimidated by the ambiguity. If Fetchit had opened doors for Negroes in Hollywood, he also endlessly repeated himself and inspired these imitators with little of his youthful political sense.

Women fared slightly better between the world wars by taking on the assertiveness expected of male characters. Hattie McDaniel, Louise Beavers, and their rivals played a generation of obstreperous confidantes and balky maids whose fortunes rose and fell with those of their mistresses. In 1939 one of them, McDaniel, won an "Oscar" for such a role in *Gone with the Wind.* But Hollywood held their range in check. Thus, many types such as tragic mulattoes had no place in movies except in occasional oddments like *Imitation of Life* (1934) in which Fredi Washington played Peola, Fannie Hurst's heroine who passed into white life.[17]

But black critics and audiences, and whites as well, were swept along by the dislocations of the Depression that helped heighten social consciousness, stimulate a taste for social realism, and bring Broadway drama to the screen, a trend that brought with it many black roles that challenged the stereotypes that had been the icons of earlier times. The black gunman in Archie Mayo's *The Petrified Forest* (1936), the less than happy slaves of *Slave Ship* (1937) and *So Red the Rose* (1935), the parallel drawn between Indians and blacks in *Massacre* (1934), the nearly lynched black in *They Won't Forget* (1937), Etta Moten's singing "Remember My Forgotten Man" in *Gold Diggers of 1933,* and the numberless blacks scattered among the disinherited in *Wild Boys of the Road* (1933), *I Am a Fugitive from a Chain Gang* (1932), *Safe in Hell* (1931), and *Cabin in the Cotton* (1932), all testified to a new liberal social order in which blacks began to find a better place.

These New Deal-inspired depictions of blacks raised up a new generation of critics that challenged Billy Rowe of the *Pittsburgh Courier,* Lawrence LaMar of the *Los Angeles Sentinel,* Harry Levette of the Associated Negro Press, and others for whom covering movies meant little more than rewriting studio press releases. This is not to cast them as entirely meretricious villains. They merely chose the actors' side of controversies rather than that of the audience. Thus, their reporting concentrated on listing the lucky actors who got two weeks' work or who travelled on location to Victorville or appeared in a closeup that survived the cutter. This, of course, required them to defend, say, *Amos 'n' Andy* for the sake of the actors, even as eastern black activists attacked the show in the 1950s. Easterners such as Ralph Mathews of the *Baltimore Afro-American* and Abram Hill of the *New York Amsterdam News,* whose readership felt more concern for the social impact of films, called for a new generation of still more socially significant black themes. Toward the end of World War II they were joined by George Norford of the Urban League magazine, *Opportunity,* and after the war by the anonymous critics of the new, nationwide, black glossy magazine, *Ebony,* both of which challenged Hollywood to use the motion picture screen as a means of broadcasting to a mass audience the liberal war aims of the Western allies.

*Paul Robeson's commanding presence and strong character portrayals pro-
vided a counterweight to the Stepin Fetchit stereotype of the shuffling, stupid
Negro. Robeson vaulted into international prominence by his performances
in* Showboat *(1927) and* The Emperor Jones *(1933).*

Momentum accelerated with such speed that World War II became
a watershed that marked the shattering of the former monopoly of
movies held by the creators of southern genre Negroes. A good half
dozen circumstances provided the high wind that carried the trend.
America's enemies cast their propaganda in racist terms—German
anti-Semitism, Italian conquests in Africa, Japanese atrocities against
Europeans in Asia—thus inviting Americans to assume the role of
anti-colonial, anti-racist knight errant. At the same time the Army
drafted one million Negroes, thereby requiring the War Department

to provide them with a reason to fight. Walter White of the NAACP carried his group to Los Angeles for its 1942 convention where he sought to impress the studios with a new sense of responsibility in keeping with the gravity of these new conditions. Coincidentally, the NAACP's special counsel, Wendell Willkie, became chairman of the board of Twentieth Century-Fox. And finally, the Office of War Information opened a Hollywood office whose director shared the views of the rapidly growing liberal coalition.

The war affected movies and racial stereotypes at their sources in Hollywood and in the War Department where documentaries were conceived. The government began to use films for wartime racial unity and harmony. A revolution in documentary films began in 1943 with the production and mandatory viewing by all troops of the Army's training film, *The Negro Soldier,* a history of blacks in America's wars written by and starring Carlton Moss.[18] *The Negro Soldier* also went into civilian release through the efforts of the Office of War Information, thereby presenting audiences with a liberal racial message cast as official government propaganda—clearly an unprecedented use of government authority to benefit a racial minority. Moss and other blacks eventually provided several such films of liberal persuasion.

Pinky *with Ethel Waters, Frederick O'Neal, and Jeanne Crain was a financially successful "message movie" reflecting the growth of conscience-liberalism in the World War II era. Blacks emerged as warm, sensitive people, and prejudice became the great enemy of American freedom.*

After World War II documentary films became very popular. Their use by classroom teachers and film societies created a booming market that attracted many leftist filmmakers of the New Deal era. Their films on "brotherhood" and "tolerance" helped reshape the tastes and racial politics of the postwar generation of schoolchildren, labor union members, and churchgoers. Sidney Meyers', Helen Levitt's, and Janice Loeb's *The Quiet One* (1948) stood out as an exemplar of the state of the art as well as a compelling depiction of black plight in a social-realism style. Hollywood films were also reshaped by the mood of conscience-liberalism that had begun during the war. Many filmmakers learned their craft on wartime projects and carried their liberal politics into a postwar era of social "message movies" that included such titles as *The Burning Cross* (1947), *Crossfire* (1947), *Gentleman's Agreement* (1947), *Lost Boundaries* (1949), *Home of the Brave* (1949), *Pinky* (1949), *No Way Out* (1950), and *Intruder in the Dust* (1949).[19]

The times promised future progress in which movie stereotypes might disappear, but new conditions demanded new stereotypes that dramatized issues, soothed anxieties, and defined changing values and new habits of mind. Postwar conscience-liberalism became a dominant mode of responding to residual racism. In a characteristic gesture President Harry S Truman created a civil rights commission that issued an urgent report in 1947 that called for overdue racial justice. At this stage, movies focused on changes in white society that required scant knowledge of black circles. Thus, they merely required inoffensive and deserving black characters whose manner promised an easy integration of American society.

Sidney Poitier, Harry Belafonte, and Sammy Davis, Jr., enjoyed lively careers as black stereotypes who gave life to the vague ideals of conscience-liberalism. Their work seemed to say that Negroes had a right of access to all sectors of American life because, after all, Negroes were merely white men with brown skins.

Their achievement would have been significant if only because they introduced stereotyping as a weapon of liberals. Although the spirit of unity, tolerance, and brotherhood—the catchwords of World War II—was endangered by the postwar conservative reaction, their work helped prolong the political life of conscience-liberalism.

Davis' work was most akin to Fetchit's; he was the ambassador who fought racism by burlesqueing it. Like Fetchit's friendship with Rogers, Davis' with singer Frank Sinatra symbolized a modest penetration into white consciousness. His nightclub routines included imitations of white stars, complete with English or Yiddish accents; his comedy thus asserted that blacks could do anything whites could do—and under handicaps. What was his handicap on the golf links, goes one of his straight lines. He was a "one-eyed, Negro, Jew"; what could be more of a handicap than that, says the punchline.

Belafonte's smaller films, over which he had some control, always taught a little homily. In MGM's *Bright Road* (1953) he and Dorothy Dandridge as teachers show that even the most sullen, abused child can be reached by warm professionalism. In *The World, the Flesh, and the Devil* (1959) he is one of three survivors of a cataclysm that has evaporated life without destroying Manhattan. In the last reel he and two whites learn to live in guarded harmony. In *Odds Against Tomorrow* (1959) a well-planned bank robbery goes awry when he and his racist partner fight amidst the pipes and valves of a refinery, only to be seared to a crisp in a fire. At the end an observer, reaching for irony, remarks that in death you could not tell which was which.

Poitier, because of his finely controlled acting talent, made the most of the trend that might accurately be named "the age of Poitier." Like Fetchit's, his characters were giving and open, even in the face of white hostility; unlike Fetchit, he stood apart—cool, reserved, and possessed of superior skills which the whites in the plot would soon need in order to avoid an awful fate. Like Horatio Alger, he earned his way to success. In their best work, Fetchit and the three liberal stereotypes eschewed sexual liaisons, as though to avoid clouding their intended ambassadorial roles by pricking white sexual anxieties that in the view of many observers seemed at the bottom of racism.

Few critics have credited Poitier with acting range, perhaps because his best work has run in a narrow channel of behavior in which a preternaturally blessed Negro wins out over merely physically strong white adversaries. In each plot he seeks survival, not hegemony, and therefore not only does not claim his fallen victim's horse and armor, but helps him up. In *No Way Out* (1950) as a doctor he struggles to save the life of a snarling bigot; in *Blackboard Jungle* (1955) he is Miller, the juvenile delinquent who helps his white teacher to survive in the classroom; in *Duel at Diablo* (1966) his blazing guns save a party of whites from attack; his Oscar-winning Homer Smith in *Lilies of the Field* (1963) is like an Arthurian knight as he builds a chapel in the wilderness at the behest of white nuns; in *Guess Who's Coming to Dinner* (1967) he is a scholarly, but sleekly social, healer in cool command of a situation that ends with a 1930s touch—he and his woman carried away in a cab to their surely happy marriage; his detective in *In the Heat of the Night* (1967) provides gentle, almost maternal, support to a narrowly limited white sheriff who grows in stature by learning to accept Poitier. Each of the movies was a message unit in a larger liberal creed that affirmed the notion of an open, racially integrated society.

Sidney Poitier's tightly-reined performances advanced conscience-liberalism in the 1960s. In Guess Who's Coming to Dinner, *as in other films, he showed the coolness, courage, and common sense that made blacks almost welcome in white homes.*

Poitier's polished performances, a little tightly reined in the eyes of his critics, ideally suited the job at hand—the presentation of Negroes to whites in disarming situations. Like Fetchit in the previous generation, he intruded into white life without threatening it. In the decade after the breakup of the coalition of nonviolent civil rights activists, Poitier's persona often seemed strained and out of place. Nevertheless, Poitier had left a legacy that black actors and writers built upon: grace and courage under pressure, guardedly cool manner, and stereotypically "white" rationalism under his dark skin, all of it covering a hint of subsurface rage. A broad spectrum of black performers owed him debts of style, manner, business, stifled smiles, flashes of silent anger, rhetorical pauses, and standing up to whites with more at his disposal than mere empty rage. Diahann Carroll's *Julia* and *Claudine,* Jim Brown's convicts, cowboys, and cops, O. J. Simpson's and Bernie Casey's simple heroes, and every single character in *Roots I* and *II* from Kunte Kinte to Alex Haley himself as played by James Earl Jones borrowed from Poitier's inventory.

Whatever its accomplishments, Poitier's era left a gap in the image of blacks. Except for *Edge of the City* (1957) and *Raisin in the Sun* (1961), Poitier's movies placed him in a white "culture of professionalism" rather than a black circle of peers—a dutiful teacher in *To Sir, with Love* (1967), a bland photo-journalist in *The Bedford Incident* (1965), a suicide-hotline worker in *The Slender Thread* (1965). His critics to the contrary, the roles were not artifically highly placed blacks, but an accurate sketch of early American racial integration that occurred first in the office, the mill, or the faculty lounge, and only later if at all in closer circles of friends and family.[20] Their failing was rather their exclusion of their characters' roots in black society.

Up to this point whites controlled the movie industry. But for a brief flash in the early 1970s white studios, eager for a means of broadening shrinking audiences, gave a few blacks an opportunity to flesh out the intricacies of black life neglected by the age of Poitier. Blacks first revealed a taste for redder meat as a result of images derived from television: the raucous street fighters of the 1960s urban riots who dramatized the rising of black nationalism among street folk for the first time since the Garvey movement in the 1920s, and the growing presence of black professional basketball players, both of these images profiting from nationwide television broadcasting. Prior to these images the makers of black exploitation films focused on sexual titilation in such vehicles as Stan Borden's *My Baby is Black!* (1965) and Larry Buchanan's *Free, White, and 21* (1963). With less success intellectuals also ventured into feature films with Gene Persson's and Anthony Harvey's film of Leroi Jones's *Dutchman* (1966), and Shirley Clarke's and Frederick Wiseman's film of Warren Miller's novel, *The Cool World* (1964). These films on the verge of the "blaxploitation" era lacked a coherent union of commerce and art. The exploitations lacked politics, the art-films lacked popular flair, and both lacked the color that television had made a *sine qua non* of commercial success.[21]

Between 1968 and 1973 Melvin Van Peebles, Gordon Parks, D'Urville Martin, and a handful of others brought together politics, flair, and color in a rash of movies that the trade papers quickly dubbed "blaxploitation." More than two hundred of them filled the American screens, with a seemingly endless variety of style, theme, and quality. Parks's and MGM's *Shaft* combined emotional ethnocentrism, flashing urban color, and sexy episodes with a conventional cops-and-robbers genre. Van Peebles' *Sweet Sweetback's Baadasssss Song* (1971) further politicized the genre in a shrill and rough-edged anti-white tract. Joseph Naar's *Blacula* (1972) films, the best of many derivations from white sources, depended on good writing and the watchful presence of the star William Marshall, to save them from low budgets and haste, and to use gothic ambience as a device for suggesting the relevance of black African culture to Afro-American life. The resulting hot box office encouraged "crossovers" designed to attract white audiences: *Sounder* (1968), *The Learning Tree* (1968), *Carwash* (1976), *Wattstax* (1973), and *Cooley High* (1975), among others. Fortunately, the movies hit during a black economic boom that saw a wave of disposable income and a black exodus to the suburbs.

In the short run, the money financed a big black audience, but in the long run after a few years the "blaxploitation" filmmakers lost touch with all but the inner city remnants of their audience, the young people who required merely simple revenge formulas rather than politics. And even they eventually turned to the more stylized, choreographed, colorful rituals of violence, the martial arts movies made in Singapore and Hong Kong.[22] The martial arts movies

Richard Roundtree's Shaft *strutted through the mean streets of urban America as the tough, savvy, and very macho black—the new look in black films of the 1960s and early 1970s.*

provided youthful, urban, black audiences with a rare instance of a political metaphor that crossed international cultural boundaries.

In a way they brought movie stereotypes full circle. Many black images in primitive silent movies had been borrowed from southern literary sources that had once helped justify slavery and discrimination. Through the medium of film they crossed regional cultural lines, and helped northern audiences develop metaphorical foundations for the ghettoization process that marked the twentieth century. Similarly, in the late 1970s martial arts movies from a foreign culture gave black youth a surrealistic (and therefore morally tolerable) expression of the violent black counter-aggression against white authorities that had marked the era after the death of Martin Luther King in 1968.[23]

At this writing, the future is unclear, except to say that various social and political forces have combined to produce an erosion of the rough edges of black characterizations. The result is that black drama in film and television has begun to draw critical fire for its growing homogeneity. As black middle-class lobbying groups, social psychologists, and journalists attack anti-social black images, the whites who control the visual industries accommodate them by writing in characters who act out conventional American values—"white" values, according to some critics. Aesthetically, the resulting homogeneity weakens dramatic conflict on the screen and makes for dull fare. Black teachers in *The Bill Cosby Show,* a detective in *Tenafly,* a petit bourgeois in *Harris and Company,* all produced little dramatic excitement, while *Roots II,* although it attracted impressive audiences, also drew criticism for its "white" rugged individualism that all but blotted out a sense of black communal life that black intellectuals had wished for. Perhaps we may expect a continuing dimunition of a rough-edged black presence, as in television commercials whose need to sell products to a general audience resulted in a continuing black presence in TV spots but in prim, muted form. It is as though the black mothers of a generation ago who shushed their children into polite silence, corrected their grammar, overdressed them on Sundays, and sent them to ballet lessons have won. Like the vestigial stereotypes that have withered away because their political motivation no longer exists, the sharp outlines of black identity may become a part of the whole, the way silt from many soils forms a delta. And like all stereotypes, it will satisfy only its audiences and will inspire intellectuals to write jargon-filled jeremiads in *Psychology Today.*[24]

NOTES

1. A good foundation for understanding stereotyping may be found in communication-theory. A good primer is Stephen W. King, *Communication and Social Influence* (1975), from which the term "cognitive consistency" is borrowed (94).

2. The post-World War II popularizing of political themes stimulated a stream of sociological literature bearing on this point. It is summarized in Thomas Cripps, "The Death of Rastus: Negroes in American Films Since 1945," *Phylon*, XXVIII (Fall 1967), 267-75.

3. For a social basis for prejudice and stereotyping, see Gordon W. Allport, *The Nature of Prejudice* (1958); an up-to-date bibliography is in George Comstock, et al., *Television and Human Behavior* (1978), 511-58.

4. Thomas Cripps, *Slow Fade to Black: The Negro in American Film, 1900-1942* (1977), Chapter 1.

5. The most complete run of the *Atlanta Independent* is in the library of Atlanta University; the most widely known usage of the term is Alain Locke, ed., *The New Negro: An Interpretation* (1925), which was dedicated to "the younger generation."

6. The references to Stepin Fetchit are from a file of ephemera on his career in the possession of the author. See also the film, *Black Shadows on a Silver Screen* (Washington, 1975). For a contrast between stereotypes in an authoritarian society in which racism was a part of public policy and one in which racism was merely inherited lore, see Fritz Hippler's *Der Ewige Jude*, "certainly the 'hate' picture of all time," in the view of David Stewart Hull, *Film in the Third Reich: A Study of the German Cinema, 1933-1945* (1969), 172-74; see also Department of Justice, Office of Alien Property, *Motion Pictures of German Origin* (1952), 20.

7. Franklin Fearing, "Influence of the Movies on Attitudes and Behavior," *Annals of the American Academy of Political and Social Science*, CCLIV (November 1947), 70-79; for "boomerang" effect see Joseph Axelrod, "German and Austrian Reaction to 'The Blackboard Jungle'," *School and Society*, LXXXV (February 16, 1957), 57-59; and Cripps, "Death of Rastus," 267-69.

8. On the "artificial relationships" between fans and stars see Sandy Banisky, "The Eyes Have It," an interview with anthropologist John L. Caughey in *Sun* (Baltimore), March 27, 1979; on Beavers, Fetchit, and other black performers and their attitudes toward their work see Cripps, *Slow Fade to Black*.

9. For a theoretical discussion of the political uses of stereotypes and a suggestion of why they should be important to minorities see Jacques Ellul, *The Political Illusion* (1967), 111-12, 128-29.

10. This theme is the subject of a work in progress by the author.

11. Cripps, *Slow Fade to Black*, Chapter 1; the strongest dissent from this view is Daniel J. Leab, *From Sambo to Superspade: The Black Experience in Motion Pictures* (1975), in which the range of roles seems only "the gamut from A to B."

12. Thomas Cripps, "The Birth of a Race Company: An Early Stride Toward a Black Cinema," *Journal of Negro History*, LIX (January 1974), 28-37.

13. Cripps, *Slow Fade to Black*, Chapter 7; Thomas Cripps, "Race Movies as Voices of the Black Bourgeoisie: *The Scar of Shame* (1927)," in John E. O'Connor and Martin A. Jackson, eds., *American History/American Film: Interpreting the Hollywood Image* (1979), 39-56.

14. On the provenance of Uncle Tom see Cripps, *Slow Fade to Black;* on *Showboat,* see Miles Krueger, *Showboat: The Story of a Classic American Musical* (1977).

15. Miles Krueger, *Hearts in Dixie* program notes, Museum of Modern Art film series (New York, n. d., mimeo.); King Vidor, *A Tree is a Tree* (1953), Chapter 16; Charles Higham, "King Vidor," *Film Heritage,* I (Summer 1966), 15-25; Thomas Cripps, introduction to *The Green Pastures* (1980).

16. Peter C. Rollins, "Will Rogers and the Relevance of Nostalgia: *Steamboat Round the Bend* (1935)," in O'Connor and Jackson, eds., *American History/American Film,* 77-96. The description of the Negro middle class is from David Gordon Nielson, *Black Ethos: Northern Urban Life and Thought, 1890-1930,* "Contributions in Afro-American and African Studies," No. 29 (1977).

17. McDaniel is one of the few black women performers to appear in the *Dictionary of American Biography.* Her few papers are in the Herrick Library of the Academy of Motion Picture Arts and Sciences; her nephew, Edgar Goff, Los Angeles, is at work on a biography. Washington's papers are in Dillard University, New Orleans. Washington had a few high moments with Duke Ellington in the short film *Black and Tan* (1929) and in *One Mile from Heaven* (1937) in which her faint Negro heritage is used as evidence by social agencies in a decision to deny her the adoption of her white foster child. For a photograph of McDaniel at the "Oscar" ceremony see Cripps, *Slow Fade to Black,* 365.

18. The theme of World War II, and specifically the film *The Negro Soldier,* as watershed is taken up in Thomas Cripps and David Culbert, "*The Negro Soldier* and Race Relations during World War II [working title]," *American Quarterly,* forthcoming, 1980.

19. The residual effect of wartime liberalism on postwar films is taken up in Thomas Cripps, "*Casablanca, Tennessee Johnson,* and *The Negro Soldier*: A Scenario for the Growth of Conscience Liberalism during World War II," a paper read before the Conference on Historical Realities and Feature Film at the Zentrum für Interdisziplinäre Forschung in Universität Bielefeld, Federal Republic of Germany, May 16, 1979.

20. No good study of this period exists. It is taken up as part of a survey in Leab, *From Sambo to Superspade,* and Donald Bogle, *Toms, Coons, Mulattoes, Mammies, & Bucks* (1973). See also Carolyn H. Ewers, *Sidney Poitier: The Long Journey* (1969); Sammy Davis, Jr., Jane and Burt Boyar, *Yes I Can: The Story of Sammy Davis, Jr.* (1965); Dorothy Dandridge and Earl Conrad, *Everything and Nothing: The Dorothy Dandridge Tragedy* (1970); Arnold Shaw, *Belafonte: An Unauthorized Biography* (1960); Alvin H. Marill, *The Films of Sidney Poitier* (1978). For a personal estimate of the times see James Baldwin, *The Devil Finds Work* (1976). For a brief survey see Cripps, "Death of Rastus." See also Jeanne Béranto et Catherine Besnard, "Sidney Poitier" (Memoire de Maitris, presenté a L'Institut d'Anglais Charles V, Université de Paris, 1971). The term "culture of professionalism," and its implied advantages and disadvangates for blacks, is borrowed from Burton J. Bledstein, *The Culture of Professionalism: The Middle Class and the Development of Higher Education in America* (1976).

21. Cripps, "Death of Rastus," *passim.*

22. The era inspired a small industry that produced essays on the phenomenon of movies-for-blacks. Collections include the black films number of *Black Scholar,* VII (May 1976); the "black image in the mass media" number of *Freedomways,* XIV (3rd Quarter 1974); Richard A. Maynard, ed., *The Black Man on Film: Racial Stereotyping* (1974); and Lindsay Patterson, ed., *Black Films and Film-Makers: A Comprehensive Anthology from Stereotype to*

Superhero (1975); and the books, Edward Mapp, *Blacks in American Films: Today and Yesterday* (1971); James Murray, *To Find an Image: Black Films from Uncle Tom to Super Fly* (1973); James Pines, *Black in Films: A Survey of Racial Themes and Images in American Film* (1975); and several pictorial compilations; as well as curiosa such as Melvin Van Peebles, *Sweet Sweetback's Baadasssss Song* [a chronicle of production] (1971). For an analysis of *Sweetback* and a fuller bibliography see Thomas Cripps, *Black Film as Genre* (1978).

23. Verina Glaessner, *Kung Fu: Cinema of Vengeance* (1974), *passim.*, is a good survey clad in a sensational cover.

24. The journalistic literature on recent television is thick but uneven. After having exhausted the pages of *The Readers' Guide to Periodical Literature, The Social Sciences Index,* and *The Humanities Index,* the subject of television stereotyping may be approached best from a behavioral point of view. Good bibliographies are in, for example, George Comstock, *et al., Television and Human Behavior;* and Eli A. Rubinstein, *et al.,* eds., for HEW and National Institute of Mental Health, *Television in Day-to-Day Life: Patterns of Use,* Vol. IV of "Television and Social Behavior," a technical report to the Surgeon General's Scientific Advisory Committee on Television and Social Behavior (Rockeville, Md., n. d.). The most recent study done in this mode is Jannette Dates, "The Relationship of Demographic Variables and Racial Attitudes to Adolescent Perceptions of Black Television Characters" (Ph.D. thesis, University of Maryland, 1979), a study that suggests informed behavioral data should lead to minority group activism against network programmers whose shows rely on racial stereotyping for humor.

2

THE ENTERTAINING ANACHRONISM: INDIANS IN AMERICAN FILM

Gretchen Bataille and
Charles L. P. Silet

Hollywood has presented an extremely distorted picture of American Indian peoples. From our childhood on, Hollywood has bombarded us with cartoons and movies which show the Indian as the "bad guy" or, at best, a tragic anachronism from out of the past.

The image of the Native American, which is a part of the history of the motion picture, evolved from stereotypes created by the earliest settlers and chroniclers of this country. The contradictory views of the Indian, sometimes gentle and good and sometimes terrifying and evil, stem from the Euro-Americans' ambivalence toward a race of people they attempted to destroy. The screen images we have today have descended from the captivity narratives of the eighteenth century, the romances of James Fenimore Cooper, and the Beadle dime novel tradition.

When the English first came to this continent they were faced with a dual problem: first, what to do with the wilderness, and second, what to do with those who inhabited that wilderness. Not only did they inherit what they believed to be an uncivilized environment but uncivilized people as well. Their task, which they felt keenly, was to subdue the wilderness and to bring order to this newly-found chaos. They wanted to create a civilized Anglo-Saxon society much like the one they had just left, because they felt that in such a society people could achieve their highest potential. One of the impediments to this progress was the Indian; so these early colonialists set about civilizing the "savage." In the end, the Native American was all but destroyed.

Initially, the impulses of the colonists, however finally disastrous, were at least well-intentioned. They wanted to Christianize the Indians into part of their social order. But the Native Americans were not easily assimilated. As Roy Harvey Pearce has pointed out in his seminal study of the Indian and the American mind,[1] by the end of the 1770s the American Revolution demanded a commitment on the part of the colonials to a new world vision of a glorious civilization, one in which the Indian would play no part. The original notion of the noble savage, a product of what Pearce calls Anglo-French primitivistic thinking, gave way to the realization that the Native American was bound inextricably to "a primitive past, a primitive society, and a primitive environment, to be destroyed by God, Nature, and Progress to make way for Civilized man."[2] Pearce notes that first the colonialists tried to understand the savage and to bring him into civilization; however, after the dawning of the Republic, the Indian became an unfortunate obstacle in the path of progress.

The transition in mental attitudes from assimilation to annihilation was not an abrupt one, and its various permutations need not concern us here. The point is that by the beginning of the nineteenth century there was public recognition of both the failure in theory and in practice of the white attitude toward the Indian. Since the Indian would not conform to the way of life of the new society, and since he could not or would not be civilized, then he must be destroyed. As Pearce writes, the whites would pity the Indian and still censure him for his failure to adapt, and in the end this pity and censure would be the "price Americans would have to pay for destroying the Indian, . . . the price of the progress of civilization over savagism."[3]

Despite the wanton destruction of the native environment and of the native cultures, Americans remained fascinated by what they regarded as savagism. The Native American was a diminishing threat to white expansionism, and by the nineteenth century Indians formed a curious object for study. The new society of which Americans felt themselves a part craved the assurances of progress and superiority—the Indian became the obvious point of comparison. The Europeans who settled this continent brought with them all the trappings of Western culture including its needs to know the past and the future. The Native American's "historyless antiquity," as Leslie Fiedler calls it, was beyond their comprehension.[4] The Indians had no past and no future in Western terms and thereby fell out of society and out of history.

The primitive life, however, was not all bad. From Rousseau, Europeans had learned about the inherent goodness of natural man and the simple life, and Americans inherited the noble savage as part of their literary tradition. As they began to create their own literature, however, they were forced to modify the noble savage to fit with the pre-existing image of the Indian in America—one to be pitied and censured. So the doomed noble savage became a part of American literature. It was easy enough to pity the Indian, especially after his fall from grace, but it was necessary to undercut his nobility as well. One could not wipe out a noble race without justification, and so the bloodthirsty noble savage emerged. Writers were also forced to admit, albeit hesitantly, white guilt as well as hatred for the Indian. Hatred and guilt mixed with celebration; the noble savage was given a peculiarly American view. The Indian was reduced to a set of contradictions: noble and ignoble, pitied and praised, censured and celebrated. In such a way Americans justified and bolstered their own barbarism. White Americans could become savage, too, in order to crush savagism to save civilization.

This ambivalence toward the Native American was reflected in the earliest accounts of life in the New World. In the journals of explorers such as Christopher Columbus and John Smith, and later in histories by government officials such as William Byrd and William Bradford, descriptions of the Indians depicted varying qualities of generosity, barbarousness, or piety.[5] During the seventeenth and eighteenth centuries the captivity narratives reinforced the existing Puritan explanation of the Indians as subhuman or inspired by the devil. One of the strongest influences on later similar works as well as on the frontier romances was Mrs. Mary Rowlandson's story, *The Sovereignty and Goodness of God . . . Being a Narrative of the Captivity and Restoration of Mrs. Mary Rowlandson* (1682). The Puritan view of the Indian remained a pervasive theme, and, although the hope of "civilizing" the Indian was often expressed, ultimately religion demanded that the confrontation between Indian and white result in Indian capitulation to white domination. Individual Indians could be "good," but the group had to be depicted as "bad" in order to justify the existing philosophies of government and religion. Relying on existing documents and stories, James Fenimore Cooper created both the noble and ignoble savages as stock characters in American literature. Cooper's *The Leatherstocking Tales* were preceded by a number of other nineteenth-century works which drew on the conventions of the English historical romance of Walter Scott as well as the prototypes created in earlier frontier accounts. Robert Montgomery Bird's *Nick of the Woods* (1837) and William Gilmore Simms's *The Yemassee* (1835) reinforced existing attitudes. These works of fiction were bolstered by the epic sweep of such historical studies as Francis Parkman's *Oregon Trail* (1849), which solidified white attitudes about manifest destiny and the role of the Indian in the expanding nation. By the mid-nineteenth century the bloodthirsty savage had become a staple of the popular dime novel and pulp weekly. Such thrillers as *Massacre!* and *The Fighting Trapper* became favorites during the same time that the enormously popular Wild West shows were playing across the country and were being exported to France and England.

Buffalo Bill was not only the most popular of the dime novel heroes, but he was also an extremely successful showman and his Wild West Show toured all over the world. His show even had a crown performance before Queen Victoria; presumably she was amused. Included among the exhibits in the show were real Indians whom Buffalo Bill paraded around the audience and used in the mock battle scenes he staged between the white settlers and the "savages." By the time Buffalo Bill was through, the Indians were firmly established as figures of entertainment like the stage Irishman and the comic Jew.[6]

By the end of the nineteenth century the favorite theme in popular fiction was Indian fighting on the Plains and the most popular outcome was another Indian "biting the dust." The gradual buildup of the Indian stereotypes from early historical accounts, captivity narratives, and frontier romances was solidified in the public mind by the end of the century. It was an easy step for these stereotypes to be transferred from the dime novels and the drama of Wild West shows to the screen.[7]

Since the Indian had high entertainment value, it seemed only natural that Edison should have shot film vignettes of Indian dances for his early penny arcade peep shows.[8] Edison's machines showed such films as the *Sioux Ghost Dance* (1894) and the *Parade of Buffalo Bill's Wild West* (1898). As Ralph and Natasha Friar put it in their book *The Only Good Indian:* "The filmic cultural genocide of the Native American begins with such commercialization as *Sioux Ghost Dance*."[9] There is no historical evidence that what was filmed was the Ghost Dance, but filmmakers, always eager to take advantage of ready-made publicity, were probably relying on the public memory of Wounded Knee only four years before. From those earliest dim flickerings of the motion picture, there continued the process of miscreating the Native American's culture and way of life. What followed for the next few years was a conscious reworking of history through the recreation (on the silver screen) of the battles of the Indian Wars. Audiences were treated to a series of films which touted the mythical, often falsified, exploits of such legendary frontier figures as Kit Carson and

Daniel Boone, plus a number of cowboys including the ever present Buffalo Bill Cody. The white heroes got the billing, and the Indians got the pratfalls.

D. W. Griffith, Thomas Ince, Cecil B. DeMille, all of the greatest of the early filmmakers, contributed to this stereotype. Yet despite the talent of these directors, the image of the Native American did not become any clearer or more historically accurate. One still saw Sioux-bonneted actors selling Navajo blankets. Even actor-writer-director William S. Hart, who prided himself on the authenticity of his westerns, spewed forth bilge about the white man's supremacy over the Indian in such films as *The Aryan* (1916). One title of this epic read: "Oft written in letters of blood, deep carved in the face of destiny, that all men may read, runs the code of the Aryan race: 'Our women shall be guarded'."[10] The threat of miscegenation was powerful.

By the time of the First World War the image of the Native American was well established in the popular film, and for the next three decades, with some minor exceptions, that image remained constant. The moviemakers expressed the same ambivalence toward the Indian that the dime novelists had. The ignoble, noble savage was still with us. There was one major difference though; because of the visual nature of the new medium, Hollywood had more opportunity to distort the image of the Native American. The writers of pulp fiction sketched in the settings and described the "red men," but Hollywood actually showed them. The resulting confusion was symptomatic of the whites' ignorance of the people they had dispossessed. Indians of the Northeast were shown wearing clothing of the Plains Indians and living in dwellings of tribes of the Southwest. Hollywood created the instant Indian: wig, war bonnet, breechclout, moccasins, phony beadwork. The movie men did what thousands of years of social evolution could not do, even what the threat of the encroaching white man could not do; Hollywood produced the homogenized Native American, devoid of tribal characteristics or regional differences. As long as an actor wore fringed pants and spoke with a halting accent, he was an Indian.[11]

The Indian had a multiple image and at the same time a partial image. *The Indian*—no tribe, no identity, almost always male—was either noble (still savage, but noble nevertheless) or bloodthirsty and vicious. There were variations of the stereotypes—the drunken Indian, the heathen, the lazy native—but still it was an image of a creature less than human without religion and lacking in morality or virtue. Usually he was viewed apart from wife or children or any family relationships; he was an isolated figure, one with a pinto pony, gliding across the plains of America, viewed always as an Indian first and an individual last. He combined all the noble virtues expressed in

The ubiquitous Indian with tomahawk and torch in hand was a stock figure in countless Hollywood B-movies, such as Frontier Woman. *These portrayals helped to reinforce a popular image of the Indian as an ignorant savage bent on obstructing progress and assailing innocent white settlers.*

a Catlin painting and the savagery of a Beadle novel.

From the beginning of the twentieth century with the publication of reviews in daily newspapers the Indian in the film has been the subject of a wide variety of articles. Even these early articles were ambivalent about the portrayal of the American Indian on the screen, some lamenting the inaccuracies and others justifying the views as accurate. Among the earliest articles dealing specifically with the Indian and the movies are several appearing in *Moving Picture World* between 1909 and 1914. The concerns voiced in these essays echo down to us through the years. They are pleas grown mute with repetition. A piece published in 1911, "The Make-Believe Indian," notes that movies do not accurately portray Indians as a "Noble race of people, with their splendid physique and physical prowess." The article mentions that a number of Indians resented the "untrue, unreal and unfair representations of themselves and their habits." The notice concludes with the hope that a series of films of "real" Indian life will be forthcoming.[12]

Unlike the pattern which developed later, American Indian people were often included as actors in the early films. This led to such reactions as Ernest Alfred Dench's in, "The Dangers of Employing Redskins as Movie Actors."[13] Because American Indians were forced to act out the image the white director had of them, they played the roles of "savages," "stoics," or drunks, many unwittingly perpetuating the stereotyped inaccuracies.

In the developing years of the movies Indian material provided exciting drama on the screen. The Indian conflicts of the nineteenth century had been settled to the advantage of the United States, and American Indians were condemned to reservations. The use of the Indian as subject for the films was successful, and even as film audiences grew and changed, the popularity of the subject continued. The western came to be a metaphor for American life—triumph over the land and the people who had once inhabited it, success of the immigrant who had sought and gained new economic and social status, and a visual representation of a colorful past of what was now perceived to be a growing nation. Especially during the 1930s and 1940s in films such as *Northwest Passage* (1940) and *Drums Along the Mohawk* (1939), audiences could applaud the demise of the warlike "savages," ignoring the conflicts emerging in their own society.

There was, however, concern about the misrepresentation throughout these early years, concern evidenced by Stanley Vestal's plea in 1936 about the racial caricatures presented by Hollywood producers. He recognized the attraction of the Indian because of our link with our past, but he was concerned lest viewers lose sight of the reality of that past in the romanticism of outdoor life and the wilderness. He was alarmed by the careless attitude of producers who seemed not to know how to construct an Indian village and actors who did not even look comfortable in their blankets and paint. In "The Hollywooden Indian" he alerted readers that ". . . in the representation of the American Indian, Hollywood has made little progress; . . . for misrepresentation, sensationalism, and all-around falsity, Indian pictures are in a class by themselves." Although Vestal has a few negative Indian stereotypes of his own, his lament was admirable for the times: "It seems stupid of producers to offer them nothing but caricatures of their race. . . . Let us hope that the Hollywooden Indian may soon go the way of his cigarstore prototype." Vestal's was an isolated voice, however, for his brief article seems not to have affected either producers or the viewers.[14]

A decade after Vestal's plea James Denton found a great deal of humor in Hollywood's use of Indian actors who had to be "taught" how to act Indian; that is, they were represented as "Indian" according to the vision of the producer.[15] Denton's essay reveals a total lack of historical perspective in portraying Indians on the screen as well as echoing the uncritical acceptance of traditional Indian stereotyping. The fact that the piece appeared in a highly successful, mass-circulation magazine reinforces once again the popular biases against American Indians. Its very existence speaks to the virulence of the cultural and racial stereotyping.

These earliest critical views of the Indian on the screen suggest some of the ambivalence which existed from the very beginning about the portrayal of Indian people by Hollywood producers.[16] Although there was a recognition of the lack of accuracy, critics were unsure about solutions to the problem. Indians had become a staple in Saturday afternoon serials such as *The Indians Are Coming, The Lone Ranger,* and *The Miracle Rider,* and necessary to the myth of the West and its portrayal on the screen. Audiences did not generally know the difference between a Navajo and a Cheyenne, so they certainly would not know the differences among tribal traditions or clothing. Producers knew this and knew also that the films would be popular despite the lack of accuracy. Because the Indian's voice has always been an isolated one, his pleas were unheeded. The few critics who spoke out against this misrepresentation during the first half of the century were equally isolated voices. Politically and socially it was all right to stereotype minority groups and women; it was, after all, entertaining and profitable. And that was what the movies were all about.

And so popular films of the last seventy years have represented the Native American as an entertaining anachronism. In spite of the sympathetic representations of Indians by photographers such as Edward Curtis and the white culture's long tradition of scientific curiosity about the Indian, it has been this distorted popular image which has dominated.

In the early 1960s filmmakers began to exhibit an ambivalence about portraying Native Americans, and the industry's concerns were reflected in the reviews of those movies.[17] Increasingly reviewers have called into question the stereotypes and misconceptions appearing on the screen. Contemporary reviews demonstrate this heightened awareness as well as the persistence of the Hollywood images. Unfortunately, many films which have presented a more balanced view of the Native American have not been received as films about Indians. For example, *One Flew Over the Cuckoo's Nest* (1975) was reviewed almost entirely for Jack Nicholson's performance with occasional references to the film's obvious use of religious metaphor. The fact that Ken Kesey's novel was narrated by an Indian was totally missing from the film version. The reviewers of *Jeremiah Johnson* (1972) made little of the Indian elements in that film as did the reviewers of *Hombre* (1967), a film which did much to create a strong and unambivalent half-breed character rather than the usual Hollywood stereotype who rises by adopting the white cultural values in dress, religion, and philosophy. Even a movie so obviously about relations between Indians and whites such as *Tell Them Willie Boy Is Here* (1969) brought

One of the new wave of pro-Indian films, Little Big Man, *starring Dustin Hoffman, evokes sympathy for the honesty and coherence of Cheyenne culture struggling against the hypocrisy, cruelty, and destructiveness of modernizing American culture, personified in George Armstrong Custer.*

forth more copy about the return of its director, Abraham Polonsky, to film work after a long forced absence because of blacklisting in the 1950s. Many films which should have been reviewed for their progressive treatment of Indian stereotypes have not received that emphasis.

It was not until the aftermath of the Vietnam debacle in the early seventies that we were treated to a series of pro-Indian films, the most famous of which were *A Man Called Horse* (1970), *Soldier Blue* (1970), and *Little Big Man* (1970). Sympathetic viewers eagerly grabbed onto what they perceived as a major shift in attitudes toward the Indian. Unfortunately, the films did little to correct the popular stereotypes. What the films did provide was a fascinating study of white America, via the movies, trying to come to grips with itself and, in some measure, with its past.

A Man Called Horse, for all its anthropological detail, became for some critics a dissatisfying study in sadism. Although the film boasts scenes graphically depicting the central character's ritualistic self-mutilation, it resolves into what one critic called just another chapter of Indian romance in a museum diorama. The interest of the film lies in director Eliot Silverstein's concern for its tone. If it was not authentic, at least it tried to be, which was something new in American popular films. The movie did make some gains, notably since the white hero accepted a love relationship with the Indian woman on her terms without forcing her to abandon her culture, and because the film did suggest diversity among Indians both tribally and individually.

For many critics Ralph Nelson's *Soldier Blue* became a theater-of-cruelty western based on a proto-My Lai, the Sand Creek, Colorado massacre of 1864. The problem with all of its slaughter, however, was that it portrayed the Indian as pretty much the stereotyped savage given to blood lust that we have seen on movie screens for years. In response to the whole problem of American self-hate Pauline Kael in her review of *Tell Them Willie Boy Is Here*[18] used the term geno-suicide to describe the apparent zeal with which the American audience was applauding the brutal exploitation of our collective guilt to be found in movies dealing with relations with the Native American.

The one film which has done consistently well with a large number of critics is Arthur Penn's *Little Big Man.* The emergence of Chief Dan George as a film personality helped to quiet the traditional complaints about the absence of Indian actors. In spite of the blood bath in the massacre scenes, the reversal of traditional western roles seems to have provided a rationale for the action of the Indians in ways that *A Man Called Horse* and *Soldier Blue* did not. The slaughter of Custer and his men was seen as a perfectly justifiable revenge for atrocities committed by the cavalry on a peaceful people. Although the perspective is decidedly mid-twentieth century, the film works. In *Little Big Man* Penn contrasts the organic culture of the Cheyenne with the confusing and destructive Anglo-Saxon Protestant society which is engulfing it. Civilization becomes disordered, hypocritical, self-seeking, and nihilistic with people living in constant fear and tension. The culture projects all of its hatred and insecurity onto its enemies. The character who bears the main burden of the destructive and death-seeking impulse of the white society is George Armstrong Custer. It is through Custer, here figuring as a vainglorious psychopath, in marked contrast to the heroic creation of Errol Flynn in *They Died with Their Boots On* (1942), that Penn strikes out at American society, but it is unfortunate that Custer bears so much of the burden because it tends to dilute the charge against American society by emphasizing one crazy individual.

That same appeal, however, provided Robert Altman with the subject matter for *Buffalo Bill and the Indians* (1976). The starring role was given to Paul Newman, which automatically focused attention on the single individual, but the debunking of national heroes has been an American pastime for years, and Buffalo Bill as well as George Armstrong Custer in their absurdity and meglomania make perfect marks for the debunking film. Because the reassessment of the Native American in the movies necessitates a revision of the entire myth of the West, broadening the scope of analysis offers the most fruitful possibilities for the future.

It becomes clear after reading the criticism on the Indian in film that reactions differ depending on the expectations of the critic or viewer. Some look for accuracy in the portrayal of cultural ways and artifacts; others are more concerned with the ethnicity of the actors and actresses. But what they are all saying amounts to the same thing —the American Indian has been and continues to be stereotyped. The stereotypes will no doubt continue as long as the Indian is portrayed only in his adversary role in nineteenth-century America. The most recent hope for a change in the portrayal may be with films such as *One Flew Over the Cuckoo's Nest* in which Chief Bromden's Indianness, although significant symbolically, is somewhat accidental. Kesey suggests in this twentieth-century version of "cowboys and Indians" that there are many victims of the American myth, and they do not all have feathers or straight black hair.

Certainly the political and social moods of the country during the 1960s and 1970s had been changing. At the same time, American Indian people were visible in the news media with the takeover at Wounded Knee, the Trail of Broken Treaties, and The Longest Walk. Perhaps producers realized that they could no longer portray the old images, that the public was becoming aware of what Stan Steiner called "the new Indians." At a time when "flower children" were searching with Don Juan and Carlos Castañada for spiritual awakening and protesters were decrying the genocide of Vietnam, new aspects of Indian existence became significant.

Philip French, even more than others, saw the McCarthy era as forcing producers to use allegory to handle sensitive issues. *Arrowhead* (1953), for example, is described by French as an "ultra-right-wing allegory of the McCarthy period in which the Indians, . . . do service for Communists, and the whites . . . for those red blooded American patriots bent on rooting out the Communist conspiracy at home and standing up to its menace abroad."[19] He cites *Cheyenne Autumn* (1964) as portraying the fairly obvious comparison between the persecution of the Indians and the German extermination camps. In more recent

Paul Newman in the debunking Buffalo Bill and the Indians *portrays Buffalo Bill as an empty, callous opportunist—the antithesis of the mythical knight-of-the-Wild-West image that popular culture manufactured from the late nineteenth through the twentieth centuries.*

films he offers comparisons with America's counterculture and parallels *Soldier Blue* and *Little Big Man* with Vietnam and My Lai. What French and others see in the contemporary films is a manipulation of the Indian image to present the political ideologies of the filmmakers, yet another form of misrepresentation.

Ultimately, it may take a non-American filmmaker to represent America to Americans, or Indian people must offer their own view of Indian experience and offer an alternative to the Hollywood image. Both alternatives are worthwhile, but neither may be practical. Europeans by and large have grown up with the same views of the American West as Americans have. Reruns of *Wagon Train,* Karl May novels, and popular culture have provided the European view of American Indians. Buffalo Bill and his Wild West Show performed the same wagon train attacks for Queen Victoria that American audiences had seen. "Cowboys and Indians" is played by children all over the world.

In this country it will be a long time before the major studios have many American Indians as employees or technical advisors. And financial backing for Native American film companies is sadly lacking. The film version of N. Scott Momaday's *House Made of Dawn* is available, but it has been shown only to limited audiences. Based on a Pulitzer Prize-winning novel written by a Kiowa Indian, directed and produced by an Indian film company, and featuring many new Indian actors, this film demonstrates what can be done despite a low budget and a lack of "Hollywood" experience. Although the film may receive criticism on selected technical issues or resentment from some Native Americans who would have preferred that the religious peyote ritual be omitted, it is generally a fine film which visually presents Native American experience as something other than the usual fare of "cowboys and Indians." Perhaps if there were more Native Americans "in the business," we would begin to receive something other than an outside view of Indian experience. The probability of this is unlikely at this time, however.[20]

The United States Commission on Civil Rights has been actively involved in studying the relationships between minorities and the visual media. In *Window Dressing on the Set* (1977) and the later *Update* (1979) the Commission confined its findings to the portrayal of minorities on television. However, the comments included by Gerald Wilkinson, director of the National Indian Youth Council, are as true for the movies as they are for television: "Indian young people will act out not what their parents and grandparents say is Indian, but what the subtleties of TV dictate to be Indian."[21] And, as the two reports show, television, not unlike its parents in Hollywood, says preciously little that is realistic about American Indians.

In another study which looks at the involvement of minorities "behind the scenes," the California Advisory Committee to the United States Commission on Civil Rights concluded that "minorities and women are poorly represented in decision making positions" and "top managers at studios have not been held accountable for effective affirmative action."[22] This 1978 study was the first major look at the employment of minorities in the motion picture industry since the hearings held in 1969, during which the Equal Employment Opportunity Commission stated that "discriminatory practices existed in both employment and portrayal of minorities and women."[23] Although the percentage of minority employees has doubled since 1969, the decrease in the total number of employees in the industry has rendered the net gains negligible.[24] Such common practices as union requirements for three members to endorse a prospective new member and questions which ask what one's father's occupation is serve to thwart minority applicants. In all categories of employment in the industry American Indians represent only .5 percent of the employees.[25] In an industry which depended for years on westerns and Saturday afternoon serials of the Lone Ranger, Red Ryder, and Indian "extras," it is deplorable that so few technical advisors or professionals are available as consultants. More accurate portrayal of American Indian traditions and a look at westward expansion and manifest destiny from a different perspective would be two major changes which might come about were American Indian people in more influential positions in the industry.

American Indian people have not been complacent about their lack

In Broken Arrow *James Stewart tenderly kisses Debra Paget, suggesting that American and Indian peoples were not necessarily incompatible. This movie with its sympathetic treatment of Indian culture represented an early break in Hollywood's depiction of Indians as savages without culture or compassion.*

of representation, nor have they silently accepted the inaccurate portrayals. In 1950 the Association on American Indian Affairs, disturbed by the continued misrepresentation on the screen, formed a National Film Committee to counteract the stereotype of the "bad, ruthless killers, schemers without honor, uncivilized savages . . ." of the movies, to focus public attention on the issues, and to provide expert information for the film producers.[26] The group claims as one of its successes the film *Broken Arrow,* one of the first films to deal sympathetically with American Indian material. The influence of this group and others such as the American Indian Historical Society in San Francisco and associations of American Indian actors provide constant reminders to the studios that American Indian people want jobs in the industry and also want to see their people's lives represented accurately.[27]

The entire population—Indian and non-Indian—is affected by the misrepresentation of Native Americans in the movies. In his study of American Indian children, Berry Brewton states that Indian children need to develop a better image of themselves, but more significant is his suggestion that non-Indians need more understanding and appreciation of the Indian so that their image of the group might also be improved. He cites evidence that the Indian's image of himself depends greatly on the image held by white society.[28] Jack Forbes in his studies of Indian and Chicano peoples echoes Brewton's conclusions: "Anglo American young people grow up in a 'never-never' land of mythology as regards non-whites and it is crucial for our society's future that damaging myths be exposed and eliminated."[29] When confronted with their own ignorance, whites respond in a variety of ways—denial of responsibility, guilt, or the adoption of a romantic view of the Native American. All of these responses have eventually found their way onto the screen.

What is the "mythology" of the American Indian? Certainly there are many "mythologies" about the people who were the first to walk the forests, climb the mountains, and plant corn in what is now America. The savage of Beadle dime novels, the romantic nomad of the forest created by Rousseau, the Indian princess with roots in Jamestown and branches as far as Dame Judith Anderson's portrayal in *Little Big Man,* the drunken Indian, the stoic cigar store vender, the old chief with the secrets of the ages in ancient mythology and oral tradition—all have remained as variants of the myth.

What better place to portray these fantasies of Americans than on the wide screen? Hollywood has managed to distort and stereotype almost every ethnic and religious group, but American Indians seem frozen in time as far as film is concerned. A few recent films use a twentiety-century setting, but by and large the Indian of the film exists in a world somewhere between the landing of the Pilgrims and the end of the nineteenth century, the primary focus being on the period between 1850 and 1900, the time when Indian people were desperately trying to hold onto their land and fighting for their lives. But because this period represents for non-Indian Americans a time of victory, of overcoming an obstacle in the way of progress, it is a glorified time. In order to justify mass slaughter and land grabbing, white producers were forced to portray Indians as savage, illiterate, and not suited for "modern" civilization. Certainly the Indian appeared primitive in the face of locomotives, repeating rifles, and the telegraph. The few who were no doubt descendants of Chingachgook, Pocahontas, or Squanto were "good" Indians. They either "vanished" or were transformed into the Tontos who knew their role in the changing society.

The images of early historians and writers still exist in the twentieth century. The noble savage who appeared as Natty Bumpo's companion was resurrected with Tonto. The scenes reproduced in Catlin paintings later appeared in *A Man Called Horse*. The drunken Indian of 1846 signing a worthless treaty was recreated in *Flap* (1970) during the 1960s. The feathered chief of Remington was still around in the 1970s, appearing as the reincarnated shaman in *Manitou* (1978).

It is difficult to know how much the distorted image on the screen has influenced generations of non-Indians. As part of a study on Indian Education, a Senate special subcommittee interviewed people all over the country. Their conclusions suggest that we all have a long way to go toward understanding the reality of American Indian life:

> To thousands of Americans, the American Indian is, and always will be, dirty, lazy, and drunk. That's the way they picture him; that's the way they treat him.

> . . . In every community visited by the subcommittee there was evidence among the white population of stereotypical opinions of Indians.

> . . . The basis for these stereotypes goes back into history—a history created by the white man to justify his exploitation of the Indian, a history the Indian is continually reminded of at school, on television, in books and at the movies.[30]

In that report Senator Edward Kennedy expressed a vision of America as "a nation of citizens determining their own destiny; of cultural difference flourishing in an atmosphere of mutual respect; of diverse people shaping their lives and the lives of their children."[31] If this is not the vision we see represented in one of the most pervasive and persuasive media of our lives, it is the vision we should be seeking.

What will happen to the filmic image of the Indian in the future is impossible to predict. If past history is any guide, films will find or develop a new stereotype, one which will accommodate a new popular image. Mass arts tend to the allegorical, preferring surfaces and types to essences and individuals, which allows them a broader or more universal appeal. And while we can expect to see Native Americans portrayed more sympathetically and with greater historical accuracy, the Indian in the popular film nevertheless will remain as one dimensional as all other types.

The cultural distortions which have been perpetuated by the motion picture industry reflect the moral obtuseness and ethical myopia technologically advanced peoples have generally exhibited toward those less advanced. After all, it was the early Greeks, the most civilized of Western cultures, who coined the word barbarian for those peoples who could not speak Greek and were therefore presumably denied access to the Greek way of life. So, too, the English tramped around the globe bearing their white man's burden with admirable tenacity, despite the reluctance of many of the peoples they conquered. It is not surprising then that white Americans allowed their sense of superiority and their allegiance to the idea of a manifest destiny to blunt their sensitivity. Unfortunately, films and television have not done much in the last few years to correct the misperceptions which were created. It would suggest an enormous insensitivity on the part of our culture to continue to produce the old films in the same old way. A reassessment is now in order.

NOTES

1. *Savagism and Civilization: A Study of the Indian and the American Mind* (1965).
2. Ibid., 4.
3. Ibid., 53.
4. *The Return of the Vanishing American* (1969).
5. The earliest graphic depictions of American Indians are contained in travel narratives dating back to 1505 and portray the Native American as a semi-naked savage. See Frank Weitenkampf's "How Indians Were Pictured in Earliest Days," *The New York Historical Society Quarterly*, 33 (October 1949), 213-21. Also see Robert F. Berkhofer, Jr., *The White Man's Indian: Images of the American Indian from Columbus to the Present* (1978).
6. For some interesting observations about the importance of the declining frontier see George N. Fenin's "The Western—Old and New," *Film Culture*, 2 (1956), 7-10.
7. For an interesting view of the popular imagery of the Native American in the 1870s see Robert A. Trennert's "Popular Imagery and the American Indian: A Centennial View," *New Mexico Historical Review*, 51 (1976), 215-30.
8. Most of the following information about the images of Indians found in early films was gleaned from Ralph and Natasha Friar's excellent book, *The Only Good Indian . . .: The Hollywood Gospel* (1972).

9. Ibid., 70.

10. Ibid., 137.

11. For a further discussion of this idea see John C. Ewers, *The Emergence of the Plains Indian as the Symbol of the North American Indian* (1964) and the same author's "The Static Images," in *Look to the Mountaintop* (1972), 107-9.

12. "The Make-Believe Indian," *Moving Picture World,* 7 (March 4, 1911), 473.

13. Alfred Ernest Dench, "The Dangers of Employing Redskins as Movie Actors," in *Making the Movies* (1915), 92-94.

14. Stanley Vestal, "The Hollywooden Indian." *Southwest Review,* 21 (1936), 418-23.

15. James F. Denton, "The Red Man Plays Indian." *Colliers,* 113 (March 18, 1944), 18-19.

16. For a lengthy and comprehensive discussion of these images see Charles L. P. Silet and Gretchen M. Bataille, "The Indian in the Film: A Critical Survey," *The Quarterly Review of Film Studies,* 2 (February 1977), 56-74.

17. A variety of the reviews of the films discussed in this section are listed and annotated in Gretchen M. Bataille and Charles L. P. Silet, "Popular Images of the Indian in the American Film," *The Journal of Popular Film,* 5 (1976), 171-82. An update of this listing is to be published in this journal shortly. See also Richard Schickel, "Why Indians Can't Be Villains Anymore," *The New York Times,* February 9, 1975, Section 2, pp. 1, 15.

18. See Pauline Kael, "American," *The New Yorker,* 45 (December 27, 1969), 47-50.

19. Philip French, "The Indian in the Western Movie," *Art in America,* 60 (July-August 1972), 32–39.

20. See Gretchen M. Bataille and Charles L. P. Silet, *The Pretend Indians: Images in the Movies,* a comprehensive collection of essays about the image of the Native American in the movies, to be published by Iowa State University Press in 1980.

21. *Window Dressing on the Set: An Update* (1979), 49.

22. *Behind the Scenes: Equal Employment Opportunity in the Motion Picture Industry* (1978), 42.

23. Ibid., 1.

24. Ibid., 41.

25. Ibid., 4.

26. Harold Mantell, "Counteracting the Stereotype," *American Indian,* 5 (Fall 1950), 16–20.

27. See Ward Churchill, Norbert Hill, and Mary Ann Hill, "Media Stereotyping and Native Response: An Historical Overview," *Indian Historian,* 11 (December 1978), 45–56, 63.

28. Berry Brewton, *The Education of the American Indians: A Survey of the Literature* (1968), 96–98.

29. Jack Forbes, *Education of the Culturally Different: A Multi-Cultural Approach* (Far West Laboratory for Educational Research and Development, 1969), 51.

30. Report #501 of the Committee on Labor and Public Welfare, U. S. Senate. Made by its Special Subcommittee on Indian Education. 91st Congress, 1st Session.

31. Ibid., ix.

3

BANDITS AND LOVERS: HISPANIC IMAGES IN AMERICAN FILM

Allen L. Woll

During recent years the developing nations of Africa, Asia, and South America have strongly criticized Western news coverage in their countries. They argue that the mass media in the United States and Europe acknowledge only the latest coups, revolutions, or earthquakes, and ignore any information which might portray these nations in a positive light. As a result, images of chaos and violence punctuate Western thinking about the Third World.

This is not a recent complaint, particularly for the nations of Central and South America. Throughout the nineteenth century, the American press considered the wars of independence, the taking of the Alamo, and the Spanish-American War as prime examples of the violent tendencies of Hispanic peoples. These images were echoed in political cartoons and popular literature as well. Hispanics in general and Mexicans in particular became characterized as violent and barbaric individuals in the media of the nineteenth century.[1]

Motion pictures easily adopted a pre-existing stereotype whenever denizens of Mexico were depicted. Although the majority of early silent films emphasized action and violence, the Mexican bandits were clearly among the vilest of the screen's villains. They robbed, murdered, plundered, raped, cheated, gambled, lied, and displayed virtually every vice that could be shown on the screen.

This image of the Mexican flowered in a series of "greaser" films, such as *Tony the Greaser* (1911), *Broncho Billy and the Greaser* (1914), and *The Greaser's Revenge* (1914). The term "greaser" swiftly supplanted "Mexican" or "Latin" as a synonym for the violent Hispanic. While the typical screen villain would primarily murder or steal, the Mexican "greaser" often carried his occupation to excess. More often than not, he enjoyed this subtle extension of the limits of violence. For example, a Mexican in *The Cowboy's Baby* (1910) threw the hero's child into a river, while the "greaser" in *A Western Child's Heroism* (1912) attacked the Americans who had previously saved his life.[2]

Not all "greasers" were violent and evil. A Mexican might redeem himself if he showed loyalty to the North American heroes. In *Tony the Greaser* (1911), Tony saves the landowner's daughter from the clutches of marauding Mexican bandits. Although he is killed, he is allowed to kiss the daughter's handkerchief as he expires. An advertisement for the film explains the incongruous aspect of Tony's character: "From force of habit, some might call him a 'Greaser'; true, he is a Mexicano, but a man of noble instincts and chivalrous nature." Tony, however, was the exception to the rule.

The Mexican Revolution accentuated the Latin image of violence on the screen as a series of pseudo-documentaries of the conflict were exhibited in American theatres. Real and fictional events soon began to blur. Indeed, one of the leading agrarian revolutionaries, Pancho Villa, signed a contract with the Mutual Film Corporation. Villa allowed Mutual cameramen to follow his exploits, and, in return, he agreed to fight during daylight hours if possible and delay his attacks until cameras were in position. Villa accepted this unusual contract because his forces needed money for munitions. Gunther Lessing, a young lawyer, arranged the deal and deposited $25,000 for Villa in an El Paso bank. Mutual also signed agreements for a second feature, a life of Villa, to be directed by D. W. Griffith. Raoul Walsh, later a noted Hollywood director, was sent to Mexico to shoot background footage and some action scenes. Griffith, however, was too busy filming *The Birth of a Nation,* so the assignment was given to Christy Cabanne. The young Walsh portrayed the agrarian hero as a youth in *The Life of Villa* (1915).[3]

Each of these "documentaries" emphasized the military aspects of the Mexican Revolution and ignored the political differences between the various power contenders. *Barbarous Mexico* (1913) seemed typical of this wartime series. The *New York Times* praised the film at its premiere, noting that "there are many scenes in which General Villa is

The image of the violent Hispanic gained some legitimacy in the Mutual Film Corporation's pseudo-documentaries about the Mexican agrarian revolutionary, Pancho Villa (extreme left in this 1913 shot). To accommodate the studio's film crew, Villa adjusted his fighting tactics.

seen directing the movements of his troops and artillery, and cavalry battles are shown with remarkable clearness. Other views show the burning of dead bodies on the battlefield."[4]

The "greaser" was briefly retired during World War I as Hollywood switched its villains to those of German descent, but he soon returned after the Armistice. By this time Mexico had had enough. It was no longer going to be ridiculed throughout the world. In late 1919, the Mexican government sent a formal letter of complaint to film producers protesting their emphasis on the "worst conditions they could find." The letter ended with a subtle warning of a restriction of motion picture photography in Mexico.

This missive did little to change Hollywood practices, so in February, 1922, the Mexican government decided to ban all films that portrayed its citizens unfavorably. A high official explained the action: "The usual portrayal of the Mexican in moving pictures is a bandit or a sneak. Ill will toward Mexico has been inflamed by these pictures to such an extent that the Mexican government found it necessary to make such a protest." It was soon realized that banning a single film would do little harm to major film producers, so Mexico proposed to ban all films produced by the company that released the offensive motion picture. The Mexican government hoped that the threat of the loss of the entire Mexican market would prevent Hollywood from reviving the "greaser" for international audiences. The strategy worked—in part. The Famous Players-Lasky offices, which had just completed a one-hundred film deal with Mexican distributors, was shaken by the pronouncement and issued a statement saying that "the wishes of the government would be respected." Panama swiftly followed Mexico's lead with similar restrictive legislation.[5]

Hispanic-Americans, unlike other ethnic groups in the United States, became the unintentional beneficiaries of international pressures on Hollywood which worked in their behalf. With the threat of the loss of a major film market (first Mexico, and potentially the rest of South America), Hollywood began to treat its neighbors to the south more gingerly. The "greaser" swiftly lost his Mexican nationality in the attempt to diffuse potential complaints, but he refused to disappear from the screen. Clever subterfuges placed an unnamed "greaser" in a new locale. Rather than use the name of an actual country and risk offending its inhabitants, screenwriters began to create mythical cities and nations. *The Dove* (1928), directed by Roland West, provided the most obvious example. The film concerned Don José María y Sandoval (Noah Beery), who considered himself "the bes' dam' *caballero* in Costa Roja." Costa Roja, as the title cards explained, was located in the Mediterranean.

This flimsy guise hardly fooled anyone. Mordaunt Hall, critic for the *New York Times,* explained: "Taken by and large, José is perhaps a screen character to which the Mexican government might have objected, for he is greedy, sensuous, boastful, cold-blooded, irritable, and quite a wine-bibber, but he does dress well. He hates to have his luncheon spoiled by a noisy victim of his shooting squad."[6] Thus, the Costa Roja subterfuge diffused possible criticism since José was not a resident of a particular Latin American country. Unfortunately, when *The Dove* was remade during the sound era as *Girl of the Rio* (1932), the screenwriters apparently forgot this distinction and situated this film in a Mexican bordertown. As a result, Mexico renewed its long-standing threat to ban motion pictures produced by companies that released films offensive to Mexicans.

The anger with *Girl of the Rio* spread beyond Mexican borders, with Panama and Nicaragua agreeing to prohibit showings of the film. Spain and several Latin American nations swiftly followed suit with a series of reciprocal treaties banning films which "attacked, slandered, defamed, insulted or misrepresented" the various nations of Hispanic origin. Repeated offenses would warrant an embargo of all feature films produced by the offending company. Nicaragua, Peru, Chile, Argentina, Spain, and El Salvador participated in similar arrangements.[7] The willingness of other nations to join Mexico's protest reflected the realization that Hollywood's "Mexican" was actually a universal Hispanic stereotype. As a result of the growing threat of economic reprisals, Hollywood's image of the Latin softened as the 1930s progressed, but certain stereotyped notions never wholly disappeared.

Warner Brothers' *Bordertown* (1935), directed by Archie Mayo, best reveals the ambivalence with which Hollywood viewed its Latin neighbors. *Bordertown* was no exception to the socially conscious films produced by Warners in the 1930s, for, in many ways, it was one of the few sympathetic portraits of the Mexican-American yet produced. Johnny Ramírez (Paul Muni) studies hard at law school and graduates at the top of his class. Yet, in his first courtroom appearance he succumbs to anger and attacks the defendant. He is ejected bodily from the court and is disbarred. He then drifts outside the law and becomes the manager of a gambling casino.

In many ways Ramírez is no different from the others in Warner's stable of Depression gangster heroes as seen in *Little Caesar* (1931) or *Public Enemy* (1931).[8] Yet, he has certain frailties which Hollywood generally considered as characteristic of the Mexican. Whereas Rico and Tommy Powers are cool and calculating, Ramírez is subject to uncontrolled fits of anger which bring his downfall. The viewer is thus asked to believe that Ramírez has studied diligently in night school for several years, but can lose his temper in his first courtroom appearance. This unexpected excitability remained a characteristic of the Latin in film. Lupe Velez became the specific exponent of this trend as a concrete demonstration that Latins are unpredictable, passionate, and uncontrollable. Her film titles—*Hot Pepper* (1933), *Strictly Dynamite* (1934), and *Mexican Spitfire* (1940)—show this clearly.

A second aspect of *Bordertown* reveals yet another common stereotype of the Latin during the 1930s. Ramírez is portrayed as a loner after his fall from grace. At last, one evening in his gambling casino, he meets the society woman who brought his downfall in his first courtroom trial. She is strangely attracted to Ramírez. After a few dates, he decides to propose. They go for a ride on a deserted country road, and Johnny pops the question. The heiress appears shocked and replies, "We aren't of the same tribe, savage!" Johnny is irate ("I was O.K. to kiss and have fun with, but not O.K. to marry"). The young woman is disgusted by his outburst and runs away from him.

In her haste she runs across the road and is hit by a car and killed. Johnny is sobered by the experience and sells his gambling casino. He then uses the money to establish a law school in his hometown. At last he realizes where he belongs—with his own people—the Chicanos. He will never try to leave again.

Johnny is thus unable to find love. The notion of a "Latin Lover," popularized in the 1920s by Valentino and Novarro, offered little solace to Latin American males on the screen during the 1930s. The image of the Latin Lover defined a Mediterranean screen character, rather than an Hispanic-American. Thus, the Latin American males on the screen during the 1930s seemed incapable of having a normal adult relationship with a woman. The Latin Lover sobriquet actually seemed more appropriate for the Hispanic women in this period. Both Dolores Del Rio and Lupe Velez typified the sultry Spanish temptress of the silver screen. Each had the uncanny ability to attract admirers by the slightest movement of an eyelash. Their favorite beaux were inevitably North Americans. In the face of the dominant

Bordertown reflected Hollywood's ambivalence about Latin people in the 1930s. Johnny Ramirez (Paul Muni) was a blend of unharnessed emotion and cool reason, criminality and honor. Both drawn to and repelled by American society and women, he found his "true" place among his own people in the end.

sensuality of the Anglo heroes, Hispanic suitors typically withdrew from the heated competition for the Latin maid. The Hispanic male remained alone and unloved.

In *Bordertown,* Johnny Ramírez turns outside the law and runs a gambling casino. Again, it seems to have been a common assumption that gambling was the Latin's favorite occupation. During the 1930s the Mexican-American actor Leo Carrillo appeared in more than thirty films. In almost half he portrayed a man involved in illicit activities, usually gambling, murder, or the rackets. Even if Carrillo had a legitimate source of money, as in *Girl of the Rio* or in *In Caliente* (1935), he still was depicted as bearing an uncontrollable urge to engage in illegal acts. Therefore, Ramírez's successful rise in the gambling business in *Bordertown* should come as no surprise since these activities were the rule rather than the exception.

The final irony of *Bordertown* was the presence of Paul Muni in the lead role. Covered in a dark shade of pancake makeup, Muni is only portraying a Latin. In order to prepare for the role, Muni haunted Olvera Street in the Spanish section of Los Angeles, but it was not enough. "I have to go swimming in tequila," he said, and traveled to Mexicali with Carroll Graham, author of the original novel of *Bordertown.* He also began taking private Spanish lessons before the shooting began.[9] Yet, it seems incongruous for North Americans of European descent to portray the major Latin roles of the 1930s while the real Latins languished in minor roles. While Ricardo Cortez may have played the romantic lead in several films of the period, his name is misleading. In reality he was Jacob Kranz of Budapest. False Latins often found the road to success easier than real Latins in the 1930s.

The basic assumption of Latin homogeneity allowed this practice to continue, as dark skin and bulging white eyeballs seemed the prime qualifications for a Latin role. More often than not, these characteristics could be supplied in the makeup room. The Latin women suffered similarly. Although, unlike their male counterparts, Latin women might achieve leading roles, there was no guarantee that they would portray a citizen of their appropriate country. The slightly darker skin seemed to allow the women to represent any minority without the slightest respect for geographical bounds. For example, Lupe Velez commented that she had portrayed "Chinese, Eskimos, Japs, squaws, Hindus, Swedes, Malays, and Javanese."[10] She came somewhat closer to home in *Kongo* (1931), where she played a Portuguese adrift in Africa, but even then her Spanish accent must have tickled Brazilian audiences. It was not until the 1940s that Lupe Velez achieved a firm screen identity as a Mexican in her *Mexican Spitfire* series.

Hollywood thus virtually ignored the Latin during the 1930s, a

Hot-blooded, hip-swaying Latin women exude sensuality in Hollywood films. Dolores Del Rio, who starred in many Hollywood romances set in Latin America, entrances Charles Farrell in this scene from The Red Dance *(1928).*

habit which changed abruptly by the end of the decade. Suddenly in 1939 films utilizing Latin stars, locales, and historical heroes flooded American screens. Such eminent leaders as Benito Juarez and Simón Bolívar were immortalized on film. Talent scouts brought planeloads of Latin American talent to Hollywood, as viewers discovered and delighted in Carmen Miranda, Desi Arnaz, and Cesar Romero. Films also began to differentiate among varying South American locales, allowing viewers to spend a *Weekend in Havana* (1941), or *Midnight in Mexico* (1948), or travel *Down Argentine Way* (1940).

This deluge of films with Latin American themes may be partly attributed to deliberate government policy. With the growing threat of war with Germany, the United States was eager to ease any remaining tensions with South American governments in order to maintain hemispheric unity as a bulwark against foreign invasion.

President Franklin D. Roosevelt thus attempted to resurrect the "Good Neighbor Policy" which had been ignored in the 1930s in the face of the Mexican government's expropriation of American oil companies and American intervention in Nicaragua and Cuba. Anxious to assuage these differences, Roosevelt explained the basis for his vigorous reassertion of the Good Neighbor Policy: "I began to visualize a wholly new attitude toward other American Republics based on an honest and sincere desire, first, to remove from their minds all fear of American aggression—territorial or financial—and, second, to take them into a kind of hemispheric partnership in which no Republic would take undue advantage."[11]

While all government agencies were expected to support the official policy of inter-American unity, a major effort was expected from the Office of the Coordinator of Inter-American Affairs and its director Nelson Rockefeller.[12] Rockefeller appointed a former associate and then vice-president of the Museum of Modern Art, John Hay Whitney, to head the Motion Picture Section of this office. Similarly, the Hays Office, the industry's self-regulatory agency which controlled film censorship, also appointed an expert in Latin American affairs in order to avoid blatant errors which might offend the "neighbors to the South." Will Hays declared that the appointment of Addison Durland to this post would "be another step in the motion picture industry's cooperation in current events to promote hemispheric solidarity."[13] This was not mere hyperbole, since Durland, director of NBC's Spanish division, spoke the language fluently and held a degree from the Universidad Nacional de Cuba.

Although the activities of the Motion Picture Section were primarily regulatory, the office also participated in the production of several newsreels and short subjects.[14] Rockefeller and Whitney were instrumental in the hiring of Walt Disney "as the first Hollywood producer of motion pictures specifically intended to carry a message of democracy and friendship below the Rio Grande." Whitney claimed that Disney would show "the truth about the American way," and another executive proclaimed him "the greatest goodwill ambassador of all time." He added that "people all over the world know Disney and love his characters." Therefore, "they would believe Disney's message of Americanism."[15] Although the Motion Picture Section proclaimed that this was "in no wise a propaganda project," memos from the executive division, published after the war, reveal otherwise. The program directors suggested a series of "direct propaganda films" couched in the simplicity of the animation medium ("If anyone wants details, let him buy a book!").[16]

In addition to these propaganda functions, both the Office of the Coordinator of Inter-American Affairs and the Hays Office provided technical assistance whenever necessary, and applied pressure if studios depicted Latins in an unfavorable light. For example, Whitney convinced Twentieth Century-Fox to spend $40,000 in order to reshoot scenes from *Down Argentine Way* which erroneously described native customs.[17] Whitney's office also encouraged Hollywood stars to travel to Latin America to spread goodwill and reassert the government's commitment to hemispheric unity. In the first flush of enthusiasm Alice Faye, Wallace Beery, and Ann Sheridan announced their intention to visit South America, but Whitney scrapped these plans after a junket by Douglas Fairbanks, Jr., proved a disaster, as the star inadvertently offended everyone he met.[18]

Thus, the onus of the production of films promoting American unity lay on Hollywood. The response of the studio executives was indeed surprising. The seven major studios were in the midst of an expensive antitrust suit brought by the government, which sought to prevent the monopolistic practices of "block booking" and "blind selling" which forced theater owners to purchase films in groups from the distributors without any knowledge of the relative merits of the films or the ability to reject any films in the package. Despite the resentment over the government's suit, Hollywood fervently responded to the patriotic call and produced Latin-themed motion pictures in unprecedented numbers.[19]

Yet, Hollywood's rationale for the resurrection of films with Latin themes betrayed a complex of motives. Patriotism, an emotion that has been muted in this day and age, seemed quite alive in the prewar era. Films not only promoted the importance of national unity in the face of a foreign threat, but also actively encouraged the entry of the United States into this hitherto European war. Despite protestations to the contrary, many filmmakers made no pretense of neutrality in the period before Pearl Harbor.

The isolationist forces in the Senate, led by Gerald Nye, brought Hollywood to task for its production of so-called propaganda films which encouraged American entry into the war. The inquiry of the subcommittee of the Interstate Commerce Committee was fortunately brief, aborted only by the attack on Pearl Harbor, which naturally stilled debates on isolationism. Nevertheless, studio executives faced this hostile inquisition with profound courage. For example, one of the first witnesses was Harry M. Warner, president of Warner Brothers, which produced *Sergeant York, Confessions of a Nazi Spy, Juarez,* and other films glorifying United States participation in wars which defended democracy and freedom. Warner, confident of his principles, claimed that he was ready to give "all personal resources to aid in the defeat of the Nazi menace to the American people."[20]

The testimony of Warner, Darryl F. Zanuck, and other studio executives ostensibly revealed a patriotic motive for the production of films designed to encourage American participation in the war. Consequently, it might be argued that studios manifested a similar disposition to produce films about Latin America in order to promote hemispheric unity.

Despite talk of such motives, a more basic economic rationale existed for the production of films with Latin themes. The coming of the war in Europe drastically lessened the influx of foreign film revenues. Certain countries, conquered by the Germans, banned American films outright. Others, such as Britain and Australia, needed foreign exchange so desperately that they decreed a fifty percent reduction in the amount spent for American films. A glance at the major foreign film markets revealed the precarious situation, since, by 1940, only Britain remained an importer of American films. In 1939 hopes for future markets centered on four areas: Japan, Holland, Scandinavia, and Central and South America. Again, by 1940, only Central and South America remained major importers of American films, owing to the changing political situation.[21] In order to compensate for lost foreign revenues, Hollywood began to look toward Latin America for economic relief and actively to seek this budding market's share of the film dollar. Thus, the film capital's Good Neighbor Policy reflected more than a patriotic gesture in response to government pressure.

Hollywood's attitude toward the Latin countries suddenly bordered on reverence. *Juarez* (1939), the first film of the South American cycle, offered a panegyric to a nineteenth-century Mexican president, and portrayed him as an equal to Abraham Lincoln. Indeed, the shadow of Lincoln haunted this enterprise. Juárez, played by Paul Muni, rarely appeared in his office without a portrait of the Great Emancipator peering over his shoulder. Similarly, forced to flee before advancing French troops, Juárez removed his portrait of Lincoln from his office before gathering any of his official documents, thus revealing the importance of the American president to him.

This dramatic link between Juárez and Lincoln leads to the suspicion that Juárez is more a symbol than a man. The film's rhetoric enforces this interpretation, as the Mexican president's dialogue transcends the historical and borders on the universal. Juárez becomes the "defender of democratic principles," and Maximilian and Napoleon III represent "the dictators who seize power illegally." Juárez's critique of European imperialism suggests an analogy with the United States in the years before World War II. Indeed, the Mexican president's climactic speech could just as easily have been delivered in Washington, D. C., in 1939 as in Mexico City in 1864: "By

Juarez was a major Hollywood contribution to the Good Neighbor Policy. Paul Muni portrayed the Mexican president as an extension of American democratic ideals and as a disciple of Abraham Lincoln.

what right, señores, do the Great Powers of Europe invade the lands of simple people . . . kill all who do not make them welcome . . . destroy their fields . . . and take the fruit of their toil from those who survive? . . . The world must know the fate of any usurper who sets his foot upon this soil." As a matter of fact, the "political parallels were so closely drawn" that the critic for the *New York Times* commented that it was not at all difficult to "read between the lines."[22]

Although *Juarez* masked an attempt to urge United States participation in the European war, the film avoided blatant stereotypes of the Mexican and revealed a newfound sensitivity toward Latin characters. Juárez was the first "Mexican" hero of the American screen, and Warners assured the Mexican authorities that he would be portrayed as accurately as possible. Aeneas MacKenzie, one of the film's three screenwriters, left for Mexico City ten months before the initial preparation of the script, although it would have been easy to prepare a scenario from Bertita Harding's *The Phantom Crown*

(1934) which Warners had just purchased. During his lengthy visit, MacKenzie read more than seven-hundred secondary sources, the President's private and official correspondence, and contemporary newspapers. As a matter of fact, a portion of the film's dialogue was derived from Congressional debates of the period.

Juarez impressed its intended audience both in the United States and Mexico. President Lazaro Cárdenas urged that the film be presented in the Palace of Fine Arts, the first motion picture so honored. The premiere audience responded warmly to the film's message, and stopped the show with applause when Juárez explained the difference between constitutional democracy and despotism. It was deemed prudent to cut only one line for the Mexican premiere. In the original version, Juárez leans over the body of the recently executed Maximilian and whispers, "Forgive me." In Mexico, Juárez bent over, moved his lips, and not a sound was heard. This reportedly headed off a confrontation with leftist elements in the audience, upset by the prospect of a Mexican president apologizing to an "imperialist aggressor."[23]

With this newfound reverence toward the Latin, Hollywood abruptly reversed old stereotypes. No longer was the Latin considered an ignorant peasant. In RKO's *They Met in Argentina* (1941) co-star Buddy Ebsen is surprised to find everyone from secretaries to ranch hands are able to speak English with only the slightest trace of an accent. Similarly, films began to portray each nation differently, each possessing an individual culture and history. Again, Ebsen is surprised to learn that Argentine immigration patterns in the nineteenth century paralleled those of the United States. Uniting these new images of the Latin was the common assumption that North America and South America were quite similar. For example, the gauchos of *They Met in Argentina* sing the same song that the North American hero sang as a youth on his Texas ranch. The similarity between the two cultures was stressed in order to accentuate the importance of Pan-American unity.[24]

Despite Hollywood's apparent good intentions, filmmakers actually succeeded in replacing one film stereotype with another. Owing to the popularity of the new Latin rhythms—the conga, the samba, the rumba—Latins became identified with their music, and would rarely appear in American musicals without singing the melodies of their native countries. These hip-swaying dances, so different from North American rhythms, gave Latin artists an increased sensuality, which Carmen Miranda, Desi Arnaz, and others emphasized in their screen performances. The use of symbolism often accentuated this image. For example, Desi Arnaz appeared bracketed in flames as he sang the main production number in *Too Many Girls* (1940), while several college coeds danced at his feet. Busby Berkeley went even further in *The Gang's All Here* (1943) by surrounding Carmen Miranda with several dancing girls with six-foot bananas on their heads.[25]

Yet, this new sensuality, an erotic compensation for years of Latin docility on the screen, rarely achieved its desired fulfillment. Despite the aura of the Latin Lover, the performers from South America rarely managed to marry the hero or heroine. In the 1933 film *Flying Down to Rio* the North American bandleader easily steals Dolores Del Rio from the arms of her Brazilian fiance, Raul Roulien. Nothing has changed by 1941, as James Ellison easily woos Maureen O'Hara, playing an Argentine, away from her boyfriend Alberto Vila in *They Met in Argentina*. The same pattern can be seen in *Too Many Girls* and *Pan-Americana* (1945), both from RKO studios. The North American still maintained a sexual superiority over the South American, despite a startling reversal in the Latin image in film.

When the war ended, Hollywood lost its extravagant and obsessive interest in Latin America, and a calmer atmosphere pervaded postwar films concerning our neighbors to the south. New motion pictures generally avoided the musical stereotypes so common during World War II and considered instead the situation of Hispanics in American society.

The film that best encapsulates Hollywood's abrupt change in attitude is *A Medal For Benny* (1945), based on a story by John Steinbeck. Benny never appears in the film. He is awarded a post-humous Congressional Medal of Honor for "killing one hundred Japs," and the townspeople of Pantera, California, have a hero on their hands. Before the war, the citizens of Pantera had ignored Benny. The only notice of his existence was in the jail records. Prone to drunkenness and violent outbursts, Benny was often arrested for disorderly conduct. In desperation the city fathers finally booted the obstreperous youth out of town.

The mayor and the town council are eager to forget this fact. As the former troublemaker becomes a hero, the town begins to take notice of its Mexican-American minority. Charlie (J. Carroll Naish), Benny's father, has repeatedly requested a loan from the bank president in order to pay off the mortgage on his humble home, but he was always refused. As soon as the news of Benny's medal is received in Pantera, the bank president escorts Charlie into his office and grants the long-awaited loan. This newfound interest in Charlie and the other Mexican-Americans of the town is based not on social justice but on mere greed. The town is eager to exploit its newfound hero in hopes that a celebration will draw tourists, business, and investment to Pantera. Suddenly, Old Charlie is described as "a member of one of the best families in the town" by the bank president. "Only this afternoon, he was doing business in my bank," he explains. Charlie's friends, who understand the true nature of this business, look on with horror and disdain. "Is he loco?" someone asks.

Charlie is moved to a palatial mansion before the ceremony, but he finally realizes that he is perpetuating a falsehood by living in this beautiful home. The pleas of the Chamber of Commerce ("You get the glory and we get the gravy.") are to no avail, and Charlie returns to his tiny home late one night. On the day of the award ceremony Charlie is nowhere to be found. The mayor and a five-star general drive to the shantytown to search for him. "You can't go there," says the mayor, "it's just a lot of shacks." "Some mighty fine Americans have come out of shacks," explains the general.

Charlie is given his son's Medal of Honor on his own doorstep. He explains to a radio audience that "Benny's house doesn't matter, because the country must depend on all kinds of people." Charlie is vindicated, and the townspeople appear foolish as the film ends.

This film is unusual in many respects. Appearing at the end of the war, *A Medal for Benny* avoided the Hollywood extravaganza approach to the life of the Mexican-American. The first half of the film is a straightforward examination of the lives of the "paisanos"—defined by the title card as "a simple, friendly people who were the original settlers of California." The loves, family relationships, occupations, and social life of these citizens are explored in the film. Joe Morales (Arturo de Cordova) experiences a love life which Johnny Ramírez *(Bordertown)* lacked in the 1930s. Here he courts a woman (Dorothy Lamour) and by the end of the film wins her hand. At last, home and family are as revered as in a film with North American protagonists.

Additionally, the Mexican-American in *A Medal For Benny* is no longer the butt of the jokes, nor is he depicted as an evil character. For the first time the Anglo citizens become the villains. The leading members of the town are seen as foolish, greedy, selfish, and intolerant. The Chicanos here display the admirable traits which their Anglo brethren seem to lack.

The attitude of the citizens of Pantera is in many ways symbolic of Hollywood's attitude toward Latin America. During the war, as European markets declined, the film industry was eager to woo Latin film dollars and exploit native talent. As soon as the war ended and former film markets reopened, Hollywood lost interest in its Good Neighbor Policy and abandoned the Latin American extravaganzas of the wartime period.

Yet, despite the reorientation of film markets toward Europe, Hollywood had not forgotten what it had learned during the war. By 1949, the twenty Latin American republics represented almost one-fifth of the total foreign markets for American films. Less than ten percent of the world population at this time furnished roughly twenty percent of foreign-earned film royalties. While Hollywood may have lost interest in actively courting this sizable segment of the world film audience, film producers tried not to offend or diminish it either. Memories of a burned-down Argentine theater after a showing of *Argentine Nights,* as well as audience riots, forced Hollywood studios to realize that they could no longer win foreign audiences if they presented stereotyped or derogatory versions of the Latin character.

Hollywood's desire not to antagonize South American audiences led the Motion Picture Association of America to establish an International Information Center in Los Angeles. Two Latin American experts assisted screenwriters, directors, and producers in the preparation of films dealing with Latin American characters. Offensive portrayals could thus be eliminated before the filming was begun.[26]

Not all unfavorable views of the Latin were removed in this reasonable and pacific manner. The Department of the Interior in Mexico seized all film shot by John Huston for the *Treasure of Sierra Madre* (1948) in Tampico. Mayor Fernando San Pedro prohibited the Warner Brothers crew from filming scenes at the Liberty Plaza and old parts of the city in which "drunks, ragged, dirty beggars, and others astride gaunt burros were depicted by the actors." Huston protested that he was portraying Tampico in 1925, not the Mexico of 1948, but it was to no avail. As a result, the bordertown sequences were considerably cleaned up to satisfy the Mexican authorities.[27]

While the advisory boards and the protests from the Latin American governments certainly tempered the Latin image on film, one additional factor eased the awkward situation. Co-productions between North American and Latin American film companies began to appear after World War II. As often as not, these films were shot on South American soil with Latin crews and frequently with Latin actors. Hollywood tended to supply the funding, screenwriters, directors, and stars. For the first time, Latin Americans had direct participation in the making of films destined for North American audiences. Complaints that could formerly have been voiced only after the film's completion could now be presented during the planning process. As a result, films that were formerly praiseworthy, now created Latin Americans of heroic proportions. *Way of the Gaucho* (1952) and *The Fugitive* (1948) were perhaps the best examples of this trend.[28]

Also remarkable in the postwar era was the fact that actual Latins were assuming leading roles in Hollywood films. For each Marlon Brando *(Viva Zapata),* there was also a Ricardo Montalban and a

Fernando Lamas. *Salt of the Earth,* directed by Herbert Biberman in 1953, shattered all precedents by casting all major parts with Hispanics or Hispanic-Americans.[29]

Unfortunately, the advances of the postwar years have not continued to the present day. Outdated stereotypes have slowly returned to the American screen by the late 1960s. The violent and bloodthirsty "greaser" has reappeared in such films as *Bring Me the Head of Alfredo Garcia* (1974), *Duck, You Sucker* (1972), and *The Good, The Bad, and The Ugly* (1968). "The Ugly" is Eli Wallach's characterization of a shifty and scheming Mexican. At the same time, the bumbling Latin has become an object of ridicule in *Viva Max!* (1970) and *Bananas* (1971). Serious attempts to consider Latin American personalities have gone awry as in *Che!* (1969), and pseudo-Latins have remained in leading roles, such as Alan Arkin's *Popi* (1975). Yet, more often than not, Hispanic characters have been excluded in recent screenplays.

This surprising reversion to former practices has its roots in a variety of motives. In an economic sense, Hollywood films have ceased to dominate Latin American film markets as they did prior to 1940. Local productions, especially in Mexico, Brazil, and Argentina, have come to rival North American products in both quantity and quality. As a result, the role of international pressure on Hollywood filmmakers has lessened considerably. On the other hand, the demands for change in motion picture images has switched from foreign countries to domestic groups, such as Ricardo Montalban's "Nosotros," which have questioned Hollywood's use of offensive stereotypes.

Hispanic-Americans have had ample reason for complaint in recent years. Although they represent almost six per cent of the American population, they have been virtually ignored by motion pictures, as Hollywood's Latins have usually been "foreigners." When films began to discover the presence of the Hispanic-Americans during the 1960s, they concentrated on only one aspect of their lives: urban violence. *West Side Story* (1961) popularized a romantic version of gang warfare, a topic which other films have tackled with gritty realism. *The Young Savages* (1961) and *Badge 373* (1973) Americanized the "greaser" as a member of a Puerto Rican street gang. Vincent Canby noted that the latter film blamed the Puerto Ricans for every evil deed that occurred in the screenplay. The Puerto Rican Action Coalition urged Paramount to withdraw the "racist" film from circulation, but Paramount President Frank Yablans refused. Despite countless complaints, this pattern has lingered into the 1970s, as both *The Warriors* (1978) and *Boulevard Nights* (1979) have continued the history of the violent Hispanic-American. Both Puerto Ricans and Chicanos argue that this is the only image of their people that films have displayed.

While motion pictures have tended to ignore topics of concern to

Hispanic-Americans in recent years, television has attempted to fill the gap. Television has repeated several mistakes that motion pictures had initiated, but it has proved responsive to demands from various organizations for the elimination of derogatory Latin American stereotypes. Both the Frito Bandito and Chiquita Banana were eliminated from commercials after repeated complaints. Similarly, during the early days of *Chico and the Man,* many Chicano organizations criticized the late Freddie Prinze's portrayal of the shiftless Chico. After several meetings with Los Angeles community groups, the portrayal of Chico was toned down and the producers agreed to increase Hispanic employment on the show. While many detective series have borrowed the Hispanic gang member as a stock villain, several shows have offered sympathetic views of the Hispanic-American. *Lou Grant,* for example, presented a 1978 show concerning the plight of illegal aliens in Los Angeles—a show which won considerable praise.

Thus, despite some hopeful signs, Latin stereotypes of nineteenth-century origin have remained rooted in the American media until the present day. Although political and economic needs have motivated modifications in the standard stereotypes discussed herein, these unflattering images have not been eradicated from American popular culture. As a result, Hispanic-Americans, the fastest-growing minority group in the United States today, need to exercise continued vigilance of the mass media's depiction of characters of Spanish origin. It is a responsibility which Hispanic-Americans view of prime importance. Max Ferra, who directs a workshop for Hispanic performers in New York City, explained this problem in a recent interview: "We want to show America what we are all about—that we are not stereotypes. Let me put it this way, we do not want to be thought of as Chiquita Bananas anymore."[30]

NOTES

1. Mark Reisler, *By the Sweat of Their Brow: Mexican Immigrant Labor in the United States, 1900-1940,* (1976), Chapter 6.

2. Allen L. Woll, *The Latin Image in American Film* (1977), 6-10.

3. Kevin Brownlow, *The Parade's Gone By* (1968), 224.

4. *New York Times,* May 10, 1914, IV, p. 7.

5. Ibid., February 11, 1922, p. 15. See also *Moving Picture World,* 40 (April 26, 1919), 532.

6. *New York Times,* January 3, 1928, p. 28.

7. League of Nations, *Treaty Series,* vol. 165 (1935), No. 3818.

8. Andrew Bergman, *We're in the Money: Depression America and Its Films* (1971), Chapter 1.

9. *Saturday Evening Post*, January 2, 1932, p. 26.

10. Jerome Lawrence, *The Life and Times of Paul Muni* (1974).

11. Bryce Wood, *The Making of the Good Neighbor Policy* (1961), 130-31.

12. For a history of this office see Donald W. Rowland, comp., *History of the Office of the Coordinator of Inter-American Affairs* (1947).

13. *Variety*, April 2, 1941, p. 14.

14. Orson Welles's *It's All True* (1942), a joint venture with RKO, was one of the Division's most renowned failures. See Joseph McBride, *Orson Welles* (1973), Chapter 8.

15. *Motion Picture Herald*, January 10, 1942, p. 30.

16. *Politics*, 2 (July 1945), 211.

17. *Variety*, February 19, 1941, p. 5.

18. Ibid., June 25, 1941, p. 8.

19. *Newsweek*, July 22, 1940, p. 12.

20. *Moving Picture Screen and Radio Propaganda*, Subcommittee of the Committee on Interstate Commerce, September 23, 1941, 338ff.

21. *Variety*, September 3, 1940, p. 6.

22. *New York Times*, April 30, 1939, IX, p. 5.

23. Ibid., July 2, 1939, IX, p. 4; and *Variety*, December 27, 1939, p. 28.

24. *Time*, November 9, 1942, pp. 96-98.

25. See Tony Thomas and Jim Terry, *The Busby Berkeley Book* (1973), 152-54.

26. *Américas*, 1 (October 1949), 3.

27. *New York Times*, February 22, 1947, p. 17.

28. *New York Times Magazine*, March 23, 1947, p. 17.

29. Herbert Biberman, *Salt of the Earth* (1965), 43-44.

30. *New York Times*, February 18, 1979, I, p. 16.

4

THE FATE OF LA FAMIGLIA: ITALIAN IMAGES IN AMERICAN FILM

Daniel Sembroff Golden

America's media heroes are wearing blue collars in the late 1970s, as the ethnic working-class experience has become a hot commodity in the television and film studios of California. And after years of either neglect or abusive stereotyping in the gangster and *film noir* genres, the Italian-American is in the forefront of this new media ethnicity. Each year's televised Academy Awards presentation documents the frail mortality of the archetypal American heroes of old—the WASP loners of impeccable chivalry and integrity, moving through a landscape of big sky and grand moral gesture. And, with the eclipse of John Wayne, Henry Fonda, and Jimmy Stewart, we witness a new cadre of Oscar nominees and recipients with names like Pacino, Scorsese, Coppola, De Niro, and Cimino.

In a way, it is not surprising that the Italian-American experience has become both a marketable and memorable topic of contemporary media. In the decade since the waning of the Vietnam war, American urban politics have been marked by a distinct ethnic signature quite different from old-style social-hall politicking, Daleyesque machinations, and neighborhood bloc voting. Rather, we have seen, to use Michael Novak's term, the rise of the "unmeltable" ethnics, a core of essentially white, lower middle-class constituencies stolidly and insistently resisting institutional incursions into their community lives.[1]

Poles, Slovaks, Irish, and especially Italian-Americans have formed lobbying units to combat federal and state governments on such crucial issues as school integration, bussing, and urban renewal. Jimmy Carter's 1976 campaign support of "ethnic purity" may well have been a public relations blooper, but it went to the heart of the issue—a pervasive fear on the part of these ethnic groups that monolithic bureaucracies were sweeping away the remnants of their communities, and the cultural values and traditions contained therein. And of all immigrant groups, Italian-Americans have most strongly valued community bonds and family loyalty. Even the most cursory examination of the history of Italian immigration to the United States reveals extraordinary replications of village and family social organization in the tenements of American cities.

The massive immigration of Italians to America occurred after 1900. Most of the immigrants came from the six provinces south and east of Rome, an area known as the *Mezzogiorno,* or colloquially as "the land that time forgot." This region, which included Sicily, had endured over ten centuries of conquest by alien peoples. The mismanagement of forest and farm resources, the crippling lease and rent systems of the absentee landlords, and the already marginal productivity of the land combined to leave the *contadini* (peasant class) in desperate poverty. Like the Irish before them, these Italian peasants sought survival in the United States, trading a primitive rural world for a complex urban experience. The southern Italian retained in the United States, however, an elaborate social system that had defended him against both destitution and exploitation in the old country. It was *l'ordine della famiglia,* which Richard Gambino defines as "the unwritten but all-demanding and complex system of rules governing one's relations within, and responsibilities to, his own family, and his posture toward those outside the family."[2] The primacy of familial kinship ties was reinforced by other institutions of social bonding, notably the selection of godparents, which admitted outsiders to the family circle, and *campanilismo,* the sense of allegiance or loyalty predicated on neighborhood or village commitment (the term literally means the village or bell tower, hence loyalties to all within the sound of the bell).[3]

Italians who came to the United States transported this complex social and familial order practically intact, like many other preindustrial immigrant groups. The *via vecchia*—the old-country way—could defend them in a world of alien languages and foods, exploitative labor bosses, and cultural discrimination and derision. To this day, urban anthropologists and sociologists point to the consoling centripetal isolation of the Italian-American family and neighborhood to explain the Italian-Americans' slow rate of assimilation into the suburban, materialistic, and ethnically homogenized American middle class. Compared to most other ethnic groups, Italians more tenaciously resisted such assimilative activities as intermarriage, the pursuit of higher education, and the movement out of center city areas.

Despite their obvious distortions and misapprehensions, American portrayals of Italians in popular magazines, editorial cartoons, films, and television over the past century capture the struggle between an isolative *via vecchia* and the centrifugal attraction of the American Dream. But these images of Italians do more than reflect the movement of the *contadini* into American culture. They also help to chart the collective imagination of the dominant WASP society of the late nineteenth century. Indeed, WASP America's obsessions and prejudices about "foreign influence" show up clearly in its images of Italians, who thus become as important a cultural mirror as the great American psychosexual mystiques of black men and women. The Italian immigrant was, in a way, a synthesized target for stereotype, susceptible on physiognomical, cultural, and religious levels. Like the earlier Irish immigrant, he was a fearsome symbol of the alien Roman church; like the Jew from Eastern Europe, his features were in radical physical contrast to the pervasive Anglo-Saxon profile.

In fact, cartoons of Italian-American immigrants were notable for caricatures of squat, swarthy men, prognathic and hunched, fitted out with earrings and daggers. This seems a visual hybridization of cartoon stereotypes of blacks, Arabs, Jews, and Gypsies, perhaps the ultimate alien in the imagination of Western Europe. Cartoons of Italians were the first visual medium to dispense widely many stereotypic aspects of caricature previously frozen in print. They anticipated and in a sense formed visual models for subsequent comic screen stereotypes—many of Chico Marx's precursors appear in the denigrating caricatures of *Life, Leslie's Weekly,* and *Judge* magazines.[4]

The taproots of American images of Italians trace back to the serious and popular literatures of England. Gothic fiction, often written by and for females, had established fairly fixed images of the Italian man and woman before 1800. Such highly popular works as *The Monk, The Castle of Otranto,* and *The Mysteries of Udolpho* posit the Italian male and female as sinister sexual, ethical, and religious threats. In time, Americans borrowed some of these images from the Gothic tradition that surveyed the degeneracy of an aristocratic and landed Italian population. Interestingly, comparatively positive images of Italian culture that predate the nineteenth century—such as Shakespeare's star-crossed Romeo and Juliet, or the fecund intellectual matrix of the Renaissance—found scanty expression in the American popular arts. Such serious writers as Henry James, Edith Wharton, and George Henry Boker (Philadelphia poet and diplomat who wrote *Francesca Da Rimini,* a brilliant imitative blank-verse tragedy) knew their Dante and Petrarch, but popular tastes were better served by a more lurid rendition of Latin passions.

Italian men in this tradition moved through the novels trailing clouds of alien Catholicism. Often priests or monks, or masquerading as such, they perenially enticed English women with the promise of exotic and arcane ritual. This line was embellished with a thinly veiled and powerful appeal to repressed sexuality—more lurked beneath cloak and cassock than a strange religion.

The Italian female also appeared in persistently sexual terms. The pallid, fragile Englishwoman competed with a "dark lady" of considerable passionate resources. The Italian woman was lush, redolent, amber or honey-skinned; her prodigious mammary endowments bespoke the confused mythic echoes of fertility goddess and terrible mother—at times she was indeed as blatant a threat to male sexuality as Kali.[5] This image of Italian woman as estrogenic wonder was consistent with other Gothic racial and ethnic portrayals: she joined the Jewish, Gypsy, and Romanian female in a broadly conceived "Mediterranean" female character.[6]

The classic and popular literary stereotypes of Italy and Italians, inaccurate enough to start with, were doubly inappropriate to the largely illiterate and unsophisticated *contadini* of the *Mezzogiorno,* a peasantry that knew little of Gothic castles and elegant seductions. The first to arrive in this country were the men, frequently under the abusive control of *padroni,* Italian-American work bosses. These immigrants joined the labor force at the most basic level, and, compared to many other ethnic groups, remained quite willingly at low-paying, unprestigious jobs well into the next two generations. Early caricatures of Italian immigrants accurately capture their willingness to work at any task in the new country. For example, in a cartoon entitled "New Year's Presents Suggested for our Newly Arrived Italian Immigrants," a *Leslie's Weekly* issue of 1873 shows a peanut stand, waffle machine, shoeshine kit, and organ with monkey.[7]

The Italian man carried with him from the old country the ideal of *rispetto*—a sense of personal worth that derived not from work-associated prestige, but from internal sources. Nothing a man did for a living mattered, for when the workday ended, he returned home with his wages and his integrity. The Italian-American male neither sought nor particularly understood social mobility achieved through the workplace; with family as the center of commitment and concern, any work that regularly put bread on the table was acceptable. Thus, the caricature of the Italian hod-carrier from the turn of this century was as inadvertently accurate as the Italian "garbage man/truck" genre of jokes from more recent popular culture.[8]

By 1883, the *Times* actually subscribed to a conspiracy theory, not about Italians, but about their fleas: "Unless the importation of this infamous insect is checked the whole country will swarm with Italian fleas. Our own native flea will disappear before formidable competition."[9] This complaint is a ludicrous example of the anti-Italianism of the late nineteenth century. Like Jews and blacks, these new aliens would corrupt the purity of all American racial stock. Even his willingness to work at any job was a negative attribute to the Italian, for he was construed as a threat to that other cherished myth of know-nothingism, the integrity of the free-enterprise system.

The first feature movies with identifiable Italian-American characters not only picked up on the image of the harmless street vendor, but emphasized the notion of a simple-minded, excitable stereotype in establishing a sentimental and musical tradition. In fact, the 1918 silent comedy *My Cousin* featured Enrico Caruso in a dual role as sculptor and lauded singer in New York's Little Italy.[10] The Fox production of 1929 encapsulated the early tendency to portray Italian-Americans in a spirit of romantic domesticity in its title, *Love, Live, and Laugh.* Edward G. Robinson appears as a sentimental hero in MGM's 1930 *A Lady to Love,* a remake of Adolph Zukor's *The Secret Hour* (1928). As Tony Patucci, Robinson is a California grape-grower seeking a bride through letter exchanges with a San Francisco waitress. How different this positive image of a prospering immigrant, seeking domestic tranquility, is from the role Robinson plays scarcely a year later that crystallizes the image of the Italian as archetypal American gangster—Caesar Enrico Bandello in Mervyn Leroy's *Little Caesar.*

That Italians rapidly are transformed in cinema from innocent buffoons, peddling arias and apples, into ruthless and driven criminals is not completely surprising. As early as 1875, with the first small influx of Italians from the *Mezzogiorno,* newspapers and magazines began to plant stereotypical notions of the Italian as criminal in American minds. An article in the *New York Times* in April, 1876 is entitled "A Natural Inclination Toward Criminality" and notes how the Italian is "fitter for intrigue than the American, by so much is he more of an artist in 'managing things'."[11]

The dominant portrayal of Italians in American film is within the gangster genre, a cinematic heritage that stretches from *Little Caesar* (1931) to its apotheosis in both parts of *The Godfather.* Initially mocked or feared for their passions, appearances, or alien liturgies (indeed, much early anti-Italianism is merely a continuation of anti-Catholicism), Italians as gangsters specifically come to represent insidious threats to the foundations of American capitalism, even as they pursue the national dream of financial success and material acquisition.

Italians were by no means the first gangsters or even the first ethnic gangsters, either in reality or on film. But a series of historical and cultural circumstances helped to enclose them in the underworld archetype. Most significant was Prohibition and the ensuing rise of criminal networks, centered in Chicago. The rise to prominence of Al Capone, who was, incidentally, a product of Brooklyn not Italian slums, received national attention, thanks to the glamorizing tabloid newspapers. The film industry seized on the story of this self-made ruthless mobster and turned out no fewer than eight versions of his intemperate life, from *Little Caesar* and Howard Hawks's *Scarface* (1932) to Roger Corman's *The St. Valentine's Day Massacre* (1967). Other underworld leaders, like Big Jim Colosimo and Johnny Torrio, were also obliquely portrayed in these and other gangster films, thus lending credence to the association of Italians with organized crime.

In terms of sex-roles, the channeling of Italian-Americans into the gangster film effectively removes them from sentimental and domestic spheres of portrayal. With only a few exceptions, Italian-American men in the movies funnel their passionate intensities into the world of crime. Glimpses of their family life—wives and children and the social order this world reflects—become rare. In fact, inasmuch as the life of crime becomes a career choice, the gangster becomes the classic work-obsessed American executive, climbing the corporate ladder of success.

Popular arts have always been a peculiarly accurate barometer of cultural obsessions. In America, the genre film has measured America's ongoing fascination with the independent man of action. War films, westerns, even musicals trace the exploits of the self-made, self-making American protagonist. And with the closing of the frontier and the 1929 shutdown of the expanding economy, the streetwise, cynical gangster becomes the new American striver, pursuing manifest destiny with machine guns. Even though many gangsters must eventually fall from the heights of their illicit accomplishments, it is their quest that puts them at the very center of an antinomian national imagination, ambivalent about the growing restrictions of urban, collectivized society. We cannot completely repudiate the modern oppositional man, for, as Jack Shadoian argues, his "continued popularity and his transformation from a figure reasonably close to historical actuality to a near-mythic condensation of forces is a sign of an entrenched moral-ethical confusion of the culture."[12]

Even the most sociopathic, or the most psychosexually flawed of gangsters seems at times to strive for a transformation of his isolated violent behavior into the systematic bottom-line activity of American business. Carnegies and Corleones alike built empires on ruthless ambition, and, whether real or fictional, each evokes admiration and envy, fear and distrust in the popular audience. As Shadoian asserts, in assimilating, the gangster truly becomes the "monstrous emblem of the capitalist."[13]

The overwhelming extent to which Italians found themselves portrayed as underworld types derived in part from the notorious activities of the Capones and Torrios of speakeasy days. Even law-abiding, Americanized Italians found themselves touched by crime in film images. If not the perpetrators, they frequently found themselves on the other side of the law as cop, district attorney, detective. This emphasis essentially displaced earlier film images of innocuous senti-mental and musically inclined Italians. The second film generation off the boat seemed to fall into crime in movies, but often because it seemed the American thing to do, not because of any innate Italian propensities. Those Italians who did not aspire to an American upward mobility were merely left by the film industry to languish in the quaint, jovial stereotypes of newly-arrived immigrants. For exam-ple, to this day, television commercials still cling to the image of the big-breasted "Mamma" in the kitchen, as if three generations of Italian-Americans had unlimited access to the same apron and black housedress.

The crucial complicating factor in the image of the Italian as criminal entrepreneur is, of course, the notion of the "Mafia," the almost mystical Italian underworld subculture. For how can the gangster be the persevering self-made American loner if he is also part of a massive system, an ethnic syndication of political marriage and byzantine alliances, directed toward subverting the most hallowed of political and governmental structures? To understand the Mafia image of Italian-Americans in film, we return again to racist pre-sumptions of those Americans who documented the wave of Sicilian and Calabrian immigrants to this country. Richard Gambino com-ments extensively on the clouded etymology and history of the actual phrase in Italy. He traces how an adjective *(mafioso)* that meant 'good' or 'admirable' came to be associated first with native Italian outlaw bands of brigands and extortionists, and ultimately with a monstrous criminal network abroad and in the United States.[14]

Indeed, some Italian-American criminals did rely on a "familial" bureaucracy of lawlessness, but most allegiances were crass and venal, without the romanticized patriarchalism with which Don Vito in *The Godfather* (1972) is imbued. There are reasons why the Mafia becomes a family in American crime cinema, with its own genetic bonds and private rituals. This allows the gangster to be doubly frightening, for, unlike the western's "bad guy," who might call upon the mercenaries of his gang for aid, the Italian gangster could enlist literal and figurative brethren in his struggle. Shrouded by differences in language and custom, *all* Italians thus could be potential enemies of truth, fair play, and American straightforwardness. In sociological terms, the Italian criminal could pursue the icons of American success without relinquishing the bonds and advantages of his extended family. So, a paradox emerges, for even as he is victimized by an assimilationist work ethic that ostensibly would isolate him from his family, the Italian gangster can have access to the consolatory surrogate of his crime "family." This is perhaps why the will to believe in the Mafia is so strong to this day, for it is a confused jealousy and resentment on the part of the viewing public estranged from its own traditions, excluded from most "old boy" networks.

Thanks to such critics as Shadoian, Robert Warshow, John Cawelti, and Stuart Kaminsky, there is a considerable body of scholarship on the formulas and rhythms of the gangster film over the years. And the strand that seems to link such critical visions of the gangster as "tragic hero," self-made man, or conglomerate wheeler-dealer is an economic one—for, like Shirley Temple, the gangster is a child of the Depression. And like the curly-haired little tap-dancer, the gangster is very much a fictive construct of the film industry, produced for our distraction, amusement, and vicarious fantasy diversion.[15]

The first Italian-American gangster to step out of the shadows and capture us with his cunning and passionate ruthlessness is Caesar Enrico Bandello in *Little Caesar*. Edward G. Robinson's portrayal of this dapper, violent, upwardly mobile hoodlum establishes the profile of the gangster figure. He is, quite literally, a "little" Caesar, extremely short, and as arrogant and cocky as he is diminutive. This image of a short, dark, overtly ethnic protagonist underscores the class structure implicit in the gangster film. The little guy on the make must confront and conquer established society, the grandchildren of all those tall, rangy cowboys that made the West a safe place for women and children. And the gangster is as undecorously aggressive as the western hero is stoically reserved. Both of these men with guns dominate genre films of the thirties, though it is no surprise to find that at the height of the Depression the underdog-loving public often misapprehended the little gangster as a latter-day Robin Hood, enacting populist revenge on the banks that have betrayed the national trust.[16]

In *Little Caesar*, Rico wants what the "Big Boy" has uptown, the icons of personal gain—clothes, paintings, jewelry. But he does not have any use for the traditional "moll," the female companion acquired as an adornment by many gangsters. Rather, Rico harbors a familiar

The archetype of the Italian gangster was created by Edward G. Robinson in Little Caesar *(1930).*

American dislike and distrust for females. Like so many American heroes before him, he instead focuses human emotion on his male sidekick, here Joe Masara, played by Douglas Fairbanks, Jr. But Joe has a girlfriend and is also a professional dancer which, according to Rico, "ain't a man's game."[17]

In fact, Rico's world of manliness is closer to the acquisitive American dream of success than the Italian paradigm for *un uomo di rispetto* (a man who has status and power). Without a past, without a family, Rico is an Italian-American adrift, with only implied and tenuous ethnic bonds to his fellow underworld types. But even the motto "friendship and loyalty" that adorns the marquee of the Club Palermo where they hang out cannot hold these men together. The film is rife with internal power struggles, betrayals, forced takeovers, and Rico's own downfall, precipitated by Joe's love for his dance partner Olga. She is the first in a long line of blond, WASPish girlfriends in the gangster film. The pale, implicitly unethnic female is especially alluring to the swarthy gangster on the make. Often taller and "classier" than their underworld benefactors, these women are social levers, opening doors for their men. Only figures like Rico, the instinctive American misogynist, recognize the banal evil in these women.

Before his demise, Rico demonstrates his casual ruthlessness in an act overlooked as significant by many critics—his assassination of his getaway driver, Antonio. This frightened young man, remorseful over his participation in robbery, has found consolation and moral focus in a sentimental scene with his mother. Tormented Antonio is convinced to go to confess all at church by his mamma, a woman outwardly old enough to be his grandmother, and thoroughly domestic in her housedress and apron. She speaks in halting stage dialect, backgrounded by Neapolitan music: "remember when you sing in the church, *caro mio?*" and she offers an appropriately ethnic antidote to despair: "I have some spaghetti on the stove . . . you feel better . . . eat somethin' . . . do you good." But Rico guns down Antonio on the steps of the church, a wide stairway that other filmmakers will visually echo as death site for James Cagney in *The Roaring Twenties* (1939) and Barzini in *The Godfather*. Rico can kill the repentant and obedient son precisely because he is offered up as rootless, a man without a family, a man without a mamma.

For the most part, Rico offers the unfortunate paradigm for the Italian-American gangster film stereotype, enough cultural signature to be affixed as Italian, but little if anything of that ethnic group's familial structures and codes of behavior and belief. Edward G. Robinson will eventually appear in over a dozen films as an Italian-American, but only in sentimental romances and comedies is his Italianness given more than surface rendering. As gangster in such films as *Key Largo* (1948) or *Black Tuesday* (1954), only his malice, callousness, and sadism are traced to his ethnicity. The pattern in Robinson's career as mock Italian demonstrates clearly that the gangster film is too immediately focused on the success ethic to stray in detail into areas of anthropological representation. It is as if the gangster becomes the first Italian-American to be victimized by an assimilationist ethic.

Up until the *Godfather* saga, most gangster films offer up characters ambiguously enacting the paradoxical American dream in pursuit of self-defining autonomy in a corporate culture. Occasionally, one of the Italian underworld films will capture the larger ethnic issues of accommodating to the customs and expectations of the new world. Such is the case in Michael Curtiz's *Kid Galahad* (also known as *The Battling Bellhop*, 1937). Here Edward G. Robinson returns as Nick Donati, Italian-American fight promoter, who isolates his kid sister and ethnic mamma on a farm in Connecticut, far from the cigar-haze corruption of the urban boxing scene. He is at the head of his family, and is intensely protective of sister Marie, whom he sends to convent schools. Ethnic crisis ensues when she falls in love with one of Nick's fighters, Ward "Gooseberry," a tall blond WASP. Nick will eventually be shot in a fight-fixing conflict and make deathbed recognition of

Marie's right to choose her own spouse. But in the course of the film, we learn of his intense Italian-American familial separatism, here underscored by the physical isolation of the Donati farmhouse retreat. At one point when he is home on a visit, Nick and his mother converse in Italian on screen, a rare event in general release commercial cinema. There is a brief moment of mother-son tenderness in the kitchen, where Nick seems to reaffirm ethnicity through a taste of mamma's minestrone soup.

Nick Donati did not want his personal and professional lives to be mixed, and only his death facilitates Marie's implied marriage to Ward and the symbolic movement of Italian-Americans through intermarriage into the mainstream American life. *Kid Galahad* is one of the earliest film features to make even tentative inquiries into the tension between Italian and American social organization. Whereas Nick's mother is the old-style immigrant mamma, queen of her kitchen but deferential to the male authority, Marie is unmarked by stereotype of silhouette or dialect, and highly Americanized in her willful independence.

In a curious way, the portrayal of Italian-American women in popular film has been a more reliable yardstick of the fate of this immigrant group in our nation than the channeling of Italian-American men into the gangster genre. From Antonio's mamma in *Little Caesar* to the overreaching Stephanie Mangano in the recent *Saturday Night Fever* (1977), Italian-American women, even when stereotyped, have been shown confronting challenges to the *via vecchia,* the old-country way, often repelling invasions into the traditional realm of the Italian family, and at times suffering painful conflict with their children over commitment to kin, work, and future.

There is a dual strand of characterization of the Italian-American women in film, which Richard Gambino notes as "the fiery, sensuous, outspoken willful 'Sophia Loren' image (indeed the actress is a native of Naples) and the jolly, all-loving, naive rotund *mamma mia* image."[18] And these images again reveal the needs of the dominant culture to create, on the one hand, an insatiable sexual creature, and on the other, a safely domesticated cook and cleaning lady. The sensuous image is, of course, consistent with the Gothic tradition identified earlier, and the Italian-American woman as passionate voluptuary can be traced in American film to its culminating figure of the widowed Serafina in *The Rose Tattoo* (1955). Here Anna Magnani begins the film still embroiled in elaborate Sicilian mourning ritual and soon discovers her sexuality has taken her over. Interestingly, she struggles especially hard to subdue not only her own passion but also that of her teen-age daughter, who is impatient and embarrassed by her mother's old-country ways.

By far the more common vision of the Italian-American woman

occurred in the domestic model of the mamma, safely distanced from sexuality in her middle age, housecoat, and hair net. And like so many ethnic mammas in media, the Italian woman is in the kitchen, brandishing a stirring spoon, and insisting that we eat, *mangia*. Here, as I have argued elsewhere, "the stereotype threatens to obscure the very real place of food and the ritual importance of meals in Italian and other ethnic communities."[19]

In such different films as *Marty* (1955), *Lovers and Other Strangers* (1970), *The Godfather,* and *Saturday Night Fever,* feast and mealtime are especially important. By the mid-1950s films of the Italian-American experience no longer relegated all males to gangster or opera singer roles, and women began to move out of the kitchen. The era seemed to encourage at least tentative media ethnic and working-class consciousness in such television shows as *The Goldbergs* and *Mama.* Social changes and GI benefits helped to break the bond of neighborhood on Italian and other city groups, and the first wave of migration began to the suburbs. The creeping Freudianism of the period also forced people to reassess personal and familial status.

Marty reveals the tensions within a superficially stable Italian-American family when the shy, middle-aged bachelor son (played by Ernest Borgnine) becomes romantically involved with a woman and draws away from his Italian mother and home. The film points up the isolation and loneliness of ethnic, working-class people.

In this nation for over seventy years, Italian-Americans were finally being shown confronting issues and problems of assimilation, and the pressures frequently surfaced at the dinner table, ostensibly the impregnable bastion of family solidarity. Problems of second and third generation begin to intrude—intermarriage, career aspirations and disappointments, generational conflicts, and the casual infidelities of the American middle class.

In *Lovers and Other Strangers,* Richard Castellano and Beatrice Arthur portray parents of two sons—one about to marry an Irish-American girl with whom he has been living, the other ready to divorce his wife, also apparently non-Italian. Castellano tries to probe for the reasons for the failed marriage (his blunt though poignant query throughout the film is "So, Richie, what's the story?"), while the audience sees clearly that his own domestic relationship is entirely based on food. His wife worries most about not offering up "veiny" veal to her husband, and in a later confession to Richie the father himself admits that the familial tradition of good eating is a shallow consolation. He asserts that he and Bea are "content" and accuses Richie at one point: "Happy? Who said you got the right to be happy? You think you're better than me?"

Paddy Chayefsky's *Marty* of almost a generation earlier underlines the interplay of food and unfulfillment in its depiction of a lonely Italian-American butcher who seems jovial only when he is providing the meat for his neighbors' weekly *pranzo* (Sunday afternoon family dinners). Thirty-six, unmarried, and living with his mother, Marty has no extended family, and his camaraderie with other single males seems forced at his age. As telling as his plight is that of his mother, played by Esther Minciotti, who seems bemused by changing times and values. She is threatened by her son's tentative romance with a lonely schoolteacher, and she sees in the plight of her sister Catherine her own potential shunting aside by future generations eager to Americanize: "It's a very sad thing. A woman, fifty-six years old, all her life, she had her own home. Now, she's just an old lady, sleeping on her daughter-in-law's couch. It's a curse to be a mother, I tell you. Your children grow up and then what is left for you to do? What is a mother's life but her children? It is a very cruel thing when your son has no place for you in his home."[20] Though the cadences of this lament are Italian, the fears of the irrelevancy and loneliness of old age are common to many ethnic parents who perceive their children rejecting the old ways.

The crisis of faith and values documented in films of Italian-American life in the past generation can be traced in many respects to the rise of Fascism and World War II. Mussolini assiduously culti-vated Italian-Americans in the 1920s and '30s, instilling an ethnic pride and sense of respectability in many of the over four million Italians living in the United States. As Angelo Pelligrini notes: "Mussolini had made America understand that Italy had had a great civilization . . . and that he was going to return the glory of Rome to Italy, re-establish the Roman Empire. . . ."[21]

Italian-Americans went so far as to rally and contribute money for the Ethiopian campaign, and even volunteer to fight in the Italian army. Up until the formation of the Axis, Italian-Americans had no difficulty supporting Mussolini and being good Americans at the same time. Once Americans were fighting in World War II, however, films document that the canny, cynical, and street-wise Italian-American was a willing part of the stereotypic ethnic cross section of American fighting men, a heroic patriot, fighting and dying for the United States. The ethnic panorama of the war film was an especially significant socializing device. It at once encouraged and glorified cultural diversity in the United States, with men from varied regions and backgrounds pooling their talents for the war effort. This was especially important in World War II, with racialism so obvious an issue—in the Pacific Americans faced a fanatical, inscrutable, and suicidal Oriental enemy, and in Europe the maniacal genetic logic of Hitler's "Master Race." The Italian-American soldier repelled these undemocratic threats with a hearty dose of cynicism for his *own* leaders and military structure. He was almost never an officer, but rather a natural leader and fighter in the ranks of his equals.

This issue of national loyalty informs the confrontation of brothers and kin in *The Godfather,* when Michael Corleone returns home to announce at the dinner table that he has enlisted in the Army. Eldest son Santino assails him, screaming: "Stupid! You fight for strangers?", which establishes the polarities of ethnic commitment in the film. Michael is the Americanized youngest son who has gone to an Ivy-League college. He will marry outside the ethnic enclave, merging his traditions with the archetypally American values epitomized in the name of his sweetheart, Kay Adams. At the wedding scene that opens *The Godfather,* Michael returns a war hero (and an officer), and further underscores his distance from *la famiglia* by arriving in uniform and reminding Kay that "That's my family, Kay, that's not me," when she marvels at the grotesque underworld milieu.

The Godfather is the single most complex and brooding disquisition on the prices of ethnic affiliation and assimilation in American cinematic history. Though he tries to disavow blood commitment and *l'ordine della famiglia,* Michael is compelled by an inarticulatable power to avenge the attempted assassination of his father, Don Vito. When he first proposes that he kill the perpetrators, Santino laughs: "Hey, Joe College, it's not like the Army, where you shoot a guy from a mile away. You gotta get up close and *bidda-bing,* you blow his brains all over your ivy-league suit!" Yet Michael does murder two men, and thus relinquishes his claim to the legitimacy of an American war hero. Brother Santino is marked for death by his own brash and uncontrollable emotionalism—he lacks the crucial element of *pazienza,* the *Mezzogiorno* ideal of a measured withholding of energies and commitment, an almost impassive reserve that is channeled into an explosion of sudden, decisive action.[22] Michael must be the inheritor of his father's position because he best embodies these old-world ideals, for Santino's bravado and male swagger cost him his life, and middle son Fredo seems almost weak and enfeebled.

In The Godfather *the strong familial bond between father (Marlon Brando) and son (Al Pacino) erases the son's education and assimilation into American life and leads him into the nether world of the Mafia. Significantly, the lawyer-like son lacks the patriarchal qualities of the father. Crime becomes a business.*

The great wave of controversy surrounding the release and success of both parts of *The Godfather* was initiated by Italian-Americans who felt massively betrayed by the very brilliant achievement of the film; it was so rich a portrait of the ethnic life of Italian-Americans, coordinated and directed by an Italian-American (Francis Ford Coppola), starring one of the few big box-office Italian-American actors (Al Pacino), that to build its presentation around the great myth of the Mafia was more than just occasion for bad publicity. It was a major wounding of an emerging Italian-American social consciousness. The film's morality and aesthetic execution were so seductive that they invited Italian-Americans themselves to believe the worst. As Joseph Papaleo writes: "In many ways, *The Godfather* finished us off because it was the most authentic portrayal (and the first made by knowledge-able Italian-American craftsmen). Italian-Americans were asked to laugh with Godfather parties, the bumper stickers reading 'Mafia Staff Car,' and many other games." More tellingly, Papaleo continues:

> All stereotypes add power to a false belief because they contain a small measure of truth. To see an inaccurate image in authentic trappings (as in the case of *The Godfather*) is often to identify with it. The ethnic becomes part of the world that is stigmatizing his very self. He gains the same view as the confused majority and holds it parallel in his mind with the truth about the variety of Italian-Americans.[23]

Coppola has said of his protagonist, "Michael is America," and in *Godfather II* (1974), the wily Jewish mobster Hyman Roth confides to Michael, "we're bigger than U.S. Steel." Both assertions touch the true meaning of the film in addressing the devastation of family and self in the pursuit of success, a quest for individual wealth and power that reaches beyond the most conspiratorial image of the Mafia. Indeed, the tonal distance between the two versions of *The Godfather* points out how old-fashioned vendetta and bloody assassination give way to a more decorous and businesslike crime world where the bosses talk like bankers. In *The Godfather,* betrayal from within the family was the result of a bad marriage, with Carlo, Connie's husband, arranging Santino's murder. But in *Godfather II* it is brother Fredo himself who sets up Michael's near death. As if this were not the destruction of the greatest bond, the blood tie, Michael pushes even further from the core of *Mezzogiorno* in fratricide, having Fredo murdered at the close of the film. But he cannot enact this horrific deed as long as any vestige of the old ways remains. He seeks his mother's counsel and asks if there is "any way a family can lose its ties." She insists that this is impossible, and Michael tells his bodyguard that as long as his mother lives, nothing must happen to Fredo. The old woman is clearly a remnant of the New York ways, and the Sicilian ways before.

The Corleone world was clearly collapsing upon itself before Fredo's betrayal. Whereas *The Godfather* opens with the joyous primitivism of Connie's wedding, *Godfather II* unfolds on the shores of a man-made Nevada lake where the only ethnicity is imported. Guest Frankie Pentangeli cannot get a glass of wine, and when he tries to stir the band into a *tarantella,* the musicians blunder into a version of "Pop Goes the Weasel." The focus of ethnic genius in *Godfather II* is relegated to the past, in the flashback scenes of Vito Corleone's arrival and life in Manhattan's Little Italy, which make ghetto slice-of-life footage from all prior movies seem paltry and two-dimensional in comparison.

Michael Corleone is a cold, calculating don without the ingratiating patriarchal quality embodied by his father, as played by Marlon Brando. In a recent interview, author Mario Puzo acknowledges that he invented the fatherly attributes that humanize Don Vito, for American criminal bosses felt no particular obligation to mete out justice on behalf of the businessmen they exploited: *"The Godfather* is really more a portrait of a Sicilian Mafia leader than an American Mafia leader. The Americans were much dirtier guys than the Sicilians. The Sicilians had a code of honor . . ."[24]

Like the individual gangster who seemed to adopt the worst attributes of his American milieu, most of Puzo's characters demonstrate the price exacted for straying from cultural and familial bonds. Connie Corleone, for example, moves from obedient, almost beatific girlishness to a sordid cheapness. By the outset of *Godfather II* she appears flashy and sluttish, dragging along her latest "fiance" to the confirmation party that initiates the film. Yet by the end of *Godfather II,* she is left hollow and tentative, having retreated into the family compound, the sombre world of her brother's shadowy dominion. Even the females in the modern Italian-American family are susceptible, no longer protected from the incursions of the world, nor functioning at the emotional center of the family.

Even with the taint of the gangster genre, *The Godfather* films are the most important, if most dramatic, treatments of the fate of Italians in the modern United States. The great irony is that the incredible financial success of both films not only resynthesized the Italian gangster stereotype as commercially viable, but also romanticized the criminal underworld into an almost Robin Hood fantasy. Don Vito Corleone sought justice, loved children, hated drugs and Negroes— indeed almost all laudable Americanisms. This was far from the image offered in the slew of spin-off imitations that followed *The Godfather*. Most offered sensationalism without Coppola's mitigating human sensibility, though *The Valachi Papers* (1972) was important in its pseudo-documentary account of Joe Valachi, the crime figure who gave investigating committees confessions about the *Cosa Nostra* (in Italian, "our thing"). Here, an insider's frightened revelations challenged the mystique of *omerta,* the ostensibly unbreakable code of silence. *The Godfather* and *The Valachi Papers* were not the first films simultaneously to depict the crime milieu and comment on the often wrenching tensions between the *via vecchia* in its broader sense and contemporary American life.

The psychological costs of assimilation were addressed in the 1961 film *The Young Savages,* in which Burt Lancaster plays Hank Bell, a New York prosecutor obsessed with deciphering the mystery behind an East Harlem street murder of a blind Puerto Rican youth by an Italian-American teen gang. Bell, formerly Bellini, grew up in these same streets and now is a zealously assimilated American, living in high-rise isolation with his daughter and blond, Vassar-educated wife (Dina Merrill). Bell is tormented by his own ethnic ambivalences, heightened by the fact that one of the suspects, the son of a former sweetheart, continuously berates his assimilated status, calling him a "fake Wop." Bell discovers that this particular youth only pretended to join in the actual stabbing, leaving his knife closed, afraid of peer repudiation.

Bell eventually builds a case that at once exonerates this youth (at the expense of his image of street manhood) and establishes a criminal complicity extending beyond the actual participants in the murder. He envisions the strong environmental determinism of the slums as the prime source of violence and death. In his own courtroom eloquence, however, he shows that at least in his generation it was possible to defeat the environment by an act of the will. Hope for contemporary youth is not so bright, partly because of the fragmentation of old familial bonds. Yet ethnic solidarity is not always beneficial. An Italian-American girl who witnessed the murder is turned in by her greengrocer father. She sneers: "What kind of a father is this who turns his own daughter into the cops," and the answer is obvious—an Americanized father, willing to trust external law and justice.[25]

In the 1962 film version of Arthur Miller's *A View from the Bridge,* the motif of entry into the new world is melded with the theme of internal ethnic betrayal. Raf Vallone plays Eddie, the dockworker who exposes a young Italian illegal alien who has fallen in love with his niece. Like Chayefsky in *Marty,* Miller reached into the assimilative experience of Italians in identifying the alienated spokesmen of mass society.

Vulnerable now to peculiarly American varieties of loneliness, despair, and guilt, Italians join Jews and blacks as post-World War II ethnic everymen. And the Italian-American, caught for so many years

Movie Italians are tough and win their fame through violence. Rocky Balboa (Sylvester Stallone) rises for a moment from his Italian South Philadelphia neighborhood to take on the champ. He survives the fight with dignity, but returns to, indeed never really leaves, his own people and his girl friend (Talia Shire) in the working-class city. Rocky (1976).

in the humiliating stereotypes of buffoon or Mafioso, has an especially difficult time finding cinematic paradigms for his increasing sense of impotence and anonymity. Agonized as he is, for example, Michael Corleone is still an icy criminal monster; Sylvester Stallone is the goofy brute, the "Italian Stallion" in *Rocky* (1976); and on television the Italian is still a gangster-gone-to-high school. Vinny Barberino (*Welcome Back, Kotter*) and Arthur Fonzarelli (*Happy Days*) strut about, wearing their machismo on the sleeves of their cabretta leather coats.

Beneath the disco glitter and polyester sensibilities of characters, John Badham's *Saturday Night Fever* at least begins to address the attenuated dreams and aspirations of the new generation of Italian-Americans. The life of the Manero family is circumscribed by economic and spiritual losses. The father, an unemployed construction worker, cannot draw on communal solidarity for either financial or moral support. He explodes when his wife suggests that she must go to work; he smacks around son Tony, played by John Travolta, for eating an extra pork chop. Again, the family dining table becomes the locus of pain and cultural disillusionment in film, rather than stereotypical site of ethnic gaiety as it remains in spaghetti sauce commercials. The food in the Manero household is neither abundant

Tony Manero (John Travolta) escapes the meanness and monotony of his Italian, working-class life by becoming the disco king on Saturday nights in Saturday Night Fever.

nor appetizing; Mr. Manero coaxes Tony to the dinner table with a wry observation: "Don't worry, your mother's sauce don't drip. . . . It don't taste, but it don't drip."

When the young disco king appears for dinner, he takes what one critic calls "prophylactic measures against his own ethnic repast," draped in a sheet and drinking his wine from a water tumbler.[26] And the arguments that course around the dinner table demonstrate a fractious and uneasy family; eldest son Frank arrives home to crystallize the dilemma with the announcement that he is leaving the priesthood. But the real center of loss in the film is Tony's, for he must come to discard his dancing, his only accomplishment of note, and hesitantly pursue a new life beyond the smothering insularity of his Brooklyn neighborhood. Inarticulate and unskilled, he trades the certainties of a tedious life as paint-store clerk, relinquishing local disco notoriety and the consolation of his male cohorts for a new life in Manhattan. His sense of personal disconnectedness is at the center of the film, but the mood of entrapment affects all the characters, especially his cadre of friends. Their random violence, drugs, and sexuality cannot fill the weekend nights, but they cannot even get across the bridge to another borough.

The deleterious effects of stereotyping are felt most tellingly when a caricatured ethnic group starts believing its own bad press. Thus Elizabeth Stone writes in a recent *New York Times* essay of Italian-Americans who feel a palpable sense of shame over their ethnicity: "Some of my friends feel they have to change even more dramatically than they've already changed in order to be acceptable. Some have even changed their names."[27] In a similar vein of self-flight and self-abuse, playwright Albert Innaurato creates in *Gemini* the slur "nigger-Italian," an epithet that captures the almost racial sense of negative ethnicity felt by Italian-Americans in contrast to the WASP world.[28]

Perhaps the single most important impediment to the removal of reductive stereotypes of Italians in movies is their very lack, until recently, of participation in the film industry. It is very difficult to identify prominent Italian-American actors or production personnel from the first forty years of cinema in the United States. The notable exception, of course, is director Frank Capra, the Sicilian-American populist, whose optimistic and folksy sentimentalism infused such films as *Mr. Smith Goes to Washington* (1939), *It's a Wonderful Life* (1947), and *Meet John Doe* (1941). Capra's belief in people and American values (he also coordinated the rousing *Why We Fight* propaganda series of World War II) was, in a way, antithetical to the old-world bondings of his immigrant kinsmen. In his 1959 movie, *A Hole in the Head,* Capra even plays around the edges of the gangster/crime world in his depiction of Frank Sinatra as Tony Manetta, hotelier with some shady dealings. But he also casts Edward G. Robinson as Tony's brother, Mario, a model of middle-class respectability who disapproves of the way his brother is raising his son.

In contrast to Capra, young director Martin Scorsese confronted his ethnicity at the outset in *Mean Streets* (1973). Here, the criminal subculture, alternately sordid and silly, is often a parody of itself. Charlie Cappa, the protagonist, is college-educated, obviously more sensitive than his street buddies, and tormented by guilts and vague self-recrimination, much of it surprisingly religious in nature, considering the rather secularized status of most Italian-American protagonists in the movies. Scorsese's true feel for his Italian-American experience shows even more overtly and sympathetically in his documentary *Italian American* (1976), part of the "Storm of Strangers" series. The film takes the form of an extended interview with his parents in their lower Manhattan apartment. They recall old-country experiences and life in New York, and Mrs. Scorsese demonstrates and discusses the making of spaghetti sauce.

These films give way to Scorsese features like *Alice Doesn't Live Here Anymore* (1974) and *New York, New York* (1977), both big commercial ventures that do not entail screen images of Italian-Americans. Other Italian-American production personnel have also focused on non-Italian topics, though Michael Cimino's *The Deer Hunter* (1978) at least suggests, in its depictions of Slavic-Americans, that ethnic experiences can in part cut across class lines in the world of male bonding, the exclusion of women, and violent rites of passage. Francis Coppola has moved in *Apocalypse Now* (1979) into areas beyond the ethnic purview of *The Godfather*. In fact, Mario Puzo has speculated that he, as well as Coppola, will not be involved in *Godfather III* unless *Apocalypse Now* fails at the box office. The sense with both men is that the ground has been covered, and the press of studio politics demands other directions. Interestingly, Puzo avers that he would want Coppola to do his fine first novel, *The Fortunate Pilgrim*.[29]

It seems that Italian-American actors and directors (and in Puzo's case, screenwriters) do not choose to or cannot wield the traditional levers of power in a profit-oriented industry to control ethnic images in their films. The general Italian-American population is, as Elizabeth Stone's essay suggests, far from unified on remedial steps to take in presenting proper screen images of their ethnic group.

Over the years in America, the Italian immigrant earned good wages, but because of his transported distrust for system and institution, he pretty much rejected education and organization as devices of social mobility. Thus, he was unprepared to engage in media politics, to campaign effectively for positive (or at least sociologically representational) film and television depiction. He had, until perhaps a decade ago, no ethnic political clearinghouse like the Anti-Defamation League of the B'nai B'rith or the NAACP. Even the first Italian-American gestures of solidarity seemed to fall into terrible burlesque. A Columbus Day rally is keynoted by Joe Colombo, known crime boss, who is then promptly gunned down after he tells Italian-Americans to fight their crime-associated media and public image.

Joseph Papaleo has asserted that the simplistic picture of Italian-Americans has usually been predicated on their emotional excessiveness. And "excess is inappropriate in American society because it is also inefficient, using too much energy for its needs. The grave sin of our society is loss of control. The Italian cries like a woman, loses his temper like a trapped animal, cowers like a rabbit in danger (if he is not a gangster), and sacrifices his potential attractiveness in competitive society by eating too much."[30]

The stoical *uomo di pazienza* (man of measured reserve) certainly was not a figure of excessive display, and it is the very lack of emotion that makes great gangster figures of all ethnic persuasion so terrifying. But as long as the dominant image of someone is primitive and childlike, he need not be taken seriously.

The difficulty of being taken seriously, and the related internal problem of not taking themselves and their situation seriously, is the true dilemma of modern Italian-Americans. In recent years, their film images have broadened to encompass at least a measure of the price they have paid for Americanization. And the loss of the Italian-American seems especially intense as he takes his place among other American isolates. He has become part of the lonely crowd by losing the consolatory *la famiglia*—something he probably always thought he would have.

There is an instructive parallel in the assimilative experiences of Italian- and Jewish-Americans. Both groups survived in the Old World through the maintenance of an almost incestuous closed society based on blood bonds. And the history of their movement into American life through intermarriage, socialization, and education is informingly contrastive, with many Jews springing eagerly into the society of their new land, while Italian counterparts resisted and maintained a *Mezzogiorno* inwardness. And ever since 1917, with the publication of Abraham Cahan's *The Rise of David Levinsky,* Jewish-Americans have documented the painful trade-offs made to merge into the mainstream. If recent films like Scorsese's *Mean Streets* and *Saturday Night Fever* are any indication, Italians are beginning to catch up in misgivings with even the most active group of Americanizing immigrants.

And the question implied in these films, and in the "new" ethnicity itself, is no longer whether or not *even* the Italian-American feels unfulfilled and cheated by the engulfing American culture. Rather, it seems that the Italian-American has come to feel even *more* intensely than many other groups the pressures of his hyphenated ethnic affiliation.

NOTES

1. Michael Novak, *The Rise of the Unmeltable Ethnics* (1971).
2. Richard Gambino, *Blood of My Blood* (1975), 34.
3. Francis X. Femminella and Jill S. Quadagno, "The Italian American Family," in Charles Mindel and Robert Habenstein, eds., *Ethnic Families in America: Patterns and Variations* (1976), 63.
4. A convenient compilation of many cartoons is in Salvatore LaGumina, *Wop!* (1973).
5. See comments by Merlin Stone, *When God Was a Woman* (1976), 143–44 *passim*.
6. For a good example of the powers of "Latin" blood as rendered in English literature see Charlotte Bronte, *Jane Eyre* (1971), 269–70.
7. LaGumina, *Wop!*, 21.
8. Andrea Greenberg collects some examples of the genre in her essay "Form and Function of the Ethnic Joke," *Keystone Folklore Quarterly*, 4 (Winter 1972), 144–61. An example of the riddle motif: "Why do they only have two pallbearers at an Italian funeral? Because garbage cans only come with two handles." (158).
9. LaGumina, *Wop!*, 67.
10. For a convenient filmography of Italian-Americans in the movies see Mirella Jona Affron, "The Italian-American in American Films, 1918–1971," *Italian-Americana*, 3 (Fall 1976), 233–55.
11. LaGumina, *Wop!*, 28.
12. *Dreams and Dead Ends* (1977), 6.
13. Ibid.
14. Gambino, *Blood of My Blood*, 273–313.
15. Especially in this last context see Charles Eckert, "Shirley Temple and the House of Rockefeller," *Jump Cut*, 1 (July–August 1974), 1, 17–20.
16. For an illuminating discussion of both the physical size and identification factors of gangsters see Stuart Kaminsky, *American Film Genres* (1977), 26–27.
17. Provocative disquisitions on the homo-eroticism of American male heroes are found throughout Leslie Fiedler, *Love and Death in the American Novel* (1966).
18. Gambino, *Blood of My Blood*, 27.
19. See my essay, "Pasta or Paradigm: The Place of Italian-American Women in Popular Film," *Explorations in Ethnic Studies*, 2 (January 1979), 3–10.
20. Paddy Chayefsky, *Marty*, in *Television Plays* (1955), 218.
21. Quoted in Maldwyn A. Jones, *Destination America* (1976), 218.
22. See further comments on *pazienza* in Gambino, *Blood of My Blood*, 129–32.

23. "Ethnic Pictures and Ethnic Fate: The Media Image of Italian-Americans," in Randall Miller, ed., *Ethnic Images in American Film and Television* (1978), 94.

24. "Dialogue on Film: Mario Puzo," *American Film,* 4 (May 1979), 38.

25. In a similar vein with opposite implications, recall the memorable opening monologue of the bereft undertaker in *The Godfather*. Here, a man who had put his faith in the American Dream must seek justice for his violated daughter from a Sicilian tribal chieftain who knows better than to leave welfare to courts and juries and strangers.

26. Patricia Ward Biederman, "Ethnic Film Fest Slated Here," Buffalo *Courier Express,* June 2, 1978, p. 15.

27. "It's Still Hard to Grow up Italian," *New York Times Magazine,* December 17, 1978, p. 43.

28. Ibid., 92.

29. "Dialogue on Film: Mario Puzo," 44.

30. "Ethnic Pictures and Ethnic Fate," 93.

5

HOLLYWOOD AND HIBERNIA:
THE IRISH IN THE MOVIES

Dennis Clark and William J. Lynch

For the immigrants who came in millions to the United States, "culture" was usually little more than "popular culture." Although at first they may have amused themselves according to their old country ways, as the attachments of the immigrant ghetto diminished, they participated actively in that mainstream of education and entertainment that was promoted by the mass media. And, for the millions, the revelations and fantasies produced by the motion picture industry during the twentieth century were powerful formative influences. Immigrants who sought social models, views of themselves, values to adopt, and frameworks with which to understand America frequently found them in the movies. This was especially true for the Irish, whose English-speaking ability and low economic status made them ready customers for Hollywood's popular-priced products.

For the Irish, as for other groups, the American motion picture has, unfortunately, been a strange mélange—part fiction, part folk drama, and part reality. The complex world of ethnic subcultures has been reflected only confusedly on the shimmering screen. Since ethnic subcultures have been deeply influential and dynamic in American life, it is important to understand how the extraordinarily powerful motion-picture medium has dealt with them.

Creative Irish participation in American films came from their rich theatrical tradition which was welcomed by the booming entertainment industry as a whole. The American film and stage producers had to battle continuous and rigorous Protestant sanctions imposed as part of the puritanical strain in the country's culture, in some ways dating back to the seventeenth century. The Irish had no such moral qualms about the movies or the stage. They brought to America a culture rich in theatrical tradition, in which music, folk dancing, and storytelling proved happy assets to the stage and screen, as the country gradually accepted popular dramatic entertainment as something other than a desecration to the soul of an essentially Protestant society. Besides, since the immigrant Irish were a socioeconomic "out-group" anyhow, they could not afford to reject paying livelihoods in such fields as the theater, no matter what alleged moral taint may have been involved.[1]

The historical range of Irish-American theatrical stereotypes and stock characters was extensive indeed. From the British theatrical tradition the American stage had inherited a series of stock Irish characters. The bumbling servant, the braggart fortune seeker, the reckless lover, and the wild Irish girl were all standard Irish types utilized by playwrights from Sheridan to Shaw.[2] That these types did not reflect the range and human dimensions of Irish character did not trouble British authors or audiences, and Americans were troubled even less, for theatrical license was accorded such portrayals since they did not offend the dominant Anglo-Saxon group in either nation.

In the American vaudeville tradition that burst forth with wonderful vitality in the 1880s, the Irish, along with blacks, became the most commonly mocked group in skits and dialect acts that kept nineteenth-century Americans amused.[3] The musical comedies of Edward Harrigan and Tony Hart set New York laughing at the caricatures of Irish politicians, fire brigade commanders, and saloon owners, among others, while the plays of Dion Boucicault added histrionic lead roles to the array of Hibernian clown characters. However, melodramas like his popular *The Colleen Bawn* (1860) simply elaborated on the prejudicial posturing that passed for dramatic presentation of the Irish. This tradition of using Irish stereotypes ran rampant in the American theater until Irish organizations protested it, at times violently, in the years before World War I. Significantly, the Irish theatrical buffoon coincided with economic exploitation, educational deprivation, widespread popular satirization, and religious and social discrimination directed at the Irish that was active in American society from the early nineteenth century. These circumstances made the public theatrical ridicule of the group a very tender point with more educated and perceptive Irish people.

When the making of films arose as a more hectic aspect of theatrical enterprise, the Irish stereotypes, still very much in cultural currency, were carried over into the new medium. The drunken "boyo," the braggart greenhorn, "Brigid" the clumsy maid, "Tim" the dumb cop, and "Paddy" the burly laborer were standard characters with a century of repeated "Pat and Mike" jokes behind them. The Irish themselves as troupers still disported to their own mockery, though giving the audience what it wanted often included debasing one's own identity. Crude silent films like *The Cohens and the Kellys* (1926) actually developed into an equally crude, but profitable, talking picture series, and along with such early sound films as *Abie's Irish Rose* (1929, 1946) played upon intergroup feelings to produce pluralist harmony by stereotyping both the Jews and the Irish as boorish, loud, stubborn, crude, and given to humorous mishandling of the English language. Such film characteristics were part of the distorted image of minority group behavior and usually did not occur in the portrayals of younger "born in America" offspring of the feuding families, such as Abie Levy and Rosemary Murphy of *Abie's Irish Rose*. Unfortunately, both poor Abie and Rosemary lost any semblance of their respective Jewishness and Irishness.

The tradition of the stereotyped stage Irishman continued through the studios' heyday, and even during their decline it was never really expunged. One interesting early exception to the "buffoon" Irish stereotype was James O'Neill, the stage matinee idol who played the title role in a silent adaptation of *The Count of Monte Cristo* (1912). He had toured the country for many years in a melodramatic stage version of the Dumas novel and always lamented the wasting of his talents in the same part for so long. His son Eugene, America's Nobel Prize-winning playwright, would use him as the model for James Tyrone, the bitter patriarch of *A Long Day's Journey into Night* (1956), which was filmed successfully in 1962. The Tyrone family members, of course, were not "stage Irishmen" in the stage or screen versions.

Though portraits of the Irish in the film studios' products were stereotypic, they were seldom consciously offensive; they also demanded a large number of actors and actresses whose background and names would be Irish or pseudo-Irish. The star system had to meet the expectations of all kinds of groups, the Irish among them. Never mind that the careers of some of these performers declined from time to time; their portrayals of Irish roles would remain nonetheless as the recognizable, though stereotyped, representations of the Irish to generations of American moviegoers. If their recognizably Irish names went upon movie house marquees for a while, that was enough for promotional purposes.

Even a partial list of performers with Irish names indicates the extensive "Irish" presence in American films. Among the silent film performers were Nancy Carroll, Maurice Costello, William and Dustin Farnum, Lloyd Hughes, Alice Joyce, Gregory Kelly, Edgar Kennedy, May McEvoy, Thomas Meighan, Colleen Moore, Tom Moore, Jack Mulhall, George O'Brien, Mary Philbin, and Hal Skelly. Talking films, through several generations of Hollywood, featured such names as Sara Allgood, Ed Begley, Peter Boyle, Walter Brennan, George Brent, James Cagney, Art Carney, Walter Connolly, Dolores Costello, Bing Crosby, Brian Donlevy, James Dunn, Irene Dunne, Richard Egan, Barry Fitzgerald, Errol Flynn, William Gargan, Jackie Gleason, James Gleason, Richard Harris, Helen Hayes, Jack Haley, Grace Kelly, Patsy Kelly, Paul Kelly, Arthur Kennedy, Frank McHugh, Erin-O'Brien Moore, Victor Moore, Lloyd Nolan, Edmond O'Brien, Margaret O'Brien, Pat O'Brien, Carroll O'Connor, Donald O'Connor, Maureen O'Hara, Dan O'Herlihy, Dennis O'Keefe, Ryan O'Neal, Peter O'Toole, Tyrone Power, Tom Powers, Anthony Quinn, Ronald Reagan, Mickey Rooney, Robert Ryan, Arthur Shields, Margaret Sullavan, Maureen O'Sullivan, Spencer Tracy, and many others with Irish surnames, real or assumed. The length and fame of this list suggest the appeal of Irishness in a business that was preoccupied with profits and often oblivious to ethnic sensitivity.

While script writers, directors, and production and financial organizers were behind the scenes, it was the movie scenes themselves that captured the public's imagination. And in the actual productions the attention was upon the actors and actresses, singers and dancers, stars and supporting players. In the calculations of Hollywood, a strategy was developed to cater to the mainstream of Anglo-America and yet patronize and celebrate the various immigrant traditions also. Irish or Irish-sounding names for performers had a special significance. While Jews, Poles, and others often sought to adopt Anglo names for screen careers, Irish names, whether real or assumed, were acceptable on movie billboards. The Irish were common coin in the country, and their names were generally pronounceable. Thus, their transfer from vaudeville and their recruitment for Hollywood were facilitated because of an advertising peculiarity relating to American group attitudes.

But Hollywood was an industry involving far more than performers. The constant generation of scripts was one of the major preoccupations of the industry after "talkies" were introduced. From the subcultural stream of Irish-American writers some luminous talent

Compared to other themes, Irish nationalism fared well in Hollywood. John Ford's masterful The Informer *set the tone. The Irish cause appears as a just one, and the Irish as a resilient, if violent, people.*

became available. Eugene O'Neill, though wary of film versions of his plays, did applaud Paul Robeson's title role in the film version of *The Emperor Jones* (1933),[4] but Lionel Barrymore as Nat Miller in *Ah, Wilderness!* (1935) and William Bendix as Yank in *The Hairy Ape* (1944) appeared in mediocre versions of O'Neill and confirmed the playwright's pessimism about Hollywood's capacity to cope with serious drama. John O'Hara's *Butterfield 8* (1960) and *Pal Joey* (1957) were more adaptable, and O'Hara, F. Scott Fitzgerald, George Kelly, and many lesser Irish-American writers participated directly in the creation of dialogue for the screen. Script writing, however, was usually only a money-making venture for major authors and never drew sufficient exercise of talent or attention to bring to the screen the keen realities of Irish-American experience as distilled in novels and plays. The writers themselves were not hired to portray Irish-American life, but to provide stock scripts, often ordered by studio moguls on an almost whimsical basis. Neither Kelly nor Fitzgerald ever worked on the screen adaptations of their own works, and, indeed, they were often given scripts to write that had little or nothing to do with their particular subject interests. Kelly, an expert at realistic dramatizations of the middle class, was once required to do a screenplay for Wallace Beery, a rural comedy called *Old Hutch* (1936); Fitzgerald's last writing assignment was a college comedy set in Dartmouth in the thirties, entitled *Winter Carnival* (1938). Such writers played the game for what it provided—ready cash—and reserved their serious efforts for their plays or novels. (It is worth noting that O'Hara, Kelly, and Fitzgerald, obviously of Irish descent, virtually ignored the Irish in their literary output, concentrating instead on the American middle or upper classes. Novelist James T. Farrell, whose *Studs Lonigan* trilogy is the classic portrayal of the world of the urban Irish, never wrote at all for Hollywood.)

The making of movies, like so much of the country's economic enterprise, grew into a full-blown business in a very disorderly fashion. Motion picture companies were a blend of theater, new technology, swift finance, and production facilities that were jerry-built and chaotic. The day of the organizer could not long be delayed. Movie companies could not run multi-million dollar businesses like one-man garment factories. Irish-Americans entered Hollywood behind the scenes, both as picture directors and as business managers. John Ford, John Huston, and Raoul Walsh directed dozens of movies during the heyday of the American film industry. Above all Hollywood directors, Ford attempted, though not always successfully, to present valid portraits of the Irish, such as those in the 1935 Academy Award-winning film, *The Informer*.[5] Too often, however, the artistic direction of films was constrained and crude, while the business direction of the industry was an arena for boisterous energy and expansion. This was especially true during the 1920s. It was during this period that Joseph P. Kennedy came to Hollywood. In 1928 he began a thirty-two month whirlwind career as film financier that would net him five million dollars. He began by promoting the talents of Gloria Swanson in an unreleased silent film entitled *Queen Kelly,* and swiftly moved through a series of ventures that culminated in the organization of the RKO Corporation. Such organizational feats reflected not only individual virtuosity, but the potential ability of Irish-Americans to manipulate their own and other ethnic colleagues and interests and to maneuver skillfully in an American culture with which they were highly conversant.[6] As in politics, the Irish were frequently to be found in roles as interpreters and intermediaries.

The fact that Jews played such a vital and extensive role in the film industry had both positive and negative effects upon Irish participa-

Versatile Jimmy Cagney as a quick-tempered hoodlum in Public Enemy *(1931), or a cool cop in* G-Men *(1935) helped make the Irish tough-guy image a staple in many Hollywood movies about crime and city life.*

tion. Jewish and Irish performers mixed freely in vaudeville, and the heavy concentration of both groups in entertainment circles in New York provided links for later Hollywood connections. But the Irish in the movies often were the Irish as seen by Jews, with the disparity and distortion that always attends one group's portrayal of another. For example, Jewish families were seen as close and peaceful, though tense, but Irish families were usually seen as rude and violent. Made for essentially non-Irish audiences, produced by staffs that were either Jewish or Anglo-Saxon, it is little wonder that the movies in which the Irish were presented were not faithful reproductions of their world. They were thrust into melodramatic adventure settings, comic argumentative family films, and sentimental "religious" pieces where their roles led naturally to stereotyping. This list of stereotypic roles related to the Irish, which Hollywood assumed, perpetuated, or enhanced with stock plots, came thus to include a set of stock backgrounds as well. The following are the basic film genres into which the Irish were forced to fit:

1. *The Gangster Film*—Since the Irish were the nation's prime contenders for criminal eminence throughout the 1920s, Al Capone notwithstanding, the action-packed Hollywood crime film, with James Cagney, Pat O'Brien, Regis Toomey, and Lloyd Nolan, became an early public offering. The Irish had long been associated with the American underworld in the city slums. From New York's Bowery to San Francisco's Barbary Coast, the Irish had dominated urban crime since the 1840s, and Dion O'Banion and Machine Gun Kelly were only the latest versions of the Irish hoodlum in their 1920s careers. Cagney, in *Public Enemy* (1931), *Angels With Dirty Faces* (1938), and *The Roaring Twenties* (1939), was the archetypal lawless urban Irish thug, whom prejudiced opinion was only too ready to associate with all of the Irish. Only the Italians have suffered as much in this area, and in recent years they have been actively protesting the film and TV presentations of their community as criminal types. Curiously, the Irish have kept silent, perhaps because their considerable security in American life in recent decades has made them less sensitive to arrant slurs.

2. *The Military Film*—Alan Hale, Victor McLaglen, Pat O'Brien, James Cagney, Peter O'Toole, and Richard Harris all made soldier, sailor, and soldier-of-fortune movies in which the Irish were invariably enlisted men. Films like *The Fighting 69th* (1940) and *The Sullivans* (1944) exemplify this kind of movie in which the Irishman is presented as a courageous, patriotic, but basically "dumb and dogged" fighter. He dies bravely, but is seldom educated or polished enough for officer material. Only George Brent, as Colonel William J. Donovan in *The Fighting 69th*, seems to have been an exception but, then, his charges were all wild Irish-Americans.

3. *The Irish Family Film*—The raucous Irish domestic scene often served as the background for the up-front plot in stock movies about feuding Irish families (for example, *The Irish in Us* (1935) and *Three Cheers for the Irish* (1940), with Sara Allgood, Patsy Kelly, May Robson, and Marjorie Main as "Irish mother" leads trying to keep peace in their brawling homes). Pictures like *A Tree Grows in Brooklyn* (1945) sometimes gave more feeling portraits, and more glamorous families, such as the O'Haras of Tara in *Gone With the Wind* (1939) or the dancing Cohans in *Yankee Doodle Dandy* (1942), were applauded, but genuine insight into the Irish immigrant family was usually lacking.

4. *Adventure Films*—Errol Flynn starred in several epics in which a lovely heroine was rescued from a plethora of perils. One of the earliest was *Captain Blood* (1935) with Flynn playing an Irish doctor, a slave on an English plantation in the Caribbean in the eighteenth century, who turns to piracy to obtain his rights. These adventure films enhanced the image of the Irishman as dashing, devil-may-care swashbuckler, an image that is often attributed to males of another culture who are migrants or exiles.

5. *The Cowboy Film*—John Wayne under a dozen different Irish names ranged the frontier relentlessly. In many of the cavalry movies, such as *Fort Apache* (1948) and *She Wore a Yellow Ribbon* (1949), there was always a tough cavalry sergeant played by Victor McLaglen, Alan Hale, Ward Bond, and even Mickey Rooney. His charges, enlisted men all, were inevitably heavy-drinking, saloon-busting Irishmen.

6. *The Religious Film*—Pat O'Brien, Barry Fitzgerald, Bing Crosby, and Spencer Tracy brought American Catholics to "goody" movies for a generation with *Boys Town* (1938), *Going My Way* (1944), *The Bells of St. Marys* (1945), and *Fighting Father Dunne* (1948). Each of these films presented the Catholic priest as a two-fisted, charming, often musical, figure who fought or sang his way into the souls of his flock.

7. *The "Old Country" Film*—Ireland, without a film industry of its own, had to rely on Hollywood to depict life on the "auld sod." Such films were often romantic, unrealistic portraits of Irish life such as *Song Of My Heart* (1931), a John McCormack musical, and *The Quiet Man* (1952), a John Wayne-Maureen O'Hara film made in Mayo. *Luck of the Irish* (1948), a Tyrone Power comedy, even featured a leprechaun, as did the Disney film *Darby O'Gill and the Little People* (1958).

More interesting have been the few films dealing with Irish politics, particularly with the efforts on the part of the Irish nationalistic movement to secure "Ireland for the Irish" by driving out the English occupation forces. In each case, with the exception of *The Night Fighters* (1960), an anti-IRA film, the sympathies of the audience are with the Irish cause. *The Informer* (1935), *The Plough and the Stars* (1936), *Beloved Enemy* (1936), *Shake Hands with the Devil* (1959), and *Ryan's Daughter* (1971) present the case for Irish freedom as a just one, though the violence employed to secure a unified Irish Republic is often questioned.

Thus, the Irish were reflected on the screen, often simplistically and at best, as in the "Irish Freedom" films, ambiguously, while behind the scenes they worked as writers, promoters, agents, directors, and publicity men. Their influence, however, was never as great in film circles as it might have been. Jewish producers and studio heads and German or Jewish directors all had a broader final impact. Although the Irish cultural connection with the movies was well established, with the exception of Joseph P. Kennedy, they were not a significant part of the financial and power structure.

In one respect the Irish did have a wide-ranging effect, albeit a negative one, on the formation of the final film product—an effect more than any single producer or director could have dreamed of in the early days of the industry. The Irish Catholics had certain religious views that were at variance with filmdom's free-wheeling use of sex in film plots. The Catholic Church in its Irish-dominated American version was highly skeptical of the moral effects of motion pictures. Films with materials about sex and marriage were especially troublesome. A public relations man from Philadelphia, named Joe Breen, was appointed chief "enforcer" of the sanctions imposed by the Hollywood Production Code, devised in 1930 and written by two Irish-Americans, trade journal publisher Martin Quigley and Jesuit Daniel Lord. The code itself, a combination of conservative rural Protestant values and equally conservative Irish-Catholicism, was a thicket of Jansenistic cautions, guidelines, and proscriptions aimed at insuring that virtue triumphed and vice was penalized, that sex would be mildly suggestive but never starkly prurient. It regulated subject matter and language more strictly than any official censor, even though it was theoretically a voluntarily accepted system. Catholic publicists would add an official and rigid film rating system which the Church imposed in a heavy-handed manner in its churches, parochial classrooms, and diocesan newspapers. Given the militant title of "The Legion of Decency," its adherence was exhorted, even demanded of American Catholics. It was strongly implied that a Catholic viewer who disobeyed it was committing a serious sin, though, in fact, the "Legion" had no moral-binding force whatsoever.

Intermittently a studio or a producer cried "censorship" and a wrangle began about provisions of the Production Code. Catholic bishops and journalists defended the rating practices while film executives groaned about the unrealistic restrictions that the code

Bing Crosby in Going My Way *exemplified the stock Irish Catholic priest of Hollywood productions–musical, charming, and big-hearted.*

imposed. Jack Vizzard, a Production Code employee for most of his life (and an ex-Jesuit seminarian), tells of the irascible Philadelphia prelate, Dennis Cardinal Dougherty, who, offended by a salacious bit of billboard advertising in the 1930s, officially forbade all Catholics in his archdiocese to attend *any* films, under threat of mortal sin. Vizzard wryly observes that the good Cardinal, in a theological "lapsus memoriae," never removed the prohibition.[7] (One shudders at the thought of the spiritual condition of the souls of Philadelphia's movie-going Catholics over the last forty years!)

The entire Irish Catholic vigilance system with respect to films fortunately began to fade in the 1950s, when such films as *The Miracle* (1950), *The Moon is Blue* (1953), and *Baby Doll* (1956) created furors but aided in breaking the prevailing puritanical prohibitions. Liberalized attitudes, greater audience maturity, and the recession of Catholic influence in areas of cultural preference all contributed to the waning of Irish-Catholic moralism as it affected the movies. So too did Hollywood's recognition that such films, which lacked Code approval, fared well at the box office during these years of declining fortunes in the movie business.

An equally sore point in Hollywood emerged in the 1950s when Senator Joseph McCarthy of Wisconsin made anti-Communism a frenzied public sport. Film stars and film writers were hauled before

Congressional committees, particularly the sensationalist and witch-hunting House Un-American Activities Committee, to testify as to whether they were or had ever been Communists. Senator McCarthy became for many Americans the personification of reactionary Irish-Catholicism, and he did in some ways reflect Irish-Catholic sentiments.[8] For years while most Americans were relatively unaware of Communist activity, Catholics were treated in their religious press to a diet of horror stories dealing with leftist excesses against religion in Russia, Mexico, China, and Spain. This publicity was a staple in Catholic schools, newspapers, magazines, and sermons, and in the testimony of missionaries who had been victimized under Communist regimes. McCarthy's contempt for the "Anglo" potentates of Ivy-League universities who were prominent in the State Department also struck a sympathetic chord among the Irish, who remembered their maltreatment and exclusion at the hands of that socially prominent elite up to and beyond the years of Al Smith. While there were many Irish-American foes of McCarthy, including bishops, to most non-Catholics he was representative as an Irish-American figure, notwithstanding the fact he was a Republican, while the Irish-Catholics were still heavily Democratic. McCarthy's career and its impact on studios caused the expulsion of liberal and leftist figures from Hollywood, but it also coincided with the decline of the Irish-Catholic opinion bloc as a factor in movie morality.

Although the Irish as part of the great American movie audience saw themselves portrayed on the screen for decades, and although their tastes and preferences were carefully adverted to by filmmakers with respect to certain moral views, the limitations of filmmaking culture did not really permit trenchant presentations of key themes of the Irish-American experience. A pleasant musical biography such as *Yankee Doodle Dandy* or *The Great Victor Herbert* (1939), based on the life of the Dublin-born composer of operettas, could be entertaining, but such movies really did not relate to the social realities most Irish people knew. *In Old Chicago* (1938) with Tyrone Power and a butchered version of James T. Farrell's fine novel *Studs Lonigan* (1956) were typical of the wide-of-the-mark movies about the urban Irish. War movies touched on a broadly-shared Irish-American experience in military service, but these movies invariably misrepresented the realities of war with mock heroics and cheap propaganda.[9] Because of Catholic taboos about sex, Irish family life was difficult to deal with on the screen, and the conservative American Catholic hierarchy would tolerate no films which would treat with real insight problems within its ranks; the studios obliged with the charming, inoffensive Crosby-Fitzgerald genre. No movie even tried to comprehend the huge subject of Irish immigration and its implications, and, as has been

The sordid, seamy side of working-class Irish life in American cities rarely surfaced in Hollywood films. A notable, and sobering, exception was On the Waterfront *with Rod Steiger and Marlon Brando both trapped by the brutal survival-of-the-fittest code of urban life.*

mentioned, "Quiet Man" portraits of Ireland itself only lent lovely natural scenery as a background for more stereotyping of Irish characters.

Nevertheless, there were a few films that showed something of the social trauma of first- and second-generation Irish families. James Dunn and Peggy Ann Garner made *A Tree Grows in Brooklyn* memorable, and *The Subject Was Roses* (1968) caught the Irish lifestyle in the Bronx with keen accuracy. Spencer Tracy in *The Last Hurrah* (1958) gave the Irish politician credibility. Probably the best of the movies showing the Irish in social contexts would include a product of Warner Brothers, *City for Conquest* (1940), with James Cagney, Anne Sheridan, Frank McHugh, Anthony Quinn, and Arthur Kennedy as the sons and daughters of working-class families caught in the toils of urban frustration. Later, *The Molly Maguires* (1970), with Sean Connery and Richard Harris, was a grimly appropriate recollection of the

Irish in Pennsylvania mining towns of the 1800s. One of the best, but most depressing, views of the Irish as victims of American urban conditions was *On the Waterfront* (1954), with Marlon Brando as an exploited Irish dockworker and one-time pugilist. The picture was a seamy depiction of waterfront American life of which even O'Neill would have approved.

After the breakup of the big studio system that dominated the movie industry until about 1950, the formulas for making films changed, and the depiction of the Irish on the screen changed as well. The accepted stock images of the Irish faded, partly because they had become hackneyed, but also because the profile of the group in American life was changing with many fewer Irish immigrants and much greater social diversity for the Irish-Americans. The new wave and individualist filmmakers, who emerged after the demise of the big studios, portrayed the Irish—if at all—in an increasingly fragmentary fashion. Individual portraits might stand out, as in Robert Shaw's fine acting of an iron-jawed Irish gangster in *The Sting* (1973), but basically there was no longer a clear social context for presentations of the Irish. What remains are adventure flops like *Murphy's War* (1970), or insubstantial, noisy shooting plots like *Kelly's Heroes* (1970) or *The Wild Geese* (1978). The old Irish stereotypes are less and less applicable; it is hard to fix a commonly acceptable image of the Irish when the group's imagery reaches from Brendan Behan to John F. Kennedy, from Princess Grace of Monaco to Bernadette Devlin. And one must ruefully admit that since the Irish have become more assimilated into the American mainstream, it is just possible that they may have lost some of their individuality and their color—two qualities essential for any dramatic medium.

In the 1970s Fellini, Truffaut, and others provided films matching the best that America produced. International influences, the revolution in candor about sex, and more explicit portrayals of violence broke inhibitions in one movie after another. The Irish-Americans remained, however, a conservative opinion bloc, flushed with bourgeois success and skeptical of the "new morality." They were unable themselves to update their image or project a new characterization of themselves, and even on fierce subjects such as the struggle in Northern Ireland they have remained dramatically and tragically mute. The British, closer to Irish talent, might cast well such films as *Ryan's Daughter* (1970), but America will have to wait more than a decade after the Ulster problem erupted to view a movie from the widely read novel *Trinity* by Leon Uris (a Jewish writer), which is due to be filmed in the near future.

Finally, it might be expected that Ireland itself and the brilliant drama it produced in the twentieth century would have had a substantial impact on American filmmakers. After all, the Irish drama was in English. However, the transfer from Ireland to America and from stage to film was simply not effected. On the whole, American films missed the gritty compactness, witty inventiveness, and historic content of Irish life here and abroad. The American film industry just moved too fast and too superficially to reveal the depth of Irish motives and mores. Part of the explanation for Hollywood's failure to assert the racy vitality and moody drama of Irish life in the movies was because of the nature of the medium itself. Writers wrote genre films, but seldom anything specifically Irish enough to require cultural fidelity. When John Ford sought to film O'Casey's *The Plough and the Stars,* studio officials refused to permit the kind of casting or accurate dialogue that would have respected the integrity of the play.[10] Films culturally explicit about the Irish would be too risky at the box office, it seemed. Because of the breadth, the complexity, and the springing ambiance of the Irish tradition, Hollywood was not able to capture more than a bit of its comic surface or a few chords of its sonorous seriousness.

It is unfortunate, but perhaps culturally inevitable, that such a refulgently oral and prodigally rich literary people as the Irish would be incompatible with American films. They figure in "entertainment" films, but very rarely in films with insight and passionate revelations of the human condition. American films would have to grow still more mature before they could adequately interpret the Irish, an ancient people addicted to contradictions beyond the simplicities on which American films have been largely based.

In summary, the Irish mark on American films was essentially creative as expressed through performers and writers, but repressive as manifested in the Production Code and McCarthyite witch-hunting. The Irish might have been a more powerful force in filmdom, but they were ultimately handicapped by their failure as a group to transmit adequately the literary and dramatic tradition native to Ireland to the peculiarly American cultural medium of films. The tragedy of Ireland's own intellectual and historical frustrations is in part responsible for this failure, for from a broken culture the Irish brought to America only such fragments as emigrants can bear away. The sad result has been that the "stage Irishman" and his screen brother have really emerged as identical twins.

NOTES

1. Awareness of a kind of "second-class citizenry" of an ethnic and professional nature may well account for the arrogant defensiveness as well as the creative drive of a personality such as playwright George M. Cohan, whose grandparents emigrated from County Cork. Cohan, though he made but two films, was the most versatile figure in the history of the American stage; he was also the subject of a memorable biographical film, *Yankee Doodle Dandy* (1942).

2. The stereotypes of the Irish are discussed in Stephen Garrett Bolger, "The Irish Character in American Fiction: 1830-60" (Ph.D. thesis, University of Pennsylvania, 1971).

3. Douglas Gilbert, *American Vaudeville: Its Life and Times* (1963), 61-77.

4. Louis Schaeffer, *O'Neill: Son and Artist* (2 vols., 1973), II, 352.

5. Ford's difficulties with his studio, RKO, in presenting honest Irish portraits are recorded in Lewis Jacobs, *The Rise of the American Film: A Critical History* (1967), 483. Even Ford was forced into Irish stereotypes, albeit delightful ones, in films such as *The Quiet Man* (1952).

6. Richard J. Whalen, *The Founding Father: The Story of Joseph P. Kennedy* (1964), 99.

7. Jack Vizzard, *See No Evil* (1970), 49-50. Vizzard's book is an amusing and informative account of Hollywood film "censorship" during the sound era. For a good discussion of the Legion of Decency see also Garth Jowett, *Film: The Democratic Art* (1976), especially 241-42, 246-56, 416-18.

8. William V. Shannon, *The American Irish* (1963), 380-81. Shannon vividly describes and explains the perverse attraction of McCarthy to the Irish-American electorate. See also John W. Caughey, "McCarthyism Rampant," in Alan Reitman, ed., *The Pulse of Freedom* (1975), 139-41. Caughey gives a close account of the effects of McCarthyism on Hollywood.

9. Joan Mellen in *Big Bad Wolves: Masculinity in the American Film* (1977), 41-42, sees John Ford and his Irish heroes as the extollment of Irish "macho types" in war and western movies.

10. Jacobs, *The Rise of the American Film*, 484.

6

BETWEEN TWO WORLDS: JEWISH IMAGES IN AMERICAN FILM

Patricia Erens

Despite their small numbers in the United States, Jews have enjoyed an advantage unequalled by any other ethnic group in America—a virtual control over their own self-image on the screen. This was made possible by the great influx of Jewish talent into all areas of film production. Indeed, Ben Hecht once commented that Hollywood experienced "a Semitic renaissance sans rabbis and Talmud."[1]

Until the 1910s when film producers gravitated west to California, moviemaking in the United States was centered on the East Coast, especially in the New York area, the heartland of Jewish-American life. The first American public screening took place at Koster & Bial's Music Hall in New York City in 1896. Thereafter, films, which soon grew from minute scenes to ten-minute one reelers, were shown in penny arcades and later in converted storefronts. In 1905 nickelodeon theaters emerged, and in 1907 the first all-film theater opened its doors. Figures for 1910 indicate that 26,000,000 Americans attended the nickelodeon each week (a little less than twenty percent of the nation's population). In New York City, however, the percentage was higher, slightly over twenty-five percent (between 1,200,000 and 1,600,000 people). Jews probably made up a large proportion of the moviegoing audience, especially as forty-two of the 123 exhibition houses were located on the Lower East Side where Jews congregated.[2]

The film producers were, of course, conscious of their potential audience and geared their films to them. The early works were short vaudeville acts, simple comedies, and predictable melodramas. From these, the Jewish immigrants received amusement after a hard day's work, an introduction into the customs of American life, especially those of the upper classes, and, from time to time, self-images sent back from the screen. Little English was necessary to follow the plot.

In the movie industry, Jews have been a dominant force as producers, writers, directors, and composers. Their participation dates back to the earliest period. But perhaps the most unique aspect of Jewish participation, that which sets them apart from any other ethnic group, has been their virtual monopoly on film producing. During the heydey of Hollywood, every major studio, save Twentieth Century-Fox, was headed by a man of Jewish origin. Jews moved into motion picture production and exhibition for the same reasons they had gravitated to such other fields as small merchandizing and the garment trades. Participation took little skill and little capital and, as a new industry, was open to immigrants; all newcomers were on an equal footing. As the Jews gained a foothold in the industry, they hired friends and relatives, and so their numbers, and influence, grew.

Following the early pioneers, a second generation of Jewish film producers emerged to build Hollywood moviemaking into a major industry. In this list are the names Carl Laemmle, William Fox, Adolph Zukor, Samuel Goldwyn, Jesse Lasky, Harry Cohn, Louis B. Mayer, the Warner Brothers, Irving Thalberg, and B. P. Schulberg, and financiers like the Schenck Brothers and Marcus Loew.

These men, the majority of whom had landed in America as poor immigrants, were driven by the need to succeed. Despite a lack of formal education, they possessed sharp business minds and an infallible instinct for pleasing audiences. Though none were overtly religious, all were unmistakably Jewish. "In certain ways, the Hollywood moguls revealed their Jewish roots implicitly, by the patriarchal style in which they ran their fiefdoms and by their close family loyalties."[3]

At the same time, these men had an overwhelming desire to prove themselves good Americans. As Philip French observes, "their commitment to the melting pot had many consequences for their work." One was a wish "to impose a certain uniformity upon their employees and their product, to advance from a notion that fundamentally everyone is much the same to a demonstration that everyone really *is* the same." Two was the "re-naming of actors and actresses capable of being identified with immigrant groups."[4] And three was a bias towards resolving scenarios with intermarriage, a circumstance which reflected events in their own biographies. These tendencies will be discussed more fully in the succeeding section.

These men constituted the second generation of Jews involved in film production. Following in their footsteps came a third generation, men such as David Selznick, Dore Schary, Pandro Berman, Arthur Freed, William Goetz, Sam Jaffe, Anatole Litvak, Joseph Mankiewicz, Joseph Pasternak, Sam Spiegel, Michael Todd, Hal Wallis, and William Wanger. Apart from Selznick and Schary, most of these men chose to work independently, rather than as part of the studio hierarchy, and to release their films through larger companies. Like their predecessors, they were hard-nosed individualists who possessed an abiding commitment to moviemaking.

Since the collapse of the "Old Hollywood" at the end of the fifties, executives have come and gone. None have had the bearing of the old moguls. None have become household names. However, in the main, these men are still of Jewish origin. American born, educated, and assimilated, they are a new breed and constitute the fourth generation of Jews active in the industry.

Jewish participation in the film industry has not been limited solely to production, however. Major artistic contributions have been made in the area of screenwriting. Again, the list is long. A recent survey indicated that seventy to eighty percent of the Screen Writers' Guild was composed of Jews, a trend dating back to the 1930s.[5] Among those writers, past and present, who have devoted themselves to scriptwriting are Julius Epstein, Phil Epstein, Carl Foreman, William Goldman, Ben Hecht, Garson Kanin, Howard Koch, Jesse Lasky, Jr., Herman Mankiewicz, Morris Riskin, and Budd Schulberg.

Jews have also made major contributions as directors. Among those whose careers span the decades are George Cukor, Stanley Kubrick, Ernst Lubitsch, Rouben Mamoulian, Abraham Polonsky, Otto Preminger, Robert Rossen, John Stahl, Billy Wilder, Robert Wise, William Wyler, and Fred Zinnemann. In addition, there are younger directors such as Elaine May, Mike Nichols, Roman Polanski, Sydney Pollack, and Steven Spielberg.

Composing has been another area of high concentration for Jewish artists. Particularly important are men such as Burt Bacharach, Irving Berlin, Elmer Bernstein, Bernard Herrmann, Marvin Hamlisch, Jerome Kern, Alfred Newman, André Previn, Miklos Rozsa, and Max Steiner.

In the first two decades of the twentieth century, Jews were portrayed quite frequently in American movies, especially as immigrant characters. Such portrayals diminished during the 1930s and 1940s as the drive toward assimilation among Jews in America was reflected on the screen. Recently, however, there has been a resurgence of ethnic identity in American life. This has resulted in an increase in the depiction of Jewish characters on the screen. But always in such portrayals two questions nag Jewish participants in filmmaking: How will the Jews appear to the outside world? How will an individual film affect the Jewish community? The history of the Jews in the American cinema is intricately tied to these concerns. What remains now is to take a close look at the films themselves and to detail the themes (which changed along with shifting social realities) and the stereotypes (which often remained constant) over a seventy-five year period.

A brief comment should be included on the subject of anti-Semitism. Despite the waves of anti-Semitism in America during this century, it has never been a state policy as in Europe nor has it taken on the proportions known elsewhere in the world. Similarly, although anti-Semitic literature has appeared in every decade, anti-Semitism has not been a dominant or even prevalent aspect of the mass media (newspapers, radio, film, television) or the fine arts (painting, literature, drama). Therefore, it is not surprising to discover that although negative portrayals of Jews exist in film, little overt anti-Semitism occurs. The large number of Jews who held the reins of Hollywood's power prevented this. Lack of overt anti-Semitism also reflected the thinking of an industry in which appeal to the largest numbers and offense to none was the order of the day. Because Jews made up a high percentage of the urban film audience, their interests could not be slighted.

A case could be made, however, against some of the early silent shorts produced by film companies in which the heads of production were not Jewish. Included in this group are many of the early comedies in which Jews appear as the butt of the joke, the scapegoat. Typical of such works is *Levitsky's Insurance Policy; Or When Thief Meets Thief*, produced by the Vitagraph Company, in which even a thief is able to best the Jewish merchant and to teach him a lesson.

In America one of the earliest Jewish screen characters appears in Thomas Edison's *Cohen's Advertising Scheme* (1904), a film based on a common vaudeville act. Cohen, a short balding man with a large nose, aggressively pushes his wares. When he discovers that one customer has no money, he gives him a coat nonetheless. Unbeknownst to the man, the back of the coat reads "Go to I. Cohen for Clothing." Cohen has outsmarted his customer, who is none the wiser.

The scheming Jewish merchant appears in many comedies up until the 1920s and possesses elements of anti-Semitic caricature. Gross features and vulgar gestures usually accompany the portrayal, a carry-over from the burlesque Jew of vaudeville, which, along with Victorian melodrama, served as the basis for early scenarios and interpretation before film writers developed their own conventions.

In addition to the burlesque Jew, early films also provide a sympathetic image, especially in melodrama. D. W. Griffith's *Old Isaacs, the Pawnbroker* (1907) offers one of the first images of the benevolent Jewish moneylender. Here the pawnbroker saves an ailing Gentile woman and her child. The story has all of the elements of pathos and sentimentality which long adhere to stories about Jewish life.

Through the 1910s the Jew appears in a wide variety of melodramas, comedies, and literary adaptations. Of this group, the melodrama is the most prevalent. Two themes emerge as dominant—the depiction of immigrant life in America and the depiction of Czarist

Al Jolson in The Jazz Singer *(1927) is caught between the ties of his Jewish family and tradition and the calls of a secular world.*

oppression in Europe. In comedy, the films tend to reproduce the vaudeville routines with little emphasis on narrative development. In the area of literary adaptation, works include *Oliver Twist, The Merchant of Venice, Ivanhoe,* and *Daniel Deronda.* Several of these stories were remade several times. The films, condensed and silent, and generally faithful to the original texts, brought to the screen anti-Semitic characters like Fagin and Shylock.

Included in the comedies, melodramas, and adaptations are a whole stable of character types. These laid the basis for the depiction of Jews on film for years to come. In each decade one or two character types have been added to this group, but in the main, the types have remained constant. Certain archetypal characters—the Jewish father/mother/daughter/son—change over the years, but the characters themselves remain fixed in number, especially as Jews tend to be defined on the screen by their occupational choices which, as in life, have changed little over the years, or by their place within the Jewish family. The character types which appear in the period before 1920 include: the scheming merchant, the benevolent pawnbroker, the stern patriarch, the prodigal son, the rose of the ghetto, the innocent Jewess, and the Yiddisher cowboy.

Three films will suffice to demonstrate the dominant characteristics and themes of the Jewish image in this early period. They include a ghetto film, a nihilist film, and a comedy.

In *A Passover Miracle* (1914), a film set in the New York ghetto, Sam goes off to medical school with tuition money earned by his sweetheart, Lena, in the sweatshops. Once away, Sam forgets Lena's sacrifices and falls for a flashy stenographer. Sam's father banishes him from the house. After much misery and reconsideration, Sam returns on Passover Eve and is accepted back into the household.

Like other ghetto films, *A Passover Miracle* focuses on educational mobility, sweatshop labor, generational rifts, and family reconciliation. Though exaggerated for dramatic effect, the ghetto films did capture the flavor and trials of the immigrant experience. *A Passover Miracle* also presents Jewish religious ritual (the Passover service) and utilizes several character types: the stern patriarch, the prodigal son, and the rose of the ghetto.

Of the nihilist films, works set in Czarist Russia, *In the Czar's Name* (1910) is typical. A young Russian nobleman, Ivan Barnoff, falls in love with a Jewess named Olga. Her father refuses the match, causing the two to elope. Meanwhile, an anti-Semite named Metchinoff stirs up trouble which eventually leads to a massacre of the Jews. The survivors are exiled to Siberia. Ivan and Olga follow in order to help the oppressed to escape. Olga's parents accept Ivan into the family and all leave for America.

The film depicts the violent persecution of Jews in Czarist Russia, suggesting intermarriage and immigration to America as possible solutions. America appears as the land of refuge in film, as it did in fact for many East European Jews. The policy of the Czarist government, however, is displaced onto an individual anti-Semite. Like the ghetto films, romance plays an important role in the narrative. Olga is one representation of the innocent Jewess. In other films, however, she is sacrificed on the altar of love or prejudice.

The comedies of this period are short and fairly sketchy. Not until the 1920s does Jewish domestic comedy emerge. *Foxy Izzy* (1911) is typical. Izzy is a peddler who is robbed at pistol point. Later he is able to reverse the situation by convincing the culprits to shoot bullet holes into his clothes. While they are distracted, he overcomes them and adds the pistol to his wares. The comedy is a good representation of the scheming merchant. Generally successful (although sometimes he outsmarts himself), he uses his cleverness to save the day. In the more anti-Semitic versions, his cleverness is a means of acquiring more money. As many of these comedies came straight from the vaudeville stage, they possess stronger negative portrayals than the melodramas which were often influenced by Yiddish stories or dramas.

The 1920s was the golden age for Jewish images. Within the decade Jews were portrayed in over ninety-five films, mostly in major roles. Like the two preceding decades, the films fall into two large groups—melodramas and comedies. The overwhelming number of films devoted to domestic life constitute a separate subgenre, a blossoming of the ghetto film from the decade before.

In a sense, the twenties began and ended with a ghetto film—in each case a blockbuster. Both *Humoresque* (1920), based on Fannie Hurst's story, and *The Jazz Singer* (1927) typify the period. Both, highly sentimental, are filled with pathos and comedy, a specifically Jewish combination. *Humoresque* deals with the rise of a young boy who becomes a famous violinist. *The Jazz Singer* focuses on a ghetto child who achieves fame as a jazz singer. Both movies depict the Jewish family, especially the relationship between a loving mother and son. In the first case, the family supports the son's goals; in the second, the father, a respected cantor, rejects his son who seeks a career as an entertainer rather than follow in the tradition. Both films reflect the Jewish struggle between traditionalism and assimilation in America—the central theme in all ghetto films of the first two decades. It also should be noted that, in contrast to *The Passover Miracle,* Jackie in *The Jazz Singer,* although reconciled with his father, does not return home to stay. As his mother says, "He belongs to the world." Also of significance is Jackie's choice of a Gentile bride. Although statistics show the rate of intermarriage among Jews in real life was very small, an overwhelming number of films in this period depict Jewish intermarriage. This tendency promoted by Jewish producers remains, even today, a strong factor in film and reflects an assimilationist ideal shared by creators and viewers alike.

During the 1920s the comedy developed into a full-blown vehicle with several stars who became familiar for their depictions of the Jew. The first to appear was Max Davidson, whose career dated back to the 1910s. The next comedian was George Sidney, whose name was to become synonymous with the comic Jewish figure for three decades. Beginning with the portrayal of *Busy Izzy* (1915), he played in films through the mid-thirties. His most famous role was Jacob Cohen, the rotund, good-natured, but inept Jew, of *The Cohens and the Kellys* (1926). The film was extremely popular and was turned into a series. (Six more films were made, the last in 1933). However, Sidney's portrayal drew much opposition from Jewish critics who saw Cohen as the perpetuation of a vulgar stereotype which was not representative of the Jewish community at large.[6]

Alongside Sidney, Alexander Carr, another Jewish comedian, made his appearance in *Potash and Perlmutter* (1923). This work also became a series. Following these men, comedians such as Sammy Cohen, George Jessel, Benny Rubin, and Harry Golden made films in Hollywood, especially at the beginning of the sound era when Jewish accents were novel and a source of humor. Al Jolson, Eddie Cantor, and the Marx Brothers also appeared in film, but aside from Jolson's appearance in *The Jazz Singer,* the first talking motion picture, none of these entertainers took parts which labeled them as specifically Jewish.

With the coming of sound in 1927, the film industry not only tackled new technological problems, but also addressed new themes. First and foremost was the emphasis on singing and dancing and the development of the musical. Then came an interest in crime stories and life on the streets.

Singers, dancers, stage directors, script writers, voice coaches, and composers flocked to California. Many of them were Jews. Hollywood now experienced its second great influx of Jewish creative talent and personnel. Like the producers before them, most of the Jews worked behind the screen. However, there also emerged a group of talented actors and actresses such as Paul Muni, Edward G. Robinson, Sylvia Sidney, and Luise Rainer. In the next decades the ranks were enlarged by the talents of Melvyn Douglas, Paulette Goddard, John Garfield, Lauren Bacall, Jack Benny, Danny Kaye, Jeff Chandler, Lee J. Cobb, Shelley Winters, Tony Curtis, and Jerry Lewis.

These actors did not think of themselves as Jewish personalities.

Most of them changed their names[7] and seldom appeared on the screen as Jews.[8] In addition, given their talent, studio publicity, and the wide range of their performances, all of them attained star status.

During the 1930s a drastic decline in the number of Jewish characters on the screen occurred. This phenomenon has three explanations. First, there was a tendency among Hollywood producers to appeal to the greatest numbers in the belief that by portraying the "average American" (a WASP) all people could identify with the image. This notion was based on the acceptance of the "melting pot" theory in which all Americans would be brothers and individual differences which separated them would disappear. This idea coincided with the efforts of many American Jews to become acculturated, if not totally assimilated.

A second factor which influenced screen portrayals was the sharp reduction in immigration beginning in 1924. This meant that the constant influx of new immigrants virtually ceased, and the Jews as a group, along with others, were moving continually towards acculturation and then to assimilation. By the mid-thirties many had completed this process. And for those who had not, the assimilated Jew was an ideal. No doubt the producers themselves, who had so recently been newcomers, unconsciously desired to project a new self-image.

Lastly, the rise of Adolf Hitler and the changes occurring in Nazi Germany created fear and tension, even in America. Although many of the men in the industry organized to fight the monstrous anti-Semitic state,[9] others felt it was not a good time to place Jewish characters and Jewishness in the foreground of films.

The moguls themselves tended to perceive their own image in terms of country, rather than religion. David Selznick went so far as to say, "I'm an American and not a Jew."[10] Likewise, Louis B. Mayer's pet project (and perhaps latent fantasy) during the 1940s was the Andy Hardy series, a portrayal of a WASP family par excellence.

In most of the films of the 1930s in which Jewish characters appear, they have a low profile, being Jewish in name only. Characters who appear in dramas or novels later adapted for film are played by non-Jewish actors: for example, John Barrymore as George Simon in *Counsellor-at-Law* (1933) and as Oscar Jaffe in *Twentieth Century* (1934). Sometimes they are de-Semitized: for example, Rabbi Ezra in the play *Winterset* becomes Professor Ezra in the 1936 screen version. Elsewhere Jews are referred to euphemistically as non-Aryans: for example, Dr. Roth in *The Mortal Storm* (1940).

A few important films ran counter to this trend. These include *The House of Rothschild* (1934) and *The Great Dictator* (1940). The former starred George Arliss, who enjoyed a huge success on stage and screen as the Jewish prime minister, Benjamin Disraeli. *The House of*

Rothschild focuses on the rise and business acumen of the four Rothschild brothers. The film highlights family solidarity, communal concerns in the wake of European anti-Semitism, and the necessity of wealth to secure physical safety for Jewish survival. As such, the film provides one of the few logical and sympathetic explanations of the Jew's concern for money.

The Great Dictator, produced, directed, written, and played by Charles Chaplin, was one of the first films to confront directly the growing threat of Nazi Germany. A few works had dealt with political problems, but without clearly relating them to the Jews. These films include *Confessions of a Nazy Spy* (1939) and *The Mortal Storm.* With slight disguise, *The Great Dictator* shows the growing power of Adenoid Hynkel (Hitler) as he imposes a policy of discrimination, then physical violence, against the Jews of Tomania (Germany). Chaplin plays the dual role of Hynkel and the Jewish barber. Developing his character of the tramp in a new direction, he sympathetically portrays the plight of the little man (this time Jewish), incorporating some elements of the traditional Jewish *schlemiel,* a clumsy and gullible character, whose good nature allows him to live in the world joyously. The Jewish barber eventually emerges as a political activist and, in the end, his speech to Tomania and those in the world beyond is a lesson in courage and humanity.

For the numbers of Yiddish-speaking Jews, particularly in New York, the 1930s also provided an indigenous cinema, Yiddish films. Produced, directed, written, and acted entirely by Jews for Jewish audiences, the Yiddish cinema provides an informative alternative to the portrayal of the Jew in Hollywood films.

The Yiddish cinema constitutes a body of approximately fifty works beginning in 1924 and running through 1961. The majority of these works appeared during the 1930s, following the arrival of sound and roughly approximating the same period in which blacks produced their own motion pictures. With the changing economic conditions brought about by World War II and the limitations on immigration, which directly affected the Yiddish speaking community, this popular form of entertainment disappeared.

Most of the Yiddish films (all of which were released with English subtitles) were produced on very low budgets and suffered from technical and directorial deficiencies. In America many were produced and directed by Joseph Seiden, who shot them in small studios in the New York area. Actors were generally culled from the Yiddish stage, then in its decline. Names such as Boris Thomashevsky, Celia Adler, and Maurice Schwartz appear on the credits as well as such singers and comedians as Molly Picon, Menasha Skulnick, Leo Fuchs, and Moishe Oysher. Scripts were either adaptations of famous Yiddish dramas or original stories with contemporary settings. In either case, the films reveal a high degree of melodrama and sentiment, often increased by the acting style of the performers. A further characteristic is the inclusion of songs, even within serious dramas. These melodies created nostalgia for a dying tradition and were eagerly awaited by the audience.

Film titles provide insight into the popular subjects. Titles like *My Yiddisher Mama, My Son, Uncle Moses, Two Sisters, Her Second Mother,* and *Where is My Child?* all deal with the Jewish family in America. Plots center on marriageable daughters, abandoned wives, orphaned children, generational conflicts, and adjusting to life in America. All tugged at the heart strings.

Produced for ethnic audiences and uninterested in appealing to non-Jewish viewers, the Yiddish cinema stresses tradition over assimilation. Representative of the Yiddish cinema as a whole is Seiden's *The Cantor's Son* (1934). Starring Moishe Oysher, the film deals with a young boy who leaves Poland and establishes himself in the New World. After much difficulty he finally succeeds in America and meets a woman who loves him. However, he cannot forget the ways of his father, and eventually he returns to Poland. He marries a girl there and replaces his father as head of the synagogue. The story is revealing, especially when compared with a similar narrative, *The Jazz Singer.* Like the other films in this genre, *The Cantor's Son* places high value on family reconciliation and the continuation of the Jewish ethos. Most specifically, it rejects intermarriage.

Lastly, one needs to mention Edgar G. Ulmer's *Green Fields* (1937), a lyrical tale of a Talmudic scholar who awakens to the beauties of life and nature. Filmed in New Jersey, the movie indicates the high artistry that might have been achieved had more money and more talent gone into these productions. As it was, the film enjoyed an enormous success, playing to packed houses in New York City for twenty weeks.

With the demise of the Yiddish cinema, the Jew virtually disappeared from the screen. In Hollywood during the next era, the Jew became assimilated beyond recognition, thus completing a tendency begun in the 1930s. Typical of Hollywood's attitude were remarks attributed to Harry Cohn and Jack Warner. Supposedly Cohn's reply to a suggestion for using a Jewish-looking actor was, "Around this studio, the only Jews we put into pictures play Indians."[11] Similarly, Warner's response to having a Jewish officer in *Objective Burma* was, "See that you get a good clean-cut American type for Jacobs."[12]

Apart from the two outstanding films which deal with anti-Semitism—*Crossfire* (1947) and *Gentleman's Agreement* (1947)—the Jew appears only as a minor character in war films until the end of the

Gentleman's Agreement, *starring Gregory Peck as a Gentile reporter posing as a Jew to expose anti-Semitism in America, was one of a growing number of post World War II films that grappled with discrimination.*

1940s. Then he reemerges in a few insignificant, nostalgic comedies like the remake of *Abie's Irish Rose* (1946) and *The Big City* (1948) or the series of film biographies based on the lives of George Gershwin (*Rhapsody in Blue,* 1945), Jerome Kern (*Till the Clouds Roll By,* 1946), and Al Jolson (*The Jolson Story,* 1946, and *Jolson Sings Again,* 1949). Only the latter two works place any real emphasis on ethnic identification.

The degree to which Jews were erased from the screen is symbolized by the remake of *Humoresque* (1947). In a rewrite prepared for Joan Crawford and John Garfield, the warm Jewish family completely disappears and nothing remains to identify the aspiring violinist as a Jew, except for Garfield's real life biography.

The war films follow a common pattern. In the main, the Jew is a low-ranking member of a platoon which includes several minority figures (Irish, Poles, and Italians). In *Air Force* (1943), *Bataan* (1943), and *Objective Burma* (1945), the Jew is generally the comedian and morale booster who keeps everyone's spirits high. A few exceptions to this pattern are *Winged Victory* (1944) and *Pride of the Marines* (1945) in which Jews assume different or larger roles.

The two most significant films of the period are the postwar works, *Crossfire* and *Gentleman's Agreement. Crossfire* deals with the murder of a Jew by a disturbed, anti-Semitic ex-soldier. The film, produced by Dore Schary for RKO Studios, centers on the violent repercussions of prejudice.

Gentleman's Agreement, adapted from Laura Z. Hobson's best-selling novel, focuses on the efforts of a Gentile reporter to expose anti-Semitism in America. Posing as a Jew, he experiences firsthand the various forms of discrimination.

Produced by Darryl F. Zanuck and directed by Elia Kazan for Twentieth Century-Fox, this film, like *Crossfire,* provoked controversy, especially appearing after Americans learned of the Holocaust. Many individual Jews and organizations like the American Jewish Committee thought that such films would disturb still waters and stimulate negative feelings about Jews. Zanuck, a Christian, and others, believed that the film would create understanding and tolerance, perhaps even change attitudes. Studies were conducted, but the results were inconclusive.[13] The tests indicated that, although attitudes could be changed, one could not be sure how long these changes would last.

However, if Schary and Zanuck hoped to create a new era of social protest on the Hollywood screen, their hopes were short-lived. Following several works such as *Pinky* (1949), a film about black-white relations, Hollywood turned its back on films which pleaded for human tolerance. In the wake of the House Un-American Activities Committee investigations, Hollywood producers decided to play it safe and returned to straight entertainment—musicals and comedies.

The HUAC hearings had a heavy impact on many talented Jews in Hollywood, and it is no secret that John Rankin, who officiated at the first investigations, was an anti-Semite. Although only three of the original "Hollywood Ten" were Jewish,[14] later blacklisting affected a high number of Jewish actors and screenwriters, including Judy Holliday, Zero Mostel, Carl Foreman, Lillian Hellman, Joseph Losey, Abraham Polonsky, Ben Maddow, and Ben Barzman.

In the 1950s Jews once again emerged as recognizable characters in Hollywood films, although for most of the decade they appear only as important minor characters who affect the central action in some significant way. Toward the end of the decade, Jews resumed center stage in a few films, especially dramas which portray the Jew as a successful, integrated member of society with middle-class standing. In addition, Jews made a major comeback as Hebrews in a deluge of

Bible films. The Holocaust, however, was carefully avoided until the end of the decade.[15]

In several films of the 1950s the Jew appears as an outsider, representative of a minority group, who teaches the main character, directly or by example, the meaning of human understanding and the difficulty of remaining true to principles. Works like *Good Morning, Miss Dove* (1955), *Home Before Dark* (1958), *The Young Lions* (1959), and *Dark at the Top of the Stairs* (1960) fall into this category.

In the latter part of the decade films dealing with specifically Jewish problems were released. In these works, many based on popular novels by Jewish authors, the emphasis was upon Jewish life or anti-Semitism. Such films as *I Accuse* (1958), *Me and the Colonel* (1958), and *The Diary of Anne Frank* (1959) deal with prejudice against Jews, while *Marjorie Morningstar* (1958), *The Last Angry Man* (1959), and *The Middle of the Night* (1959) deal with being Jewish in America. Whether Jews were played by Jewish actors did not seem of great importance. Danny Kaye and Paul Muni take the leads in *Me and the Colonel* and *The Last Angry Man*, but non-Jews like Jose Ferrer, Natalie Wood, and Gene Kelly were cast as Jews in *I Accuse* and *Marjorie Morningstar*.

The most significant aspect of the 1950s was the appearance of films set in Israel and the creation of new character types—the Israeli warrior and his female counterpart. The first film in this genre was *The Sword in the Desert* (1949). This was followed by *The Juggler* (1953), starring Kirk Douglas, a story of the Holocaust refugees who fled to Israel after World War II. But most important was Otto Preminger's epic production, *Exodus* (1960), which established henceforth the image of the proud Israeli with a gun in hand. This image lent dignity to the Jewish character who had for so long been depicted as a victim. In a subtle way, pride in Israel and the new Jewish image also altered the defensive posture of many American Jews and allowed for a new openness on the screen.

During the 1950s, Hollywood studios began releasing Biblical epics. This trend was aided by the success of the first Cinemascope production, *The Robe* (1953). Several of these works were based on Old Testament stories. *Samson and Delilah* (1949) came first, followed by *David and Bathsheba* (1951). However, the success of *The Ten Commandments* (1956), starring Charlton Heston in the role of Moses, solidified studio commitment. *The Ten Commandments* was followed by *Ben Hur* (1959), *Esther and the King* (1960), *Solomon and Sheba* (1960), and *The Story of Ruth* (1960). It is interesting to note that in all cases the Jews overcome formidable enemies and emerge as victors. Such narratives carry a latent message about Jewish survival and serve as a necessary antidote after the horrors of the Holocaust.

By the end of the 1950s the Jewish presence in film was quite significant, although there still remained a tendency to underplay the Jewish element, to de-Semitize the characters, or just to ignore the entire question of ethnicity. Thus, *A Hole in the Head* (1959), a Broadway comedy about Jews, becomes Italian when it is filmed. Elsewhere, movies like *Houdini* (1953), *Compulsion* (1959), and *Murder, Inc.* (1960) simply sidestep the question of Jewish heritage. *Houdini*, starring Tony Curtis, is quite revealing, especially when compared with *The Great Houdini* (made for television, 1976), wherein the conflicts between Jewish mother and Gentile daughter-in-law become one of the film's major themes. The film also offers one of the screen's few heartfelt defenses for marrying within the Jewish faith.

With the opening of the 1960s the stage was set for a full return of the Jewish character. The films are numerous and cover many genres—drama, comedy, biography, war films. Beginning in 1968, several films highlight Jewish issues, Jewish humor, and Jewish performers, as even minor characters take on a pronounced ethnicity. Reflecting the new sense of ethnic identity (if not strict religious observance) felt by many groups throughout America, these films form a prelude to the 1970s, an era so filled with Jewish characters that I am tempted to call it the Second Golden Age rivaled only by the 1920s.

It is also in the 1960s that Hollywood addressed itself to the full impact of the Holocaust. Only after a distance of fifteen years did producers and audiences feel ready to confront the emotional and intellectual significance of such an event. *Judgment at Nuremberg* (1961) raises the question at the beginning of the decade, and although the film lacks any Jewish presence, except for the bodies in the documentary footage, the film does confront the issue. The major contribution, however, was *The Pawnbroker* (1965) which focused on the scars of the survivors. Both films were produced independently.

For the first time since the 1920s Jewish domestic comedy reappears. In these films Jews play leading roles and growing up Jewish becomes a central theme. The genre begins with *A Majority of One* (1961) and is followed by *Come Blow Your Horn* (1963), *Enter Laughing* (1967), *Bye, Bye Braverman* (1968), *I Love You, Alice B. Toklas* (1968), *The Producers* (1967), *Take the Money and Run* (1969), and *Goodbye, Columbus* (1969). Most works poke fun at the Jewish family, the overbearing mother, the weak father, the confused son, and the Jewish drive for success and money. What had been sentimental in the 1920s now emerges as gross and reprehensible.

The mystique of Israel continues as a fascination in films like *Judith* (1965) and *Cast a Giant Shadow* (1966), a fictionalized biography of Colonel Mickey Marcus.

Other biographies were made on the lives of Arnold Rothstein (*King of the Roaring Twenties,* 1961), Moss Hart (*Act One,* 1963), Sigmund Freud (*Freud,* 1962), and Fanny Brice (*Funny Girl,* 1968). All openly acknowledged the Jewish heritage of their subjects.

Several films during the period feature important minor Jewish characters such as Jack Kruschen's physician in *The Apartment* (1960) and Milton Selzer's talent agent in *The Legend of Lylah Clair* (1968). Doctors and film producers became favorite Jewish subjects. In most cases, the doctors are dedicated and bright, the producers hardnosed and materialistic. In an article in *Commentary* (1965), critic Robert Alter notes the tendency in the literature of the 1960s to sentimentalize the Jew.[16] This same trend appears in film as well. *The Apartment* is one case in point. But the engaging protrayal of Fagin in the British musical production *Oliver* (1969) confirms the issue. One has only to recall the offensive caricature in David Lean's 1951 dramatic version, *Oliver Twist,* to appreciate the shift. In part, the new images were the result of Jewish writers looking back on their past with much nostalgia.

The year 1968 serves as a watershed. A quick glance at the film dates mentioned above indicates the number of significant movies which appeared that year. Also, it is important to note the appearance of Barbra Streisand in *Funny Girl,* George Segal in *No Way to Treat a Lady,* and Woody Allen in *Take the Money and Run,* for all three are quintessentially Jewish in name, features, and personality. The success of these performers as specifically Jewish stars paved the way for others like Richard Benjamin, Elliott Gould, Dustin Hoffman, and Richard Dreyfuss, all of whom define their screen characters by the infusion of their own off-screen personalities.

During the 1970s Jews appear as major characters in several dozen films and as minor characters in an endless list, where their Jewishness serves as a quick indicator of other traits (intellectualism, drive for success, a mother complex and its accompanying affliction—sexual problems). In other cases, the Jewishness seems gratuitous and hardly matters in the development of the character.

There are several reasons for the increase in Jewish portrayals. One is the growing concern with ethnic roots experienced by all minority groups during the 1970s. As one Hollywood producer observed, "Jewishness is an eminently marketable commodity." Two is a desire on the part of Hollywood producers to expose what had been suppressed in earlier films—sexuality, profane language, and ethnic identification. Three, the new producers and writers, mostly Jewish, no longer felt insecure about their place in American society. Totally assimilated, there was no question of belonging nor any need to hide their religion. Some critics, especially those from Jewish organizations, have looked with skepticism at the new portrayals, many of

In 1967 Mel Brooks' outrageous The Producers *ridiculed the Jewish drive for success with its unlikely tale of two Jewish producers (Gene Wilder and Zero Mostel) staging "Springtime for Hitler," a musical comedy based on the life of Adolf Hitler. With plots such as this, Jewish self-deprecation was well underway.*

which are negative and self-deprecating. Films that have prompted severe criticism are *Goodbye, Columbus, Portnoy's Complaint, The Long Goodbye, Lepke,* and the Canadian production, *The Apprenticeship of Duddy Kravitz.* Some critics believe that these fictions constitute a new form of anti-Semitism based on Jewish self-hatred.[17] The producers argue that it is a healthy sign when Jews can laugh at themselves in public. The success of Woody Allen's films based on insider jokes seems to prove their point. But Allen Rivkin, the former head of the Jewish Film Advisory Committee (a group established in the 1930s to police new projects), says simply of the new films, "Who needs it?"[18]

Perhaps the most visible Jewish characters have appeared in light drama and comedy. In these films, the emphasis has been on being Jewish in America. Here young women and men, almost all in their twenties, come to terms with their heritage as they try to solve their personal problems and interpersonal relationships. In most cases, heritage translates as family, the single most significant aspect of

Jewish-American life. In some films, the ethnic aspect is clearly prominent; in others, it is only implied. But in all cases, the central characters and their families are Jewish, although Gentile lovers remain a constant preoccupation, especially for Jewish heroes. The list is long and includes: *Move* (1970), *Where's Poppa?* (1970), *The Hospital* (1971), *Jennifer on My Mind* (1971), *Minnie and Moscowitz* (1971), *The Steagle* (1971), *Such Good Friends* (1971), *Play it Again, Sam* (1971), *Portnoy's Complaint* (1972), *Blume in Love* (1973), *The Heartbreak Kid* (1973), *Save the Tiger* (1973), *The Way We Were* (1973), *The Gambler* (1974), *Sheila Levine is Dead and Living in New York* (1975), *Shampoo* (1975), *Next Stop, Greenwich Village* (1976), *Annie Hall* (1977), *The Big Fix* (1978), *Girlfriends* (1978), *I Never Promised You a Rose Garden* (1978), *The Bell Jar* (1979), *Fast Break* (1979), *Norma Rae* (1979), and *Manhattan* (1979).

On the whole, the young heroes are oversexed, confused young men who are nevertheless accomplished in their fields. The heroines are graceless young women determined to find a man. The older generation comprises jaded businessmen or professionals and over-

As Hollywood Jews became more secure and assimilated in American society, they indulged in some self-deprecation. Woody Allen's urban Jewishness was a principal focus in many of his films, including Annie Hall, *but it was sometimes a source of embarrassment and self-doubt as he courted the affections of a WASP woman (Diane Keaton).*

bearing mothers. Not a pretty picture, although *The Way We Were* and the films of 1978 and 1979 do provide alternative stereotypes.

A new phenomenon has been the appearance of the Jewish gangster. Although several Jews were prominent in underworld activities and the ghettos bred their own crime, in the past Jewish criminals were carefully kept off the screen. A few exceptions exist in the early 1930s: *Four Walls* (1928), *Public Enemy* (1931), and *Lawyer Man* (1932). However, with the new openness of the 1970s, several films depicting Jewish gangsters appear. Included are *The Hot Rock* (1972), *Hit* (1973), *The Gambler* (1974), *Godfather II* (1974), and *Lepke* (1975), the most ethnic criminal to appear in recent years.

Several of the productions in the last decade have focused on an earlier world or the situation of Jews in other countries. Of interest are *The Angel Levine* (1970), about an elderly Jewish couple in New York; *Romance of a Horse Thief* (1971), set in Czarist Russia; the enormously popular *Fiddler on the Roof* (1971), which depicts the Jewish *shtetl; Cabaret* (1972), the portrayal of life in the waning days of the Weimar Republic; *Hester Street* (1976), about immigrant Jews at the turn of the century; *Voyage of the Damned* (1976), which charts the plight of Jewish refugees from Nazi Germany; *The Hiding Place* (1975), a film about Jewish sympathizers and their concentration camp experience; and *The Magician of Lubin* (1979), based on Isaac B. Singer's Polish tale.

In addition to these dramas, several works have been released which focus on Israel. *The Jerusalem File* (1972), *Rosebud* (1974), and *Black Sunday* (1977) all highlight the current Middle East problem. *The Man in the Glass Booth* (1975) provided a fictionalized account of the Eichmann trial and the Entebbe films cashed in on the spectacular daring of the news event. *Diamonds* (1975), on the other hand, simply used Israel as a backdrop for a conventional caper film.

Several Jews provided material for film biographies. Reflecting the new sensibility, all were clearly identified as Jewish, although ethnicity did not always play an important role in these films. Included in the list are *The Assassination of Trotsky* (1972); *Funny Lady* (1975), another feature about Fanny Brice; *Lenny* (1976), the story of Lenny Bruce; *All the President's Men* (1976), featuring Carl Bernstein; *The Last Tycoon* (1976), a fictionalized account of Irving Thalberg; and *Julia* (1977), a film about Lillian Hellman.

Again, it is in the area of minor characters that Jews have proliferated on the screen. As film producers, they have appeared in *Gable and Lombard* (1976) and *Hearts of the West* (1975); as Jewish mothers in *The Poseidon Adventure* (1972) and *Diamonds* (1975); as psychiatrists in *Bob and Carol and Ted and Alice* (1969), *Portnoy's Complaint* (1972), and *An Unmarried Woman* (1978); as merchants in *Klute* (1971); as doctors in *House Calls* (1978); as lawyers in *The End* (1978); as rabbis in *Everything You Wanted to Know About Sex and Were Afraid to Ask* (1972); as policemen in *The Exorcist* (1973); as painters in *An Unmarried Woman;* as a lesbian in *A Different Story;* and finally as a madame in *For Pete's Sake* (1974). They have turned up in the Old West in *Blazing Saddles* (1974) and *The Duchess and the Dirtwater Fox* (1978). No place seems beyond their reach.

In summary, the Jews, both on screen and off, span the entire history of Hollywood cinema. As producers, screenwriters, directors, composers, and actors they have virtually built the industry and continuously provided for its creative sustenance. As characters on the screen, the Jews reflect the dominant aspects of our social history and the Hollywood tradition. Their presence in and contribution to America has been richly documented on the screen, although their virtual disappearance during three decades (1930-1960) is a great loss. Despite the stereotypes which appear in an overwhelming number of works, the films do reveal a truth about the American-Jewish experience. The Jews' struggle between traditionalism and assimilation was the creative tension of Jewish participation in the movies, as it was also in America.

The new visibility of the screen Jew and his animator, the Jewish performer, is significant. It registers current attitudes towards ethnicity and individual differences. Streisand's nose, Gould's wavy hair, and Hoffman's five o'clock shadow are icons on the silver screen. These images present a personal point of view—private jokes now public property. Such a phenomenon hopefully bespeaks a basic health in the American body politic.

NOTES

1. Norman Zierold, *The Moguls* (1969), 254.
2. Robert Allen, "Motion Picture Exhibition in Manhattan, 1906-1912: Beyond the Nickelodeon," *Cinema Journal,* 18 (Spring 1979), 4.
3. Tom Tugent, "A History of Hollywood's Jews," *Davka,* 5 (Fall 1975), 6. Family loyalties were also extended through marriage, e.g., David O. Selznick was married to Louis B. Mayer's youngest daughter. Other such marriages in Hollywood included Samuel Goldwyn, married to the sister of Jesse Lasky, and William Goetz, married to Mayer's eldest daughter.
4. Philip French, *The Movie Moguls* (1969), 106-107.
5. Tugent, "Hollywood's Jews," 7.
6. See N. L. Rothman, "The Jew on the Screen," *The Jewish Forum* (October 1928), 527-528.
7. Muni Wisenfreund became Paul Muni, Emanuel Goldenberg became Edward G. Robinson, Sophie Josow became Sylvia Sidney, Melvyn Hesselberg became Melvyn Douglas, Paulette Levy became Paulette Goddard, Julius

Garfinkle became John Garfield, Betty Perske became Lauren Bacall, Jack Kubelsky became Jack Benny, David Kaminsky became Danny Kaye, Danielovitch Demsky became Kirk Douglas, Ira Grossel became Jeff Chandler, Leo Jacobi became Lee J. Cobb, Shirley Schrift became Shelley Winters, and Bernard Schwartz became Tony Curtis.

8. There are exceptions particularly in the case of John Garfield. Further, since the 1960s, almost all of the actors have played Jewish characters in at least one film.

9. In 1936 several Jewish actors and creators organized the Anti-Nazi League of Hollywood, which drew members in the thousands.

10. French, *The Movie Moguls,* 105.

11. Tugent, "Hollywood's Jews," 5.

12. French, *The Movie Moguls,* 109.

13. See Irwin C. Rosen's "The Effect of the Motion Picture *Gentleman's Agreement* on Attitudes Toward Jews," *The Journal of Psychology* (October 1948), 525-536.

14. Albert Maltz, Samuel Ornitz, and Herbert Biberman.

15. *The Search* (1948) did depict Jewish war orphans.

16. Robert Alter, "Sentimentalizing the Jews," *Commentary* (September 1965), 71-75.

17. See articles by Fred M. Hechinger and Dan Isaac in *The New York Times,* July 16, 1972, and September 8, 1974.

18. This organization, originally known as The Motion Picture Project, was supported by national Jewish organizations. The committee is no longer in existence.

7

STELLAAAAAA......!!!!!!!!: THE SLAVIC STEREOTYPE IN AMERICAN FILM

Caroline Golab

A caricature of an Italian or a Jew on a vaudeville stage would be as readily recognized as that of an Irishman. Is this true of any Slavic type?[1]

Unlike the Jews, Italians, Irish, or blacks, the Slavs were not, until quite recently, popular victims of Hollywood's fascinating propensity to stereotype. Of the thousands of movies produced in the past sixty years, probably less than two dozen contain Slavic-Americans as major or minor characters.[2] What is missing in quantity, however, is made up for in quality. American film not only helped to perfect the Slavic stereotype, but was largely responsible for nationalizing it. It found the Slavs in the small, isolated towns of Pennsylvania and the gritty cities of the Great Lakes and distributed them throughout the nation. By the time Hollywood was finished, everyone could identify the Slavic stereotype even though most people had never encountered a living Slav and probably would not recognize one if they did.

135

The Slavs' historical relationship to America, and to themselves, is the primary explanation for their absence from the screen. It has been difficult to get a handle on the Slav because, in reality, "there is no such person . . . any more than there is such a person as a Teuton or a Celt. All Slavs are primarily members of some distinct nationality; they are Russians, Poles or what not, as the Teuton is a German or a Swede or an Englishman."[3]

In reality, Slavs comprise at *least* sixteen different nationalities: they are Poles; Slovaks; Croatians and Slovenians; Ukrainians (Ruthenians or Russniaks); Czechs (Bohemians) and Moravians; Bulgarians, Serbians, and Montenegrins; Russians; Dalmatians, Bosnians, and Herzegovinians. And to this official list[4] must be added two others—Hungarians and Lithuanians. Technically not Slavs, either racially or linguistically, these two groups nevertheless inhabit the same part of the world as the true Slavs and in terms of culture, religion, history, and experiences in America (including stereotyping) are very similar.

The various Slavic peoples were keenly aware of their differences. Americans and members of older immigrant groups, however, rarely were appreciative or even cognizant of these differences. They tended to lump all Slavs together under one rubric; Hun, Hunkie ("whether or not they ever saw or heard of Hungary"), and Polak ("whether the name has any application or not") were the most popular epithets.[5] From the very beginning, Americans sought a least common denominator in order to bring order out of a seemingly endless and confusing conglomeration of peoples. The need for a stereotype was already present.

Secondly, Americans were generally familiar with the Latin and Hebrew peoples, including their histories and geographies, but were not familiar with the Slavs. One could point to Italy, Spain, and ancient Israel on the map, but there was no place in Europe that one could point to as a composite homeland of the Slavs. "Slavland," like the Slav, did not exist. Educated Americans were probably familiar with countries such as Russia, Poland, and Bohemia, but who, educated or not, had ever heard of Bosnia, Herzegovina, Carniola, or Croatia? Could anyone locate these places on a map? ("Southeastern Europe is in something of a snarl.")[6]

Moreover, the classic tradition of Western civilization came to northern Europe and, hence, to America via Greece and Rome. Plato and Aristotle, in other words, were not bequeathed to us by way of Warsaw, Moscow, or Dubrovnik. Italy was also the home of the Renaissance and the seat of high culture in painting, sculpture, and music. Rome, not Kiev or Buda-Pest, was a mandatory stop for upper-class Americans doing the grand tour of Europe. A Christian

nation, historically dedicated to the Bible, America was also familiar
with the history of the Jews. In addition, Jews were present in the
United States before its founding and were a familiar group in all the
countries of Europe at some point in history. In short, as Emily Balch
observed in 1910, "Italian and Hebrew immigrants stand against a
background of familiar history; we know something of their homes,
their literature and their racial characteristics. This is much less true
of the Slavs."[7]

Finally, despite their large numbers, Slavs were not as conspicuous
as other immigrant groups because their work and settlement patterns were significantly different. This, perhaps, is the most important factor accounting for the Slav's lack of visibility—on or off the
screen. Quite simply, the American public had little contact with Slavs
because these immigrants, unlike Jews or Italians, did not perform
work which brought them constantly and conspicuously into public
view. Jews were often peddlers, merchants, small manufacturers, and
skilled craftsmen operating their own businesses; they ran grocery,
clothing, and department stores and were independent carpenters,
bakers, tailors, and metalsmiths. Americans were familiar with their
pushcarts, their shops, and their services, coming into contact with
them on a daily basis. Rare was the city or town, North or South, big
or small, that did not have its Jewish shopkeepers.

Italians, too, were frequently self-employed businessmen and
skilled craftsmen who provided services to the general public—green
groceries, restaurants, tailorshops. Moreover, if not self-employed as
shopkeeper or craftsman, the Italian was visible everywhere and
anywhere as construction laborer. This form of work, facilitated by
the railroad, gave him great visibility because it could take him to any
part of the city or country on a given day. Finally, Jews and Italians
were very likely to locate their colonies in the most central portions of
the city, directly adjacent to the downtown. Anyone coming into or
going out of the city, as shopper, commuter, tourist, or worker, had
great opportunity to see them in their neighborhoods.

The Slavs, in contrast, were very rarely merchants, shopkeepers,
manufacturers, or skilled craftsmen.[8] Their history, experiences, and
personal inclinations did not point them in these directions; nor did
they become, like the Italians (or Irish before them), the majority of
workers in the ubiquitous construction industry. The work which the
Slavs performed had precise locations and was the type of work which
never brought them into constant or frequent contact with the general public.

Slavs were primarily and overwhelmingly unskilled laborers who
eventually formed the bulk of America's industrial proletariat in the

first half of the twentieth century. They performed the most basic types of work associated with newly industrialized enterprises. They were miners of all sorts—coal, iron, mercury, lead; steelworkers; slaughterers and meatpackers; leather workers; sugar and oil refiners; stevedores and longshoremen. Such work required little skill, little or no training, but much strength and endurance. It flourished in the smaller towns and cities of Pennsylvania where coal mines and steel manufacture made this state a "Titan of Industry"; or in the cities of the Industrial Heartland—Chicago, Milwaukee, Cleveland, Detroit, and Buffalo, where metal and related manufacture was again the primary industry. Slavic women, too, had low visibility. Domestic service (cleaning) and keeping lodgers and boarders were their most popular forms of work. Keeping lodgers brought them into contact with no one but fellow Slavs; cleaning did little better. Because of strong Irish and black dominance in private households, Slavic women tended to clean offices, hotels, hospitals, and other institutional buildings rather than private homes. Since they tended to work at night, their ability to confront large audiences was limited.[9]

Finally, because their work had precise locations, the Slavs formed their colonies or neighborhoods right on top of or adjacent to their places of employment. These neighborhoods were often removed from the most central portions of the city and were normally not subjected to the traffic of strangers passing through. Moreover, these neighborhoods were self-contained in that they provided the inhabitants with their own churches, schools, newspapers, and fraternal and beneficial societies as well as shops and services. With little or infrequent need to leave these enclaves, the Slavs were further removed from public sight. And, if the immigrants had little need or desire to venture out of their "ghettos," most other Americans had absolutely no need or desire to venture into them.[10]

The Slavs' low profile and limited visibility did not prevent American society from forming opinions about them. Through occasional newspaper articles, travel memoirs, and a general font of popular folklore brought with their ancestors from Europe, Americans had formulated a generalized image of Slavs by the early nineteenth century. According to this popular belief, Slavs were "common, coarse . . ." with "low, square forehead, heavy brows, prominent cheek-bones, flattish nose, with broad nostrils and full lips."[11] Former barbarians mongrelized by Asiatic blood, they were a passive, unaggressive people: "They seem to lack some element of aggressiveness, something of the instinct to retaliate."[12] Furthermore, they lacked the capacity for leadership, cohesion, or state-building; prone to anarchy, they were forever destined to be subjects rather than masters: "Since the curtain of history rose, the Slavs have been anvil rather than hammer."[13]

The most popular Slavic image, however, was that of the "peasant," a serf only recently freed from slavery.[14] Peasants, in the American mind, were inferior peoples of the lowest possible social standing who lived little better than animals: "To be a peasant means to be addressed by a personal pronoun which is a mark of inferiority; it means to be bound by customs which are as irksome as an 'iron shirt'; it means to be the butt of the ridicule of stage fools, who, after all, only mimic the fools in real life."[15] They were crude, coarse (". . . with the coarseness of those that have to deal with nature not mainly as the source of aesthetic emotions but of a good litter of pigs and a proper production of manure. . ."),[16] stubborn,[17] filthy and, like animals, were super-fecund, with "a rather gross attitude towards sexual morality."[18] A brutal people, living by force untempered by reason, they beat their wives and children as a matter of God-given right ("He

Joe Radek (Paul Muni) in Black Fury *was a "typical" Polish miner—hardworking but simple and ignorant. He became the dupe of labor racketeers, but emerged as hero of sorts in the end. His heroism, however, was born of peasant ignorance and innocence rather than steely, modern realism.*

who does not beat his wife is no man.")[19] They drank themselves into unconsciousness: "The Slav does not know how to enjoy himself save by getting drunk; he does not know how to show kindness to his friends save by making them drink."[20] In sum, Slavs ". . . reveal the propensities of a rude, undeveloped people of undisciplined primitive passions."[21]

By the height of the Slavic immigration to America (1905–1914), the Slavic image had been perfected: the Slav as a crude, muscle-bound, sexually powerful but hard-working peasant. He performed the most onerous and distasteful jobs that America had to offer.[22] He was dull, easily led (". . . with his brain wherever the stronger brain leads him")[23] and, above all, not too bright.[24] Docile ("like sheep")[25], patient and obedient when sober, he was a wild, violent animal when drunk (a frequent occurrence at their weddings and christenings).[26] Finally, the Slavic peasant was clannish[27] and definitely of low—very low—social standing:

> "In the communities visited," reports the Industrial Commission, "farm-ers of German, Scandinavian, Irish, Bohemian, Belgian, Swiss and American origin were found living in juxtaposition to Poles. In virtually every instance the Pole was considered one degree lower than his neighbors. Neither the Poles as a body nor the others desire to fuse socially, and the Bohemians felt well above their Slavic brethren." The farmers look down on the Poles as uncleanly, intemperate, quarrel-some, ignorant, priest-ridden, and hard on women and children. When a few Poles have come into a neighborhood, the other farmers become restless, sell out, and move away. Soon a parish is organized, church and parish school arise, the public school decays, and Slavdom has a new outpost.[28]

Thus, by 1914 the components of the Slavic stereotype were already floating around in the American psyche.

In its heyday, vaudeville made frequent use of the caricatured Jew, Italian, and Irishman. The Slav made infrequent appearances, if he made any at all. Only in the Yiddish theater did he reappear again and again, usually as the poor, dumb, easily duped peasant. As we have seen, the Slavs, although numbering in the millions, were in many ways an invisible minority because of the nature of the work they performed and its location. Moreover, the Slavs' entry into the American economy was at the lowest level, causing them to fuse and to be identified with America's burgeoning working-class proletariat. In its formative years, American film, like the rest of society in general, paid little attention to the life and problems of the working class. Slavs simply were not the stuff of Hollywood's dreams. The

Slavs' transition to the film, therefore, depended largely on the availability of good, interesting stories which appeared first in other forms, such as the novel, play, or newspaper story. Only in the 1970s do Slavs become a serious (and not-so-serious) film subject, projected to the screen by writers and directors without the aid of previously published materials. By this time, however, the Slavic image had matured in the public mind, and Hollywood was eager to give its version of working-class America.

> *Stella:* Stanley is Polish, you know.
> *Blanche:* Oh, yes. They're something like Irish, aren't they?
> —Tennessee Williams, *A Streetcar Named Desire*

Joe Radek is an ignorant, jovial, Polish miner who enjoys the whiskey bottle and is popular with his fellow workers. Submissive, hardworking, often drunk, but loyal and, above all, innocent and unsuspecting, he becomes the dupe of gangsters from a local strike-breaking agency. His innocence, so cleverly manipulated by racketeering agents, precipitates a fatal split in the union. During the subsequent strike, Radek's best friend, Mike Shemanski, is brutally clubbed to death by Pennsylvania's infamous coal and iron police. Bludgeoned into submission by these cruel automatons, the miners return to work on company terms. Joe, realizing his mistake, barricades himself in the mine, threatening to blow up both himself and company property unless the miners get a better deal. He succeeds, but he never fully understands the crisis in which he played so important a role. (*Black Fury*, 1935)

Frank Wieczek is a young Chicago youth, not very bright or articulate, who is convicted of killing a cop in a tavern holdup. Innocent, but unable to prove it, he is sentenced to ninety-nine years in prison. His mother scrubs floors for ten years to save a $5,000 reward for anyone producing evidence which will prove his innocence. A newspaper reporter discovers that Wieczek was duped—framed by a corrupt (Irish) police department. The helpless victim is freed and awarded $24,000 by the state for this "miscarriage of justice." (*Call Northside 777*, 1948)

Frankie (Majcinek) Machine is a young, not too smart, drug addict living in the heart of Chicago's "Division Street"—Polacktown. Frustrated, poverty-stricken, and confused, he would be totally degenerate were it not for the love of Molly Novotny, a local stripper and hustler who, in the end, effects his cure. Frankie's Slavic friends (and enemies) are venal, distasteful, and corrupt. Despite all his problems

In Call Northside 777 *Frank Wieczek (Richard Conte) is a dull-witted Pole from Chicago who is wrongfully convicted of a robbery. Only the sharp non-Slavic reporter (James Stewart) can unravel the mystery and free the innocent Pole.*

and weaknesses, however, Frankie is not unlikeable or unattractive; he is simply a victim of his environment. (*The Man with the Golden Arm*, 1956)

Stanley Kowalski is a "Polak." Brawny, brutish, ape-like, crude, primitive, and amoral, he exudes animal magnetism and revels in sensuous pleasures—eating, drinking (both to excess), sex, and any other pleasure of the moment. ("Stan is the epitome of the pleasure an animal enjoys with his body, an aggressive, indulgent, powerful, and proud expression of sex."[29]) He lives by instinct and violence (he slaps his pregnant wife and rapes her sister), not by intelligence or reason. A former master sergeant in the Engineering Corps, he works as an auto mechanic and lives in a New Orleans slum. His car, his radio, poker, drinking with the boys, and bowling (including gaudy bowling shirts) are his favorite possessions and pastimes. Although portrayed on the screen as an animal and barbarian (his sister-in-law, Blanche, compares him to a caveman bringing meat home to his mate), his is a complex personality. When sober he is capable of great feeling and tenderness. His wife, Stella, however, sees the light and leaves him. (*A Streetcar Named Desire*, 1951)

Joe Lucasta is the tyrannical head of an impoverished and raunchy Polish family living in a small Pennsylvania milltown. Filthy, crude, ignorant, he leers incestuously at his curvaceous daughter, *Anna.* (Joe Lucasta could easily be Stanley Kowalski in late middle-age). *Frank,* Lucasta's son-in-law, is a conniving, money-hungry brute, domineering and despicable, who tries to use Anna as bait for his money-grabbing schemes. Anna, however, although a fallen woman, is at least honest and foils his schemes. (*Anna Lucasta,* 1949)

Steve Nowak, immigrant's son, big, brawny, inarticulate (he has very little to say throughout this entire movie), and not the brightest guy in the world, wants to be accepted by the elite of American society. Innocent and unsuspecting, he goes off to play football—the key to fame, glory, education, and acceptance—at a major southern university. Although determined to play hard and study hard (engineering), he falls prey to his teammates' pressures, a tyrannical coach, and an unscrupulous alumnus who sees only dollar signs instead of young men in football jerseys. Steve succumbs to corruption and is soon on the verge of despair. He is saved from total obliquity by a nice "proper" southern girl and a strong-minded, foreign-born papa. (*Saturday's Hero,* 1951)

Stephen Maryk is another immigrant's son, strong and stolid, who sees the Navy as his way to success in America. Never good in school (C- average) and intimidated by intellectuals and those who are more articulate or learned than he, he becomes the very competent, but square-headed and simple-minded executive officer of a minesweeper during World War II. Exceptionally popular with both crew and fellow officers, he is duped by a comrade into believing that the ship's captain is insane. Maryk relieves the captain of command during a typhoon. Court-martialed, but acquitted through the expert legal trickery of a clever Jewish lawyer, his naval career is forever ruined. (*The Caine Mutiny,* 1954)

Johnny Kovak, son of Hungarian immigrants, is rough, tough, and amoral, but determined to become the head of the largest teamsters' union in the nation ("everything on wheels belongs to me"). Weaned on violence (he beats a man to death with an axe-handle), he lives by force and instinct, not intelligence. On his way to the top he partakes in all forms of sordid corruption, aligning himself with gangsters and racketeers. Again, like Kowalski, Kovak is a complex character, also capable of great tenderness and deep feeling, as seen in his marriage to a pretty Lithuanian girl. Feeling, though, is the key. Kovak, like Kowalski, is all physical force and emotion and little brain. (*F.I.S.T.*, 1978)

Jerry is a big, muscle-bound Polish-American from the working-class slums of Detroit. He, along with two black buddies, works the assembly line at an auto factory. All yearn for the material rewards of the American Dream, which always seem to elude them. Increasingly frustrated, they sink deeper and deeper into debt. (Jerry moonlights at a gas station in order to buy braces for his daughter's teeth). The three pals decide to rob their local union, only to discover evidence of illegal doings rather than ready cash. Attempts to blackmail the union fail. One pal is killed, the other is bought off by promotion to shop steward, and Jerry turns stoolie for the FBI. The Pole and his surviving black friend end up hating each other. Management and union together deliberately encourage racist feelings in order to divide the workers and keep them in line. (It's a modern version of the "divide and conquer" strategy used by bosses in the early twentieth century to keep the immigrants from organizing. Instead of immigrants fighting immigrants, today it's working-class white ethnics confronting blacks.) (*Blue Collar,* 1978)

Michael Vronsky, prosperous, unionized steelworker from Clairton, Pennsylvania, is a powerful, virile, inscrutable specimen of humanity who carries the extension of his sexuality, his rifle, at his side. Beyond the need for women (or incapable of intimacy with them?), he prefers the company of men and those pleasures which are decidedly masculine—drinking to excess at the local bar, or deer hunting, where the proof of manhood lies in bringing the buck down with one clean shot. Aloof, he lives by his own personal code of fanatical loyalty to his companions and responds to things by instinct. He lives in a town in 1960s America which is dirty and run-down, apparently imprisoned by the local steelmill. The town's inhabitants are mostly Ukrainians and Russians, who drink hard, play hard, and fight hard. Their celebrations end in drunken brawls, their fathers are women-beating tyrants, and their women are sluts. Everyone, however, loves America, so much so that they are willing to die for it in the far-off jungles of Southeast Asia. (*The Deer Hunter,* 1978)

The image of the Slavic male presented in these films is consistent and predictable: physically strong, hardworking, but often submissive, easily duped or manipulated; brutal, crude, sexually powerful, non-intellectual, and inarticulate; prone to drunkenness and violence; stubborn and amoral, but loyal to a fault, even clannish. At his worst,

Jerry, The Pole, becomes the symbol for white, ethnic, working-class rivalry with blacks in Blue Collar, *a movie about the despairing, sordid world of the assembly line.*

the Slav is a primitive animal and barbarian (Kowalski) or a corrupt amoral, violent maniac (Kovak). At his best, he is hardworking but not too bright, a victim of circumstance, environment, or manipulation (Radek, Wieczek, Maryk, and Frankie Machine). Hardly ever is he the master of his own destiny. Never is he intellectual or highly cultured; he is the football hero (Nowak), never the smart lawyer or class valedictorian. The image of the Slavic woman, too, is consistent and straightforward. She is a prostitute—Anna Lucasta or Nellie in *Let No Man Write My Epitaph* (1960); a loose woman—Molly Novotny; or a sex symbol, all body and no brains—Sugar (Kowalczyk) Kane, portrayed as only Marilyn Monroe could do it in *Some Like It Hot* (1959). At her best, she has some personal honor and redeeming value— Lucasta and Novotny; at her worst, she is stupid and sluttish, as portrayed in *The Deer Hunter.*[30]

The major difficulty in analyzing the Slavic, or any group's image, is that film, by its very nature, lends itself to stereotyping. Film cannot capture nuances of meaning or character in the same way, for example, as the novel. There usually is no narrator to serve as interpreter. The audience—each individual member of the audience—is the interpreter. Moreover, film does not portray reality, only *images* of reality. A person's hand, a crowd, a chair, a flower—all are inanimate objects when put on the screen. Because it deals with images of reality and not with reality itself, the film seeks to define everything—people, places, and events—as simply as possible; it seeks the least common denominator to present to the audience. For this reason, film has to deal in stereotypes because it cannot go beyond them. The film, in essence, is the media of metaphor and stereotyping is necessary because it produces metaphor. Indeed, it is often difficult to know where stereotype ends and metaphor begins.[31]

The inability of the motion picture to transcend stereotypes is further complicated by the fact that, with few exceptions, most movies (especially those cited here) are adapted from novels, plays, or real-life biographies. In the course of translation to the screen, myriad shadings, details, and deeper meanings are often lost, or deliberately sacrificed. Major changes often have to be made in plot or character, for what works in the novel, play, or real life, does not work in film. What is left is the least common denominator for audience identification. Complex characters, situations, or events are reduced to symbols, or metaphors.

For example, when it first appeared in 1935, *Black Fury* was intended as an explosive political and social indictment of immigrant worker exploitation by American business and its allies. (It was considered inflammatory by the New York State Board of Censors and was banned in many places.) The film is based on a novel of the same name by a Pennsylvania judge, Michael Musmanno (he also wrote the screenplay), who was an unrelenting crusader for miners' rights. Recognized as the foremost expert on working conditions in Pennsylvania's mines and mills, Musmanno waged continuing warfare, in fiction and in the courtroom, against the corrupt and cruel coal and iron police. The novel, in turn, was based on true happenings: Shemanski's death and the events leading up to it were real, recorded for posterity in local newspapers. The coal and iron police were, in reality, cruel and calculating. Racketeering agencies did sow dissension within peaceful unions in order to break strikes and return workers to the mines on company terms. The majority of coal miners at this time were Slavic immigrants and their children. Like Joe Radek, they tended to be innocent, unsuspecting, illiterate and easily led—or misled. Like Joe, they tended to drown their joys and sorrows in whiskey. In *Black Fury* Joe Radek may be a Slavic stereotype, but he is also a metaphor for all the miners who lived, worked, and died in the small coal towns of Pennsylvania. Radek, however, emerges the hero. Innocence prevails. He alone accomplishes what the union and all the striking miners could not do.[32]

Call Northside 777 is based on a series of true newspaper stories written by Chicago reporter James McGuire. In real life Frank Wieczek was Joe Majczek, a young Polish boy who was, in fact, framed by corrupt police and served eleven years for a murder he never committed. His mother really was a scrubwoman and really did work ten years to save the $5,000 reward. A pictorial essay in *Life Magazine*

(1948) neatly shows the real and fictional characters side by side. If *Life* is to be believed, the real life participants are more stereotypic than those portrayed in the film. Richard Conte as Wieczek and Kasia Ozazewski as his mother are more appealing than the real ones.[33]

The Man with the Golden Arm is based on Nelson Algren's novel of the same title. It was a ground breaking book (and movie) for its time because it dealt with the forbidden subject of drug addiction and the seedy world that spawned it. (The National Censors had problems with its "stark portrayals of reality.") Like *Call Northside 777,* its setting is Chicago's Polish ghetto, an area Algren knew well because Chicago was his hometown. The jacket blurb for the 1951 paperback edition by Pocket Books announced: "This is the story of the lost and damned of a great American city. It is the drama of men and women and children drained by poverty, frustration and despair, of their hopes and struggles and defeats." The movie may not have succeeded as well as the book, but that is the difficulty in taking complex works of fiction and putting them into film. The subtlety and complexity of characters get lost in translation. Frankie Machine, on the screen, becomes the metaphor, in Slavic garb, for all "the lost and damned of a great American city" who have succumbed to drugs. In the book, Frankie commits suicide, but what works in the novel does not work in the film: he is cured, cold turkey, by his faithful girlfriend who locks him in her room for several days. The movie, like the book, is not without its final message: it is the slums, with all their poverty and suffocation, that are on trial. Frankie and his venal, corrupt, and often distasteful friends are victims of their American environment. And the Chicago of the 1930s and 1940s, in many minds, was the synonym for slums and corruption. Chicago at this time, however, was a Slavic city. The old cliche about more Poles than Warsaw, more Czechs than Prague . . . was not without its point of truth.

There is no better example of the problems of translation than those illustrated by Tennessee Williams' play, *A Streetcar Named Desire.* The same actor, Marlon Brando, played in both stage and screen versions; the same man, Elia Kazan, directed both. In his *Notebook* Kazan said of *Streetcar:* "[Williams] sees the play as a conflict between two civilizations—the dying aristocracy [represented by the southern belle, Blanche DuBois, Kowalski's sister-in-law] and the vital, modern, cynical democracy [Kowalski]. Williams sees the situation as a parable of the fall of Rome to the blue-eyed marauders from the North, of the destruction of all beauty by brutality." Kazan expressed the theme of the play as "a message from the dark interior. This little twisted, pathetic, confused bit of light and culture [Blanche] puts out a cry. It is snuffed out by the crude forces of violence [Kowalski], and this cry is the play." When asked what the message of *Streetcar* was, Williams

Stanley Kowalski (Marlon Brando) was Tennessee Williams' metaphor in
A Streetcar Named Desire *for the working-class slob. Kowalski's passion,*
his violence, his boorishness, his "Polishness" are Williams' warnings of
civilization's imminent collapse.

allegedly replied, "If we don't watch out, the apes will take over!"[34]
Apparently, Stella Kowalski agrees. In the movie, she leaves her
husband—and we are glad; in the play, she stays with him—and we
are glad.

How are we to interpret Stanley Kowalski? Is Kowalski simply a
Polish stereotype gone wild? And why is he Polish in the first place?
Why not Italian, Irish, or Jewish? Why is the Polish theme constantly
reappearing, from direct references to "stupid Polak" to subtler
elements, such as Stanley's polka-dot underwear and the powerful
polka music which escalates in intensity whenever Blanche is leaping
towards madness?

The key to understanding Kowalski is to realize that Williams was
using him as the representative for all the baser, lower forms of
human life. Stanley Kowalski, quite simply, is a working-class slob.
Over time, the Slavic image has evolved to connote all that we
associate today with the term "working class." Working-class men are
strong, macho, physical, tolerant of violence, hard-drinking, anti-

intellectual, TV addicts, sports fanatics (football, wrestling, and bowling, never tennis or golf); in love with their cars; politically conservative, pro-union, super-patriotic, and bigoted. They prefer the company of men to that of women who, in turn, are crude, loud, sluttish, and stupid.

Slavs have such low social standing that, more often than not, they are portrayed as being one thin line above blacks in the American social hierarchy. (The crudeness, even indecency, of the "Polish Jokes" in *Rabbit Test* (1978) and *The End* (1978) attest to this evaluation.) In many parts of Pennsylvania's coal and iron regions, Slavs were referred to as "white niggers" because they lived so cheaply (too cheaply, according to some), and performed work that "no white man would do."[35] It is no coincidence that Philip Yordan's *Anna Lucasta,* in original novel form, dealt with a sordid Polish family in a murky Pennsylvania town, but was first brought to the stage with an all black cast (1944); or that the first movie production (1949), which again dealt with a Polish family, was followed ten years later by a remake starring Eartha Kitt and Sammy Davis, Jr. When dealing with themes of poverty, prostitution, and lower-class life, it appears that Slavs and blacks are interchangeable. It is also no coincidence that *Blue Collar,* a story of contemporary factory life, should feature a Pole as its representative of the white working class confronting black America. The white working class is increasingly cited as the "enemy" of black progress. If the archetypal working-class image is the Slavic-American, then it follows that the Slav, of course, is a racist.[36]

By the 1940s, if not decades earlier, the image of the Slav, especially the Pole, as working class had been cemented in the popular mind. In looking for a synonym for "working class," Williams came up with Kowalski just as Philip Yordan came up with Lucasta and director Paul Schrader came up with Jerry in *Blue Collar.* If one wishes to show a crude, brutish, semi-civilized creature, if one wishes to convey the baser forms of lower-class life destroying higher forms of culture and refinement, if one wishes to portray bigotry in any form, one automatically chooses the metaphor that everyone is most likely to know—the "Polak." Stanley Kowalski, Polak, Slavic stereotype *par excellence,* is a metaphor. The instant the audience realizes that he is a "Polak," the play and the film need to say no more, for the stereotype says it all. Each member of the audience can now draw upon a personal reservoir of meaning and image.[37]

Thus, Kowalski had to be Kowalski. A Caparelli, Murphy, or Feinstein would not have conveyed the same message. The Italian, Irish, and Jewish metaphors are different, and the audience knows that. The Irish by this time had moved up in the American social hierarchy and were not always readily thought of as working class; the

Jews were never even contestants for the title. Italians, the other major working-class group, would not do because they lacked the connotation of being big, brutish, sexually potent, uncivilized and dumb—all wrapped up together. Moreover, there was still something romantic about Italians; but where was the romance in a semi-civilized, slavish brute or a dumb, muscle-bound peasant? Finally, Italians generally came packaged with strong families—doting mothers, endless siblings (usually brothers), and old-world papas. Slavs were usually portrayed as loners, either family-less or family haters. For Slavs, this was a particularly ironic distortion because, in fact, they cherished their strong family ties.

Indeed, so strong has the association between Slavic-American and working class become that the three most recent works—*F.I.S.T., Blue Collar,* and *The Deer Hunter,* all products of the 1970s—are the only major films dealing with Slavic images that are *not* based on novels, plays, or nonfiction news articles. *The Deer Hunter* came out of the mind of its director, Michael Cimino, and is his particular conception of patriotic white Americans gladly off to war; *Blue Collar* is a product of Paul Schrader's interpretation of contemporary factory life; and *F.I.S.T.* is Sylvester Stallone and Norman Jewison's version of working-class union life from the 1930s through the 1950s—as seen through the eyes of the 1970s. All chose Slavic characters—Vronsky, Jerry, and Kovak—to make their points. All pulled these men out of their own imaginations, i.e., out of the popular image already existing in the public mind. More than in the earlier movies, the metaphor in these films of the 1970s is undisguised, even blatant. Nonetheless, they are following the pattern established by Tennessee Williams in *Streetcar,* for it was Williams, more than anyone, who perfected the use of the Slavic stereotype as metaphor for the working class. It was Williams who first tapped the public reservoir and gave us Stanley Kowalski.

If we are upset with the nature of ethnic portrayals, the solution lies not in changing the stereotype in the film, but in changing the public metaphor. As we have seen, stereotypes exist in the popular mind long before they reach the screen. Film does not create them, it only distributes or nationalizes them. And how do we change the public metaphor? Only by replacing it with another one or by making the current one inapplicable. It would be helpful to remember that, historically, the image of Slavs as working-class slobs and dolts was preceded by the image of the Irish as working-class slobs and dolts. Today, however, that image, for the Irish at least, is no longer meaningful. As metaphor, it no longer works because the pieces of reality upon which the stereotype was based have gone out of existence. The Irish are no longer the bulk of America's industrial

*Slavic, working-class male camaraderie dominated even the wedding in
The Deer Hunter.*

proletariat. They are not seen as crude peasants, just off the boat,
bringing their crime, disease, and drunken habits. They have moved
up in the American socio-economic hierarchy and changed their
visibility in the process. Hence, the stereotype, too, had to change.
Furthermore, as the Irish moved up, they were replaced by new
groups who fit their old image much better than they did—Italians
and, of course, the Slavs, especially the Poles.

Stereotypes, then, have several characteristics worth noting: they
have historicity, they are dynamic, and they are always images of
groups, not individuals. A group's historical relationship to the
majority or dominant group is the key to understanding the creation
and subsequent evolution of ethnic stereotypes.[38] Most groups which
entered the American system did so at the bottom, beginning as
indentured servants, slaves, conquered subjects, or unskilled workers.
The Slavs, as a group, formed the bulk of the nation's industrial
proletariat from the late nineteenth to the mid-twentieth century. In
many areas of the country they continue to be highly concentrated in
working-class occupations. In fact, with the flight of middle-class
urban Americans to the suburbs, their visibility has actually
heightened; they are one of the few white groups remaining in
increasingly black and brown cities.

The Slavic stereotype as portrayed in the film will change only as the Slavs, like the Irish before them, move up the social ladder. America, for all its pretensions to classlessness, is a very status conscious society. Those higher up on the ladder need those lower down in order to secure their superior positions. It makes no difference if there are many Slavs with great accomplishments in America, or many who have left their working-class roots far behind: it is the public image of the *group* which must change, and only time and history can do that. Finally, there are, on the horizon, new candidates for the working-class stereotype. Blacks, Puerto Ricans, and Appalachian poor whites may be the Polaks of tomorrow.

NOTES

1. Emily Greene Balch, *Our Slavic Fellow Citizens* (1910), 6.

2. Among the more accessible are: *Black Fury* (1935); *Clash by Night* (1944); *Call Northside 777* (1948); *Anna Lucasta* (1949); *Knock on Any Door* (1949); *Saturday's Hero* (1951); *A Streetcar Named Desire* (1951); *The Caine Mutiny* (1954); *The Man with the Golden Arm* (1956); *Task Force* (1958); *Some Like It Hot* (1959); *Let No Man Write My Epitaph* (1960); *West Side Story* (1961); *The Great Escape* (1963); *How Do I Love Thee?* (1970); *The Deserter* (1970); *The End* (1978); *Rabbitt Test* (1978); *F.I.S.T.* (1978); *Blue Collar* (1978); *The Deer Hunter* (1978).

3. Balch, *Our Slavic Fellow Citizens,* 6.

4. These are the Slavic groups, in order of numerical importance, as officially recognized by the U.S. Government and its Department of Immigration, c. 1900-1915.

5. Balch, *Our Slavic Fellow Citizens,* 7; Peter Roberts, "The Sclavs in Anthracite Coal Communities," *Charities* (December 3, 1904), 215-16. One would never think of confusing Swedes with Germans or Englishmen, but this, in effect, is what happened when one lumped Bulgarians with Russians or Poles. Of greater interest: until Americans got to know them better, Italians, too, were often thrown in with Slavs and were referred to as "Hunkies" or even "Polaks."

6. Balch, *Our Slavic Fellow Citizens,* 6.

7. Ibid.

8. The only major exception is the Czechs (Bohemians) who, unlike the other Slavic nationalities, were often highly skilled and likely to be merchants. In fact, this whole discussion of Slavs, including the following portions on stereotypes, does not apply to them at all. They are the only Slavic group to be exempted from the stereotype.

9. For a discussion of Slavic, Jewish, and Italian work patterns see Caroline Golab, *Immigrant Destinations* (1977).

10. Golab, *Immigrant Destinations,* Chapter 6 for a discussion of Slavic neighborhoods, their locations, and characteristics.

11. Bayard Taylor, *Travels in Greece and Russia* (1872), 306. The very next line of text reads: "With the addition of a projecting mouth, many of the faces would be completely Irish."

12. Balch, *Our Slavic Fellow Citizens,* 20; Edward A. Ross, *The Old World in*

the New (1913), 120; Edward A. Steiner, *The Immigrant Tide, Its Ebb and Flow* (1909), 210; Steiner, *On the Trail of the Immigrant* (1906), 183.

13. Ross, *The Old World in the New,* 120; Steiner, *The Immigrant Tide,* 210; Steiner, *On the Trail of the Immigrant,* 183; William Futhey Gibbons, "The Adopted Home of the Hun. A Social Study in Pennsylvania," *American Magazine of Civics* (September 1895), 316: "Their conquerors had said of them in a former age, 'to suffer injuries is their duty; to resent them is a crime worthy of punishment.' . . ."

14. At one time, all Slavs were serfs. As a whole, they were the last group in Europe to be freed from this medieval slavery. Some Slavs (very few) were freed as early as 1807; others in 1848; but the majority—Poles and Russians—remained the physical property of their masters until the Emancipation of 1865.

15. Steiner, *The Immigrant Tide,* 205; Balch, *Our Slavic Fellow Citizens,* 37: "A peasant [in America] seems to be understood as a synonym for a member of the lowest possible social class; a being devoid of all claims to respect who takes a great step up when he becomes a factory employee." See also Kate Holladay Claghorn, "Slavs, Magyars and some others in the New Immigration," *Charities* (December 3, 1904), 204. To Poles, the term "peasant" is the most derisive slur that can be applied to them today.

16. Balch, *Our Slavic Fellow Citizens,* 44.

17. "I have described the Slav's quality as brittle; perhaps stubborn would be better. You can lead him to the water and can also compel him to drink; but he will stop drinking when you are not looking, and 'kick' besides." "On the other hand, once he understands and endorses an ideal, he will be loyal to it; stubbornly loyal." Steiner, *The Immigrant Tide,* 213.

18. Steiner, *The Immigrant Tide,* 210; Ross, *The Old World in the New,* 129-30; Roberts, "The Sclavs in Anthracite Coal Communities," 220; Frank Julian Warne, *The Slav Invasion and the Mine Workers; A Study in Immigration* (1904), 65-83; Paul Fox, *The Poles in America* (1902), 71-72, 86-87.

19. Ross, *The Old World in the New,* 129-130; another proverb: "Strike a wife and a snake on the head." Wedding song: "Strike your wife only with good cause and when she has greatly vexed you." Popular Slavic song: "What sort of husband are you to me? You do not pull my hair, nor do you strike me!"; see also Steiner, *On the Trail of the Immigrant,* 187-88.

20. Roberts, "The Sclavs in Anthracite Coal Communities," 219; there isn't one observer who could be found that did not comment on the excessive drinking of the Slavs.

21. Ross, *The Old World in the New,* 127.

22. Balch, *Our Slavic Fellow Citizens,* 282: "No work is too onerous, too exhausting or too dangerous for them"; Ross, *The Old World in the New,* 125: "For these manful Slavs, no work is too toilsome and dangerous"; Steiner, *The Immigrant Tide,* 208: ". . . of rugged physique and docile temper, [the Slav] is regarded a valuable workman, performing the hardest task uncomplainingly, facing attendant dangers courageously, and enduring hardships and sufferings stolidly and without murmur."

23. Steiner, *The Immigrant Tide,* 207; Balch, *Our Slavic Fellow Citizens,* 42: "It is part of his world that there should be a God in heaven, and masters *(Herrschaften, Pani)* on the earth."

24. Ross, *The Old World in the New;* "These people haven't any natural ability to transmit," said a large employer of Slavs. "You may grind and polish dull minds all you want to in the public schools, but you never will get a keen edge on them because the steel is poor." p. 138; He continues, p. 139: "A

steel-town superintendent of schools finds the bulk of the children of the Slavs 'rather sluggish intellectually.' They do well in the lower grades, where memory counts most; but in the higher grades, where association is called for, they fall behind." A popular study was frequently cited to show the intellectual inferiority of Slavs as compared to native-born Americans and members of other immigrant groups: "Of 23,000 pupils of non-English speaking fathers, 43.4 percent were found to be behind their grade; . . . but for the Poles, the retardation was 58.1 percent, and for Slovaks 54.5 percent."

25. Steiner, *The Immigrant Tide,* 208; Gibbons, "The Adopted Home of the Hun," 316. "Docile" was a very popular word used to describe Slavs.

26. Balch, *Our Slavic Fellow Citizens,* 366-67: ". . . such occasions too often turn into debauches, and too often they end, not unnaturally, in brawls. This does more to injure the reputation of Slavs in this country than everything else put together . . ." Balch goes on to compare the drinking of the Slavs with that of the Irish; the Irish are always intemperate but the Pole does "spasmodic hard drinking." The Irish are alcoholics, the Poles are drunkards. The Irish lose time from work because of their drinking; the Poles never do (367-68). Moreover, "the Slavs do not seem to have any characteristic national weapon of offence like the Englishman's fists, the Irishman's shillalah, the Italian's stiletto, the Negro's razor or, most deadly of all, the American's revolver. Men who are very gentle when sober, when maddened by drink will strike with anything that comes to hand—chairs, lamps, knives." (And, we might add—radios. Balch could easily have been describing Stanley Kowalski's drunken scene in *A Streetcar Named Desire* where, in a rage, he hurls his radio out of the window.) Margaret Byington, in her "The Mill Town Courts and their Lodgers," also tells how gentle and peaceable the Slavs are when sober and how terrible they are when drunk; she also tells of one police officer who reported that "in all his experience he had never arrested a sober 'Hunkie' . . ." *Charities,* 21 (February 6, 1909), 913-22.

27. "One million Poles outnumber all the rest of the Slavs in America, and the Poles are very much clannish. When they settle in groups there is little association between them and their neighbors." Ross, *The Old World in the New,* 135; see also Steiner, *On the Trail of the Immigrant,* 196; Gibbons, "The Adopted Home of the Hun," 316; and Florian Znaniecki's chapter on the Poles in Henry Pratt Fairchild, *Immigrant Backgrounds* (1927), where he talks about how Poles tend to isolate themselves in America.

28. Ross, *The Old World in the New,* 135-36.

29. Signea Lenea Falk, *Tennessee Williams* (1961), 81; see also Francis Donahue, *The Dramatic World of Tennessee Williams* (1964), 36: "Kowalski is the embodiment of animal force, of brute life . . . He is all muscle, lumpish sensuality and crude energy. He is the unwitting anti-Christ of our time . . ."

30. In 1978 on network prime-time television a three-day special related the story of a small town Polish girl who moves to the big city and becomes a high class call-girl. TV's Lenny Kolowski of *Laverne and Shirley* is a modern version of Stanley Kowalski.

31. See Maurice Yacowar, "Aspects of the Familiar: A Defense of Minority Group Stereotyping in the Popular Film," *Journal of Popular Film,* 2 (1974), 129-39.

32. See Andre Sennwald's review of *Black Fury, New York Times,* April 11, 1935, p. 27.

33. *Life* (March 1, 1948).

34. Nancy M. Tischler, *Tennessee Williams: Rebellious Puritan* (1961), 137-39; Donahue, *The Dramatic World Of Tennessee Williams,* 37.

35. Ross, *The Old World in the New,* 142-43.

36. This theme was also implied in *West Side Story* (1961). Tony (Anton, the Polish form of Anthony, is his real name) and the other members of his largely Slavic gang, the Jets, are not portrayed as sympathetically as the rival gang of Puerto Ricans and obviously are anti-Puerto Rican. The Jets exhibit other aspects of the working-class image: rough, tough, crude, they inhabit the slums of Hell's Kitchen, believe in force and fists, and have little use for schooling, preferring to play hooky. It is also interesting that Tony, in this modern version of Romeo and Juliet, is deceived—another common Slavic theme—and, as a result, is killed.

37. In making its point, however, the movie went further than the play. The movie Kowalski was blown out of proportion and made larger than life. Possessing little if any redeeming social value, Stella had to leave him because the audience could not have accepted any other ending.

38. A helpful book in showing the historical context out of which stereotypes grow is William Newman, *American Pluralism; A Study of Minority Groups and Social Theory* (1973), especially Chapter 5.

8

DEUTSCHLAND, USA: GERMAN IMAGES IN AMERICAN FILM

Daniel J. Leab

"Those damned Dutch"—which is how many Americans incorrectly and angrily referred to immigrants from Germany—came to America in large numbers during the eighteenth and nineteenth centuries. The Germans settled in both rural and urban areas, in most parts of the United States. In 1909 Albert Faust, estimating on the basis of the 1900 census figures, asserted that in twenty-five of the forty-eight continental states and territories "Germans were more numerous in 1900 than other national stocks." And a recent immigration history reviewing the 1900 census figures points out that the Germans "were the most prominent ethnic group in eight of the nation's ten largest cities; only in Philadelphia and Boston were the Irish more numerous."[1]

Being of German stock did not necessarily mean that a person identified with the German community in America. Many immigrants chose assimilation. John Hawgood in his seminal study of German America found that especially "where individuals or families settled away from their fellow Germans they were usually very easily assimilated." The only thing that remained German about these men and

156

women was their family name, and often that too became Americanized—Schmidt became Smith, Hilgard became Villard, Steinveg became Steinway, and Pfoerschein became Pershing.[2]

Significant numbers of Germans, however, did not become assimilated. Whether living in a rural or urban environment, they clung to their language and to Old World mores, even unto the second or third generation. Thus, there were many places that had "Little Germanies." New York City, for example, had its *Kleindeutschland* where a traveller from Germany found that "life is almost the same as in the Old Country. . . . There is not a single business which is not run by Germans. . . . The resident . . . need not even know English to make a living."[3]

In the Middle West, whole areas were "Teutonic in character." By the mid-nineteenth century some 50,000 Germans lived in a section of Cincinnati known as "Over The Rhine." And Milwaukee vied with Cincinnati for recognition as *the* German cultural center in the United States. In these cities, as elsewhere in America, there were hundreds of singing societies, gymnastic clubs, benevolent associations, workingman's groups, and societies devoted to lectures and discussion. This organizational mania existed wherever there was a significant German presence and tended, as one scholar has put it, "to leave German communities as islands in a sea of Americanism."[4]

This self-imposed cultural isolation does not alone explain the Germans' failure to play a political or social role in America commensurate with their numbers. The German immigrants had only their language in common. They were split in many different ways, and they represented a wide range of political and religious beliefs as well as varying vocations. To use the perceptive analogy of Daniel Moynihan and Nathan Glazer, the German immigrants in America "reflected, as it were, an entire modern society, not simply an element of one [and] the only thing they all had in common were the outward manifestations of German culture: language for a generation or two, and . . . a fondness for certain kinds of food and drink. . . ." The Germans were rent by internecine quarrels and factional disputes of every kind. It was said that "wherever there are four Germans there will be five opinions." Nowhere was the division among the Germans more discernible than in the clash between Catholics and Protestants, who had a bitter history of strife in Central Europe stretching back to the 1500s. Indeed, in 1883 on the 400th anniversary of Martin Luther's birth, a Baltimore German Catholic newspaper, with a national readership, ran over fifty articles strenuously attacking Luther, the Reformation, and Protestantism.[5]

American society paid scant attention to these clashes and struggles.

For the average American, all Germans were alike, marked by their clannishness, attachment to a foreign language, and strange ways. But overall the general attitude was not hostile. Indeed, in 1908, reports John Higham, "a group of professional people, in rating the traits of various immigrant nationalities, ranked the Germans above the English and in some respects judged them superior to the native whites." Still, tensions did mark and mar the relationship between American society and unassimilated German elements. Outright condemnation was unusual, but qualified praise was not. Germans were admired for being thrifty, honest, industrious, but were also called materialistic, authoritarian, stubborn. Their love of education was favorably commented upon, but they also were accused of being unimaginative and plodding. The German-American *hausfrau* was considered a role model because of her many virtues, but she was also considered to be too willingly subject to her husband.[6]

There were also some tensions which were friction-producing. The Germans, as Richard Krickus indicates, "were the first serious exponents of Marxism in America," and many in the United States were put off by German radicalism and by what Richard O'Connor describes as "the anti-clerical and anti-religious among the German-Americans . . . [who] were aggressive partisans" of nonbelief and freethinking. Other areas of tension had to do with the German community's understandable opposition to the rising tide of Prohibitionism and with "the German Sunday," which was merry and a far cry from the traditional dour Sunday observance. Also irritating was the Germans' superior attitude toward American culture, which they dismissed as crude, uncouth, naive, bumptious, even "bizarre." And after the establishment of Wilhelmine Germany in 1871, and its rapid rise as an industrial and military power, chauvinism of a sort marked the attitude of many Germans with regard to "the Fatherland." As a recent history of the German-Americans shows, it became "characteristic" for them "to glory in the achievements of the new German Empire."[7]

As a group, then, the German-Americans prior to 1914 were respected and admired, at times emulated, and occasionally feared. But even though there were few tangible frictions, they were not well-liked, despite the varying positive statements made about them by public opinion leaders in the United States. Ethnic stereotyping is a sound measurement of popular opinion in a free society, and the stereotypes of the German prevalent in American culture for a generation prior to 1914 measure that lack of affection. The stereotypes were not unkind, but they were condescending, disparaging, and even occasionally ridiculous. Popular verses and songs mocked German "traits," and the stage, burlesque, and vaudeville abounded with pigheaded, comically bellicose Germans, all of whom, according to one show-business history, had "padded stomachs, wore chin whiskers, blond wigs, small brown derbys, checkered trousers, big shoes, fancy vests with heavy watchchains, and murdered the English language."[8]

German fracturing of the language also occurred in the newly developing newspaper comic strips, especially *The Katzenjammer Kids,* which almost immediately after its debut in 1897 attained enormous popularity. Openly based on the German cartoonist Wilhelm Busch's *Max und Moritz,* the illustrated adventures of two quite mischievous young boys, *The Katzenjammer Kids* depicts "the guerilla war conducted by Hans and Fritz . . . against any form of authority and indeed against society itself." Rudolph Dirks, the strip's creator, made very effective use of an Anglo-German pidgin. Thus, for the boys "society ist nix" and their chief targets include "die Mama" (their mother, a rotund middle-aged stereotyped German-American *hausfrau*), "der Captain" (their adoptive father, a shipwrecked sailor rescued by die Mama), and "der Inspector" (a long-white-bearded truant officer, resembling the stereotyped German civil servant of the time, who apparently came for the boys and stayed).[9]

Stereotypes such as these quickly found their way into the films of the day. Commercial production of motion pictures began in the United States during the mid-1890s, and by 1917 the movies had become one of the most important forms of mass entertainment in the country. Because the movies drew heavily on the contemporary popular culture, the image of the German-American found in these early films retained somewhat negative connotations. As I have pointed out elsewhere, "the German-Americans were not cruelly libeled in the manner of many other ethnic groups, but they were ridiculed and made the butt of nasty humor."[10]

Prior to America's entry into World War I in 1917, the image of the male German-American, for example, had few positive qualities. Younger men were often presented, as in Cecil B. DeMille's 1915 melodrama *Kindling,* as tenement dwellers with limited imagination: "Honest" Heinie Schultz and his family, whatever their prospects, are at the low end of the social spectrum. A good example of the German-American as middle-aged man is the 1916 comedy-drama *The Man Who Stood Still,* in which Lew Fields (one of the better known "Dutch comics" of the day) repeated his stage role—"an old-fashioned unprogressive German, the owner of a small jewelry store" who wants his unwilling daughter to marry the son of his old friend Otto Spiegel. And Fields's interpretation was the selling point of the film according to the *Motion Picture News,* which found the plot "simple and seemingly trite . . ." The older generation of German-Americans did not escape scorn. At a time when blacks were usually objects of contempt and ridicule, a black serving woman in the 1904 Biograph comedy *A Bucket of Cream Ale* is shown dumping a bucket of beer on the head of a white-haired, pot-bellied, pipe-smoking, beer-drinking, mustachioed, obvious burgher.[11]

Indeed, an examination of some other Biograph films further indicates how popular sentiments about the German-American were translated to the screen and obviously reinforced the already prevalent stereotypes in such matters as dress, language, and vocation. Among the most interesting of the Biograph films treating German-Americans is the 1909 drama *The Voice of the Violin,* because it touches on fears that became rampant during and immediately after World War I. Herr von Schmitt comes to the United States from Germany and makes a living teaching the violin. In Germany, he had become imbued with the doctrines of Karl Marx. One of von Schmitt's pupils is Helen Walker, the daughter of "a wealthy capitalist." He declares his love for her and is spurned, "of course, owing to the disparity of rank." Enraged by this state of affairs, he agrees to join with his radical friends and blow up "a certain monopolist." While the bomb is being placed in the monopolist's cellar, he stays outside on watch and suddenly hears his "own violin composition being played within." Helen is in danger. He determines to stop the bombing but is overpowered and left in the cellar bound hand and foot and with the lighted bomb. In a stirring climax, "he crawls with supernatural effort towards the bomb and with his teeth bites the fuse in two as the fire is within inches of igniting the bomb." And then, as the Biograph plot synopsis concludes, "Well, you may guess what the finish will be . . . they lived happily ever afterwards."[12]

Happiness, however, was not to be the fate of the German-Americans. And the catalyst which would destroy them as a community was World War I. At war's outbreak in August, 1914, President Woodrow Wilson had appealed to all Americans, whatever their background, to "be impartial in thought as well as action. . . ." But many of the dominant elements in American society were Anglophiles and neutral neither in thought nor in deed. The leaders of the German-American community sought to counter pro-Allied influences. They saw nothing wrong legally or morally in this activity: they believed "Germany is our mother; Columbia our bride" and asserted, to use one historian's words, that it was "not necessary . . . for a man to forsake his mother in order to be loyal to his bride." They proved to be in error.[13]

The American road to war was a winding one upon which this

country trod slowly, but in time public sentiment came to favor the Allies. In part this change in attitude from one of neutrality was due to the intelligent and intensive British propaganda campaign waged in the United States, and in part the change was due to ill-conceived German actions which included the violation of Belgian neutrality, unrestricted submarine warfare periodically resulting in the sinking of passenger vessels and the death of noncombatants (as was the case with the *Lusitania*), and the occasionally destructive but ultimately ineffectual attempts by German agents to sabotage American industries producing war material for the Allies.[14]

The movies were not immune to these stirrings and changes in American public opinion. Social scientists and others concerned with the impact of film on public opinion are sharply divided as to whether movies influence an audience, or whether they mirror its ideas. Whichever side one agrees with there can be no gainsaying that by 1914 a burgeoning American film industry had found that war "figured importantly in providing the type of escapist entertainment demanded by audiences." The themes varied between 1914 and 1917,

Hollywood contributed heavily to the Hate-the-Hun campaign of World War I with potboilers such as The Battle Cry of Peace *(1915), in which the Germans display their barbarism and lechery toward women and children.*

but however the movies dealt with the subject of war, the Germans in the main came off badly. They, or villains with German-sounding names or German-style uniforms, committed dastardly deeds. The on-screen image of Germans between 1914 and 1917 went from the liberal, graceful young man in *Old Heidelberg* (with the rising star Wallace Reid as the peace-loving heir to the throne who finds happiness only while a student at the university) to *Womanhood, the Glory of the Nation* (whose plot dealt with the American woman's response to an invading army of 150,000 "Ruthanians"). German-Americans vigorously attempted to deal with this situation, but to little avail. Garth Jowett is correct in his judgment that "the cinemas were mobilized against Germany well before Wilson led the nation into war."[15]

The cinema's anti-German bias notwithstanding, movie audiences between 1914 and 1917 did have some opportunity to see the German point of view—mainly in films dealing with fighting at the front lines. Indeed, according to a recent study, such films were "highly successful and were widely shown in pre-war America." Among them was the 1915 film *The German Side of the War,* which was a tremendous success. Trade journalist Terry Ramsaye remembered that in New York City "lines awaiting the attention of the box office extended for four blocks." The film was a "sensation." But given the Allies' control of communications between the United States and Europe, such films were few and far between.[16]

The German-Americans' failure to counter pro-Allied propaganda and the spate of anti-German films boded ill for German-Americans. Because of their well-known strong cultural, social, and emotional ties to the Fatherland, the changing movie image of the Germans affected American society's view of the German-Americans as well. This change occurred in a "second-hand" fashion, but occur it did. In the process the movie image of the German-Americans became forever subordinate to that of Germany. Henceforth, it would be the latter's image that would dominate the American moviegoer's imagination. And whatever chance there might have been of reversing this subordination died with the collapse of organized German America after the American entry into World War I. This collapse came partly because of the shock among German-Americans that the United States was at war with Germany. John Hawgood alleges that "cases of suicide in the draft camps were not unknown among the sons of German homes, for whom this conflict . . . proved unbearable." In general, as Frederick Luebke has indicated, "German-Americans of all kinds were bewildered by the onset of war."[17]

Bewilderment gave way to fear as a wave of anti-German hysteria swept across the United States in 1917 and 1918. Every possible manifestation of German influence in America came under attack.

The syndicators of *The Katzenjammer Kids* found it expedient temporarily to rename the strip *The Shenanigan Kids.* Renaming became a popular pastime: sauerkraut became "liberty cabbage," hamburgers became "liberty sandwiches," German measles became "liberty measles," and of course dachshunds became "liberty pups." In many instances renaming was necessary for economic survival. The Germania Bank of Milwaukee became the National Bank of Commerce, the Germania Life Insurance Co. became the Guardian Life. Historian John Higham, in discussing the widespread attack on the German language, reports that "a campaign to eliminate German from the public school curricula made considerable headway [and] before the war ended, some whole states . . . banned the teaching of German." Operas, symphonic music, even hymns of German origin became suspect and were boycotted. Churchmen, who should have known better, joined in this chorus of hate: one Brooklyn Congregational minister described the Lutheran Church as "not the bride of Christ but the paramour of Kaiserism." Patriots saw German conspiracies everywhere: German-American Red Cross volunteers, for example, "were widely believed to be putting ground glass in bandages and food sent to soldiers."[18]

As brutal intolerance filtered through every level of American life, the German-American organizations found that they could not survive. *Vereins* of one sort or another everywhere in the country dissolved. The German language press, "the glue which held the ethnic community together," suffered grievously. Nearly fifty percent of the total German language publications disappeared by 1920, and the survivors had much reduced circulations. Because of continuing acts of violence against German-Americans, name changing became a common occurence. Milwaukee court records show two hundred such changes in the first four months of the war alone. The persecution of the German-Americans came to an end shortly after the war, but by then it was too late for organized German-Americanism. As John Hawgood has observed "the German-Americans as German-Americans did not emerge from the war at all. The war had so enhanced the distance between the German and the American that no hyphen could stretch from one to the other."[19]

The propaganda-oriented American film industry participated with a vengeance in this extraordinary hate campaign, not only attacking Germany vehemently, but also stigmatizing German-Americans as disloyal and a threat. Thus, in *The Hun Within,* a 1918 melodrama, the German-American Karl Wagner returns from Berlin (where he had been sent to college) "a changed man," according to one synopsis of the plot. He plans with the aid of "a traitorous sailor Krug" to conceal a bomb in the hold of a ship carrying American troops to France. Happily, this "treachery" is foiled at the last moment. In other feature films German-Americans were shown planning to destroy an American munitions factory, to spread pro-German propaganda that would undermine the war effort, and to pass vital secret information to the enemy. German agents—usually German-Americans—seemingly were everywhere in the United States, operating on all levels of society.[20]

Among the most striking hate films, and among the earliest such films, was *The Little American,* released in July, 1917. The heroine was portrayed by Mary Pickford, "America's Sweetheart," and the German-American Karl is in love with her. But upon war's outbreak in 1914 he goes to Germany to report for military service. The Mary Pickford character, as the result of what can be described only as an extraordinary series of circumstances, arrives at the family chateau in France just before the Germans overrun it. And soon afterward on a dark night she is assaulted and nearly raped by Karl "who in his lust and the dark does not recognize her until it is almost too late." The shock of recognition followed by renewed association at the chateau with "the little American" leads Karl to repent. But for their love it is too late. The Mary Pickford character has become involved with French espionage (her firsthand knowledge of German cruelty, she declares, had led her to abandon neutrality). She is found out; he becomes involved; they face a firing squad together; she escapes death; he does not.[21]

The little American had witnessed the drowning of women and children as the result of a callous U-boat attack, the burning of priceless antiques by German soldiers in need of firewood, and the execution of civilian hostages by heartless German officers. This catalogue of nefarious German activities was typical of what the movies depicted during the next two years. In the First World War a highly effective Allied propaganda campaign made "Hun" a common and derogatory synonym for German, and upon America's entry into the war, the movie industry in the United States became a very active part of the Hate-the-Hun campaign. The Hun behaved with unbelievable brutality on screen. In the 1917 melodrama *Bitter Sweet,* characterized by one critic as "a typical account of Belgium's distress," a 14-year-old girl suffers dreadful hardships at the hands of the Germans before finding refuge in America. In other such melodramas a French mother is humbled by the Prussians, Belgian children are shipped to the Fatherland to work as whipped and starved slaved laborers in war industries, and an American nurse who goes to France is captured by the Germans and raped. D. W. Griffith's film *Hearts of the World* (1918), much of which is set in a French village, depicted what a *New York Times* critic described as "Prussian brutality" and "the horrors of German occupation."[22]

One of the most sensational of the atrocity films was *My Four Years in Germany* (1918), based on the best seller of the same name by James W. Gerard, who served as American ambassador in Berlin from 1913 to 1917. The first important Warner Brothers success, this ambitious film included some scenes supposedly taking place in German prisoner-of-war camps (but actually filmed on the East Coast of the United States.) People were shown being beaten, set on by vicious guard dogs, and scrambling for scraps of bread. British soldiers are thrown in with Russian soldiers suffering from typhus; when an American asks why the sick Russians are not quarantined, he is told that "they're Allies, let them get acquainted." A trade journal admiringly stated: "there is no stone left unturned to arouse the audience to a sense that the German manner of conducting war is synonymous with barbarianism." A recent viewer of the film found "the simple-mindedness of the film . . . beyond belief."[23]

My Four Years in Germany was not kind to the Kaiser, and in many films he became the focal point for anti-German propaganda; indeed, he became the personification of the Hated Hun. The Kaiser perfectly fit the stereotypes of the German in American eyes, with his arrogant stare, upturned moustache, and arched eyebrows. Cartoonist Winsor McKay's animated one-reeler *The Sinking of the Lusitania* (1918) ends with the title "the man who fired the shot was decorated for it by the Kaiser!—AND THEY TELL US NOT TO HATE THE HUN." And in movie after movie the Hun in the form of the Kaiser was punished. He was assassinated by a bastard son (*The Kaiser's Finish,* 1918), was literally sent to Hell (*To Hell With The Kaiser,* 1918), was killed by a lightning bolt (*Why America Will Win,* 1918), and in the most grotesque of the "Get-the-Kaiser" films (*The Kaiser—The Beast of Berlin,* 1918), he was at war's end "stripped of all his glory" and "handed over to the people of Belgium. . . ."[24]

The war came to an end on the morning of November 11, 1918. American audiences, overjoyed by the ending of the war, almost overnight lost interest in the kind of film which had dominated the nation's screens for nearly two years. The movie industry found it difficult to sell movies that had been planned and made in a different atmosphere. Films were exhibited as "NOT a war film." Yet *Behind The Door,* one of the box office hits of 1920, was a war film, albeit one very different from its predecessors, especially in its treatment of German-Americans. Oscar Krug (played by Hobart Bosworth, a well-known star of the time) is a veteran skipper who retires to Maine. When America enters the war, he is viewed with suspicion because of his ethnic background and is forced to fight for his life. Later he weds the much younger Alice Morse, joins the navy, and receives command of a ship. Jane Novak, who played Alice, years later described the rest of the plot to a fascinated interviewer:

> Bosworth was my husband . . . and we were on a ship, during the war, going to Europe, and the ship is bombed by this submarine. . . . Bosworth and I were in a little lifeboat, and then we see the periscope and the submarine comes up . . . and it's Wallace Beery. They take me aboard . . . Bosworth, they kick over, and submerge with me down in the submarine. I don't remember how he was saved—somebody saved him, because he vowed "If I ever meet you again, I will skin you alive." After I had been on the sub for I don't know how long, and they were all tired of me, they put me in the torpedo thing and out. Then Hobart did meet the German captain later, and he did skin him alive. At the end of this picture was this thing hanging—Oh! It was ghastly. . . .

Given the hysteria of the wartime years the treatment of the Bosworth character is interesting. Krug is shown to have been dealt with unfairly by the Maine townspeople. And later, after his new command has destroyed Beery's U-Boat and captured him, Krug unjustly comes under suspicion from his crew when he is closeted with the Beery character. The crewmen do not know what is going on behind Krug's closed door—they only know that at first German is being spoken. Finally they decide to confront Krug; when the door opens, they see him bloody, with straight razor in hand, and the shadow of the skinned-alive German on the wall.[25]

Behind The Door was unusual not only for the relatively sympathetic manner in which Krug was presented, but also for the fact that the movies depicted a German-American, or for that matter any German. By 1920 such types had just about disappeared from movies made in the United States, and with few exceptions remained absent until the mid-1930s. *The American Film Institute Catalog of Feature Films, 1921-1930* deals with more than 6,000 films but records fewer than 150 features that in some way touched on Germany and the Germans. And the Germans were much more visible than the German-Americans, although those few films in the 1920s and early 1930s that did depict German-Americans softened the prewar stereotypes. Thus, the male German-Americans were still burgherly, family-oriented types, but whether as barber (*Sins of the Children,* a 1930 melodrama), bootlegger (*Sins of the Fathers,* a 1929 drama), or bank cashier (*The Way of All Flesh,* a 1927 star vehicle for Emil Jannings, a well-known German actor), the stereotype was no longer ludicrous or repugnant. Although treated as types, the German-Americans were treated sympathetically—a dramatic change not only as regards World War I, but also the prewar years. A notable exception was *Greed* (1924) whose main protagonist McTeague married into a Swiss-German family. Their flaws are highlighted in this tale of avarice, treachery, and decay. But such films with German-American characters were few and far between.[26]

The reason that I have spent so much time on the German-American image prior to the 1920s is that thereafter one really only finds a German image in American film. That image also improved during the 1920s and early 1930s. True enough that some films still showed the Germans as "bloody Huns." *The Four Horsemen of the Apocalypse* (1921), for example, portrayed the Germans as barbarians killing for the love of killing. But soon movies dealing with World War I, while still showing Germans as the enemy, no longer presented them as Huns. By the end of the decade, war movies reflected America's disenchantment with the crusade to "make the world safe for democracy." Hate had given way to sympathy and compassion. *Four Sons* (1928) poignantly recounted the plight of a German mother who lost three sons during the war, and who finally finds peace with the son who had emigrated to America. The film had some ugly German military types in it, but the tone of the film is indicated by the scene where an American doughboy watches one of the four sons dying and asking for his mother: the title reads "Oh, dem guys have got mothers too." In *Young Eagles* (1930), to note another instance, there are again some unpleasant German militarists, but the chief German, an ace pilot, is shown to be an honorable man.[27]

Of the various American movies dealing with World War I produced at this time, none had the impact of *All Quiet on the Western Front* (1930). Based on the powerful, heart-rending novel by Erich Maria Remarque, this deeply moving film dealt with seven callow youths who rush to join the army at the outbreak of war, and instead of realizing their patriotic visions of glory find only futility, horror, and death. As Bosley Crowther remarked years later, "more strongly than by any previous war film . . . the viewer was pulled into this experience [and] made to identify almost totally with . . . soldiers in German uniform. . . ." Although the intent may have been to be universal, the story in effect was told from the German side. There were also unflattering German military types in this film, but the emphasis on the youths overshadowed them, as "with simple eloquence" the film "made the point that the German soldier suffered, bled, went hungry, laughed and loved too [and] when he was killed there was no stirring martial music . . . just agony and terror, and the terrible sense of a young and unfulfilled life wasted."[28]

Other kinds of movies with German characters in them during the 1920s and early 1930s also projected a kinder, more pleasing image.

Pointing in this direction was D. W. Griffith's 1924 film *Isn't Life Wonderful*. Although ostensibly about Polish refugees in postwar Germany, this film could not help but create sympathy for the inhabitants of that wracked country. As two Griffith critics point out, "the director makes it abundantly clear . . . [that] the Germans themselves are sharing in the agonizing hardships with which the picture deals." By 1927 it was not necessary to be so indirect, and a movie could preach against anti-German prejudice. In *His Foreign Wife* (1927) a doughboy who married a German girl brought her back to the United States, and when he found her encountering resentment, denounced "the false patriotism" that engenders such prejudice. And ultimately Germany became just another locale with varying types. Thus, in *Grand Hotel* (1932) a hateful industrialist with all the unpleasant characteristics usually attributed to screen Germans is offset by a winning gentleman jewel thief and other more attractive types.[29]

The treatment of the Germans on film reflected the subtle changes in American public opinion about Germany in the years after the Armistice. While a positive approach was long in coming, the anti-Hun hysteria subsided almost immediately as new targets came under frantic and fanatical attack. "The German element" as one historian quite correctly observes, "was replaced as a topic of conversation by the Blacks and their 'new' ways. . . [by] the withdrawal into isolationism, and [by] the Bolshevik Menace." This menace especially captured public attention, and it took some time before the "red menace" became a "tiresome broken record" (to use Paul Murphy's apt phrase).[30]

Some within the once extensive German-American community sought to take advantage of the shift in focus. The Steuben Society was formed in 1919. Among the expressed objectives of its founders was the determination "to enlighten the public on the important part played by the Germanic element in the making of America." The Society's campaign to rehabilitate German-Americans and Germany was helped immeasurably by the writings of the journalists and scholars who came to be known as the "revisionists." Although by no means all pro-German, the revisionists cast serious doubts on the official histories of the war which assumed Germany's guilt for its outbreak. Moreover, American economic interests benefitted from the German acceptance of American-devised plans to deal with the difficult problem of reparations. Despite occasional strains, then, at the beginning of the 1930s Germany's reputation in the United States was "sound." As a consequence, there was some small resurgence of German-American life. Americans of German extraction began to reenter public life, and clubs of various kinds began to reappear. But compared to such activity prior to World War I, this resurgence was at best weak.[31]

Adolf Hitler's accession to power in 1933 and the ensuing Nazification of Germany resulted in another swing in public opinion, this time against Germany. But the initial response was limited, as was the response of the German-Americans to the Nazi takeover. Despite everything that was reported about what the new German government euphemistically called "excesses," many German-Americans, as a recent study concludes, "were reluctant initially to criticize. . ., [and] unwilling to believe what was really happening. . . [in] the ancestral home, plus [there was] pride in the new respect Germany secured among the world's nations." However, as the decade progressed, pride gave way to other feelings. In part this change in attitude was due to the increasingly outspoken hostility of the American public to Nazi Germany. Gallup in December, 1938, found that ninety-four percent of the sample he polled disapproved of Nazi Germany's racist policies. German-Americans feared that a failure on their part to speak out against Hitler and Nazism would be construed as support and might result in another wave of anti-German hysteria similar to that of World War I. But neither should the feelings of revulsion and contempt aroused in the German-American community by Nazi Germany's domestic and foreign policies be overlooked.[32]

There were some in the German-American community who became outspoken adherents of Hitler and the "New Order." But in the main, as John Hawgood noted in 1940, "the swastika was carried into German America mainly by actual German citizens, assisted by a relatively small number of native-born Americans of German stock. . . ." Subsequent scholarship has confirmed Hawgood's assertion. The Nazi movement in the United States had virtually no success because it failed to receive more than marginal German-American support. The best known manifestation of that movement, the German-American Bund, attained considerable notoriety in the late 1930s because anti-Nazi groups invested it with more power than it had, because of the open meetings it organized, and because the FBI linked it to the German espionage network in the United States. But by mid-1939 the Bund was disintegrating precisely because of its failure to gain support from German-Americans.[33]

By 1939 there was pronounced anti-Nazi sentiment in the United States. Shortly after World War II broke out in September, 1939, Gallup found that sixteen percent of a sample he polled were ready to go to war against the Germans, and he found forty-four percent who believed that if the Allies faced defeat the United States should intervene; moreover, eighty-four percent wished the Allies to win,

In 1939 Hollywood handed down its first indictment of Nazism. Confessions of a Nazi Spy *clearly stamped the subversives threatening America as Germans by adorning them with all the cruelty and duplicity of the Hate-the-Hun images. It signalled Hollywood's break with American isolationism on the eve of World War II.*

and only two percent wanted a Nazi victory. Such sentiments not-withstanding, the American movie industry exercised great caution in its approach to the subject of Germany. One could view the 1934 film *The House of Rothschild* as an indirect swipe at the Nazis. In this film about the economic and social rise of the multi-national Jewish banking family during the latter part of the 1700s and the Napoleonic Wars, Boris Karloff, of all people, portrayed an anti-Semitic German nobleman, who ultimately is put in his place. But not too much should be made of one film at a time when nearly 500 films were produced by Hollywood annually.[34]

Hollywood also dealt only sporadically and very carefully with the developments in Germany that led to the success of the Nazis. Thus, *Little Man, What Now?* (1934) is a bowdlerized version of German novelist Hans Fallada's tough-minded book about the tribulations of the middle class in Weimar Germany, and *The Road Back* (1937) is a weak version of Remarque's novel about what happened to German veterans who returned home after World War I. What happened to another Remarque novel dealing with veterans in Weimar Germany illustrates the studios' attitude towards Nazi Germany throughout much of the 1930s. The original script for *Three Comrades* (1938) contained incidents which *Time* considered "a corrosive arraignment of Nazi Germany." Thanks to the direct intervention of MGM head Louis B. Mayer, these incidents were softened or removed. Joseph Mankiewicz later recalled that MGM, for the sake of its German market, appeased the Nazis: "MGM . . . kept on releasing its films in Nazi Germany until Hitler threw them out. In fact, one producer was in charge of taking anyone's name off a picture credit if it sounded Jewish."[35]

Obviously, the lucrative German market (which after mid-1938 included Nazi-annexed Austria and after mid-1939 included occupied Czechoslovakia) was a factor in the industry's hesitancy in producing films dealing with Nazi Germany. But one should not forget that the bulk of the industry's production was governed by a principle summed up in a typical Samuel Goldwynism— "If you have a message, send it Western Union." Nor should the strength of isolationist sentiment in America be underestimated. As late as the autumn of 1941 a Senate committee began an investigation of the industry, because as one Senator put it, "when you go to the movies, . . . before you know where you are you have actually listened to a speech designed to make you believe that Hitler is going to get you if you don't watch out." He referred to the overtly anti-German movies released during 1940 and 1941. Hollywood produced only a handful of such films until mid-1941 when the industry, having been thrown out of Germany and German-occupied Europe, and recognizing the political drift in the United States, began to produce in somewhat greater, but still limited numbers, the kind of films the Senator had described. Finally, the very excesses utilized in caricaturing Germans on the screen during World War I and the fuss made about this propaganda during the 1930s militated against any easy or immediate acceptance of similar films.[36]

The Warner Brothers movie *Confessions of a Nazi Spy*, which was not released until spring, 1939, was the first major studio film to be outspokenly anti-Nazi. Based on an actual 1938 case in which the FBI broke a German spy ring, this film, which today would be called a "docudrama," was more indictment than entertainment. It attacked the Bund as a nest of subversives and spies, asserted that German consulates in the United States served as command posts for espionage, and declared that the Nazis waged a clandestine war against America. Although it was what Otis Ferguson called "a hate breeder," the film did specify that there were only a few bad guys and thousands of good non-Nazi German-Americans.[37]

The Warner Brothers film represented a breakthrough of sorts. No longer was it necessary for the studios to refer to the spies menacing the United States as agents of an unnamed foreign power, although it still took some time before all these agents went from having German names to a clearly defined German identity. Nor did the movies now hesitate to comment on contemporary politics. This commentary could be somewhat elliptical, as in the unprepossessing swashbuckler *Son of Monte Cristo* (1940), in which the count's son saves a mythical nineteenth-century Middle European country and its pretty ruler from a general who looks German, talks Nazi, and has a variety of henchmen who do both. Anti-Nazi comments could even be found in Charlie Chan movies: in *Charlie Chan in the City of Darkness* (1939) the fabled detective, learning that British Prime Minister Neville Chamberlain intends to fly to Munich to confer with Hitler (which actually happened at the time of the Sudeten crisis in September, 1938), aphorized "when spider send invitations to house, fly better beware."[38]

A few more outspoken films were made in 1940 and 1941, all of them uncompromising in their treatment of Germany. Thus, *The Mortal Storm*, MGM's 1940 filming of Phyllis Bottome's best-selling novel, related "the story of a non-Aryan professor and his family in Germany from the time of Hitler's appointment as chancellor to the professor's death in a concentration camp and the shooting of his daughter as she seeks to escape across the border." This film and others, such as *Underground* (1941) in which dedicated Germans conspire to defeat the Nazis and *Escape* (1940) in which sympathetic Germans aid an American in rescuing his German mother from a concentration camp, presupposed that there were decent Germans opposed to the Nazi evil.[39]

But it was the evil that was emphasized in the myriad number of anti-German films that were produced by the American movie industry once the United States entered the war in December, 1941. As might be expected, these propaganda vehicles presented a highly negative image of Germans and relied heavily on certain kinds of stock characterizations. Is there a viewer of such movies on television who does not know that World War II Germans spoke with guttural accents, heiled Hitler, shouted "Schweinhund" at the slightest provocation, and enjoyed tormenting old people and pretty young women? The officers and upper class were presented as cultured swine willing to bleed Russian children to obtain plasma for German troops, or to shoot innocent hostages; German noncoms and middle-echelon types were presented as libidinous, sadistic bullies given to rape and torture. Russell Shain believes that the "highest number" of Nazi wrongdoings in any one film "per minute" took place in *Hitler's Children* (1943): "the picture had the Nazis transgressing against individual freedom, motherhood, true love, religion, free expression, family, bodily integrity, and life" in less than eighty minutes. Yet, for all the unpleasantness displayed by Germans in various films of this period, for all the American film industry's yahooing, the "nasty Nazi" theme of World War II never approximated the vicious proportions of the Hate-the-Hun campaign of World War I.[40]

The guidelines laid down by the Bureau of Motion Pictures of the Office of War Information were largely responsible for the more sensible approach undertaken in World War II. Sophisticated in its approach to propaganda, the Bureau, for example, urged the American film industry to make a distinction between Germans and Nazis: "don't make blanket condemnation of all Germans . . . as this country does not regard the German people as our enemies, only their leaders." Thus, although the Nazis, and the Germans, often were presented irrationally or virulently in many of the American movies produced during the war, even the staunchest anti-Nazi film could contain a decent German. Because of the nature of total war, however, they might often prove to be casualties of our side, as happens

This sinister interrogation scene from Berlin Correspondent *(1942) evokes terror from the audience and reminds Americans of the sadism and brutality of the Nazis.*

to the kind, lonely officer in *The Moon Is Down* (1943), the movie version of John Steinbeck's uneven story of the difficulties faced by the German occupiers of a Norwegian town. More often than not the good German could be found in films dealing with life inside Germany, for such characters demonstrated that even Hitler's behemoth was not monolithic. The protagonist of *The Seventh Cross* (1944) escapes from a concentration camp prior to the war; he avoids capture as well as crucifixion and is able to escape Germany only because there are still decent Germans willing to help him. Such films carried the message "don't hate the Nazis because they are German, hate those Germans who are Nazis." Of course, the distinction between the Germans and the Nazis sometimes blurred, but whether blurred or not the distinction deserves emphasis because of the break it marks with the depiction of Germans in World War I era films. Over a generation after the end of World War II, the existence of this distinction caused a West German film critic to note with some awe that "even during the height of the war, films were released in which 'good Germans' were presented sentimentally and respectfully, as if Hitler and the war did not exist."[41]

German-Americans on screen were also treated differently during World War II. In considerable part this was due to the fact that there was none of the hysteria which their forebears had faced a generation earlier. In this war there was little fear on the home front that people of German descent owed a divided allegiance, and, as one history relates, "tolerance was displayed . . . to citizens of German . . . descent and they encountered little public animosity." The depiction of German-Americans on screen reflected this attitude. In the main they appeared as superloyal in such potboilers as *Nazi Agent* (1942), in which a loyal, naturalized German-American at the risk of his life takes the place of his twin brother who had come to the United States to wreak destruction, and *They Came To Blow Up America* (1943), in which German saboteurs find they cannot count on any assistance from German-Americans. In some movies such as *The House on 92nd Street* (1945), a psuedo-documentary, some traitorous German-Americans are shown, but the hero of this film is "an American of German parentage."[42]

The immediate postwar revelations of Nazi atrocities inside Germany and elsewhere in Europe tended to keep people from avowing ethnic pride in being of German descent, and the already diminished German-American community suffered accordingly. Nor were new recruits to be won from the postwar German immigrants to the United States. These immigrants were interested in melding rapidly into American society, and this they did. The German-American community, deprived of new blood and suffering from the stigma imposed by Nazi actions, virtually disappeared as an organized entity, except for ceremonial occasions and a very limited, constantly diminishing social subculture. What then has happened to the American of German descent? Historian Richard O'Connor has an interesting and compelling answer to that question. He maintains that they have been absorbed into the mainstream of American society, that there has been "a merging of what had been separate Anglo-Saxon and German entities into a new Anglo-Teutonic amalgamation," and that "together the old breed of English, Welsh, and Scotch-Irish and those of German origin are in a position of unassailable dominance . . . lords of government, industry, business, science, agriculture, education, and the military establishment."[43]

However one may react to O'Connor's argument, there is no question that the film image of the German-American for some time now has been extinct. But the movie image of the German has undergone some startling permutations since World War II. At war's end it became tragically clear that Allied propaganda, including American movies, had seriously underestimated the horrific extent of the Nazi atrocities. The offenses against humanity committed by some Germans understandably resulted in a blanket but unthinking condemnation of Germany and its populace. But the exigencies of postwar international politics very soon resulted in reassessments as Communism almost overnight replaced Nazism as the supreme evil threatening the American way of life. And the principal European foe, Germany (or at least that portion of it not under Communist control), became America's staunchest ally, while the former comrades-in-arms, the Russians, became the new *bête noire*. Critic Dwight Macdonald justifiably must be excused his incredulity in marveling at how "the Russian blockade of Berlin in the winter of 1948-49 produced a dramatic reversal of . . . wartime roles . . . as . . . the population of Berlin . . . were transmuted from cowardly accomplices of one kind of totalitarianism into heroic resisters of another kind."[44]

The American movie industry's exculpation of Germany began toward the end of the 1940s as movies dealing with Germany drew a distinction between what has been described as "the good German who fought for his country and the Nazi fanatical beasts who were the cause of all difficulties." Thus, in a film like *Berlin Express* (1948) a German statesman returning to his country from exile abroad to help plan the future of the defeated Germany is kidnapped by Nazi fanatics intent on bringing back "the good old days" of the Third Reich. The situation borders on the absurd in *The Sealed Verdict* (1948) in which the good German turns out to be the former mistress of a high-ranking convicted war criminal, whose hanging finally makes it possible for her to find peace in the arms of the American army officer who sees to it that the German does not score a moral victory by cheating the hangman. Films such as these set a pattern which has continued since then as almost every segment of German society has been refurbished by the movies, and other media, and made a victim of rather than an accessory to the Nazis. As one disgusted critic recently put it: "we've worked overtime to make beauties of the beasts."[45]

In the course of this transmutation during the 1950s and 1960s, the good Germans depicted differed significantly in social class from those presented in the wartime films. No longer were the good Germans "the little people" so prominent in films like *The Seventh Cross*. Rather, as in *The Desert Fox* (1951), the highly idealized film version of the last years of Field Marshal Erwin Rommel's life, it is the upper classes who serve as the center of resistance to Hitler and to the social-climbing, socially undesirable Nazis. And even when not a field marshal, the good German comes from a better-than-average family. In *Decision Before Dawn* (1953) the handsome and intelligent young German prisoner of war who decides to spy for the Americans is the son of a doctor. The sophisticated evil of the less than physically attractive Walter Slezak (who portrayed the commander of the German forces occupying an industrial town in the 1943 melodrama *This Land Is Mine*) gave way to the duty-must-be-done attitude of a glamorous John Wayne, who portrayed an avowedly anti-Nazi but patriotically noble ship captain in the 1955 adventure film *The Sea Chase*. This change in the treatment of the good German is inextricably tied up with the changing attitude motivated by political necessity. Thus, the very traits which during World Wars I and II had been condemned as Prussian vices now came to be regarded as German virtues to be feted in our joint alliance against Communism. No longer were the Germans condemned as militaristic; we now hailed their soldier-like qualities.

Hollywood has never been known for its faithfulness to the literary materials it purchases or adapts for screen fodder. In the context of the changing depiction of the German, some examples are especially instructive. *The Enemy Below* (1957) is a suspenseful film about a cat and mouse chase between an American destroyer and a German submarine which ends with both vessels sunk and the crews cooperating while in the water; and in the very end, aboard another American ship, the German and American captains eye each other with respect. The novel of the same name has basically the same plot except that the destroyer was British and that at the end the shipwrecked German and British sailors were "a waving sea of arms and legs . . . locked in deadly combat." Equally insidious was the change in

The refurbishing of the German image began after World War II with James Mason in Rommel—The Desert Fox *(1951). Mason played Rommel as an aristocrat who deplored Nazi excesses, fought for country not ideology, and secretly plotted the overthrow of the déclassé Nazi thugs.*

the structure of Irwin Shaw's massive novel *The Young Lions,* which was filmed in 1955. In the novel the main German character was a nice guy who during the war is turned into an unredeemed Nazi; in the movie he is a confused but patriotic idealist who over time becomes disillusioned and dies needlessly. One critic correctly described the movie character as a "curiously clean romantic . . . a vulgarized American version of a Teutonic hero."[46]

There were, of course, some films which still showed Germans and/or Nazis in a bad light or at least without a halo. Films such as *Hitler* (1962), *Hitler: The Last Ten Days* (1972), *Marathon Man* (1976), and *The Boys from Brazil* (1978), zeroed in on the Nazi leader and his entourage. The 1961 film *Judgment at Nuremberg,* dealing with one of the lesser war crimes trials, was a well-meaning but ponderous attempt to address the question of German responsibility for the Nazi evil. It fails to accomplish the screen writer's stated intention of explaining how "men who had been the bulwark of what many thought to be the most enlightened culture in Europe . . . could . . . have gone along with the Nazis." Whatever its shortcomings, *Judgment at Nuremberg* was not a sensation-seeking film. But there are films, such as the American-financed *The Night Porter* (1974), whose quality and intent is summed up by Andrew Sarris' reference to them as "sado-masochistic spectacles" and "kinky nostalgia."[47]

By the mid-1970s the pendulum had swung so far that movies were produced in which it was obvious that audiences were meant to root for the Germans against the Russians (*Cross of Iron,* a 1977 film that has been described as "the first Nazi Western, about those poor devils on the Russian frontier led by a spit-and-polish, by-the-book officer who can't cope with a war where you get your boots muddied"), and against the English and Americans (*The Eagle Has Landed,* a 1977 film which revolves around a German plot to assassinate Winston Churchill and which includes a firefight between German and American troops in which the audience is manipulated to root for the Germans). In ten years the movie industry had come a long way from that paean to bad taste—*The Producers* (1967). Mel Brooks had put his considerable talents to use in composing a story about two Jewish producers who stage as a musical a play by an insane Nazi fanatic about Adolf Hitler. "Springtime for Hitler," as this musical within a movie is called, includes a fey Hitler played by a hipster, and a production number that includes a chorus line of female SS troops. It is not a large jump from *The Producers* to *The Eagle Has Landed* or *Cross of Iron.* Indeed, television long ago managed to trivialize the horrors of World War II in *Hogan's Heroes,* a TV situation comedy laid in a prisoner-of-war camp in Germany. However, TV is beyond the scope of this essay. Suffice it to say that the German image differs little from that on the large screen, except for the occasional World War II movie which still gets shown.[48]

It is not easy to predict future trends with reference to media images. But it probably is fair to say that there will be no significant resuscitation of the once-familiar German-American film stereotypes. As for the movie image of the German, which has been subject to such violent fluctuations during the last eight decades, who can say how the projection of that image will be affected by life situations. The Nazi, over a generation since the end of World War II, still serves as a convenient shorthand symbol, but the stereotype increasingly is becoming divorced from the German image. How the future will alter that image depends most of all on our relations with West Germany, and in the near term the outlook is for continued friendship. The patterns for both a negative and a positive image are there, and only time itself can serve to develop that image.

NOTES

1. Thomas A. Bailey, *Voices of America: The Nation's Story in Slogans, Sayings and Songs* (1976), 14; *Historical Statistics of the United States, 1789-1945* (1949), 33-36; Leonard Dinnerstein, Roger Nichols, and David Reimers, *Natives and Strangers: Ethnic Groups and the Building of America* (1979), 9. A great deal has been written about the Germans in America; two very useful bibliographies are Henry Pochmann, *Bibliography of German Culture in America to 1940* (1953), and D. H. Tolzmann, *German Americana: A Bibliography* (1975).

2. John Hawgood, *The Tragedy of German America: The Germans in the United States during the 19th Century—and After* (1940), xiv.

3. Karl Thedor Griesinger, *Lebende Bilder Aus Amerika* (1858), in Howard Furer, ed., *The Germans in America 1607-1970* (1973), 125; Griesinger, *Land und Leute in Amerika* (1863), in *ibid*, 118.

4. Arthur M. Schlesinger, *Paths to the Present* (revised and enlarged ed., 1964), 69; Hawgood, *Tragedy of German America,* xiv.

5. Nathan Glazer and Daniel Moynihan, *Beyond The Melting Pot: The Negroes, Puerto Ricans, Jews, Italians, and Irish of New York City* (2nd ed., 1970), 312; quoted in G. A. Dobbert, "German-Americans Between New and Old Fatherland," *American Quarterly,* 19 (1967), 665.

6. John Higham, *Strangers in the Land: Patterns of American Nativism, 1860-1925* (corrected ed., 1963), 196; Frederick Luebke, *Bonds of Loyalty* (1974), xiii.

7. Richard Krickus, *Pursuing the American Dream: White Ethnics and the New Populism* (1976), 47; Richard O'Connor, *The German-Americans* (1968), 314-15; Dinnerstein, Nichols, and Reimers, *Natives and Strangers,* 108; LaVern J. Rippley, *The German Americans* (1976), 83.

8. For examples of songs and verses, see Maldwyn Jones, *Destination America* (1976); Mark Sullivan, *Our Times,* vol. III, "Pre-War America" (1930), 388, 390; Abel Green and Joe Laurie, Jr., *Show Biz: Variety from Vaude to Video* (1951), 7.

9. Maurice Horn, ed., *The World Encyclopedia of Comics* (1976), 421. For examples of the strip in its heyday see Rudolph Dirks, *The Katzenjammer Kids,* with an introduction by August Derleth (1974).

10. Daniel J. Leab, "Goethe or Attila? The Celluloid German," in Randall Miller, ed., *Ethnic Images in American Film and Television* (1978), 64.

11. *Motion Picture News,* November 4, 1916, pp. 2863-64; for more detail on *A Bucket of Cream Ale* see Daniel J. Leab, *From Sambo to Superspade* (1975), 35-36.

12. For examples of some Biograph films see *Biograph Bulletins 1908-1912* (with an introduction by Eileen Bowser, New York, 1973), 709, 304; and Robert Henderson, *D. W. Griffith: The Years at Biograph* (1970), 11. *Biograph Bulletins,* 73.

13. Wilson quoted in Bailey, *Voices of America,* 330; Luebke, *Bonds of Loyalty,* 48-49.

14. Americans were ambivalent for a long time. In 1916 Wilson re-election slogans included "War In The East! Peace In The West! Thank God for Wilson! (Bailey, *Voices of America,* 331).

15. Timothy J. Lyons, "Hollywood and World War I, 1914-1918," *Journal of Popular Film,* 1 (1972), 17; Kevin Brownlow, *The War, the West, and the Wilderness* (1979), 79-80; Garth Jowett, *Film: The Democratic Art* (1976), 66.

16. Brownlow, *The War,* 82; Terry Ramsaye, *A Million and One Nights* (1926), 686.

17. Richard A. Oehling, "The German-Americans, Germany, and the American Media," in Miller, *Ethnic Images,* 54; Hawgood, *Tragedy of German America,* 301; Luebke, *Bonds of Loyalty,* 234.

18. James R. Mock and Cedric Larson, *Words That Won the War: The Story of the Committee on Public Information* (1939), 214; Higham, *Strangers,* 208; Mark Sullivan, *Our Times,* vol. V, "Over Here 1914-1918" (1933), 467, 469.

19. Luebke, *Bonds of Loyalty,* 271, 282; Hawgood, *Tragedy of German America,* 297.

20. Jack Spears, *Hollywood: The Golden Era* (1971), 29; *Motion Picture News,* September 7, 1918, p. 1599, December 1, 1917, p. 3857, October 12, 1918, p. 2445, October 19, 1918, p. 2594.

21. Richard A. Oehling, "Germans in Hollywood Films," *Film and History,* 3 (May 1973), 1.

22. In 1900 Kaiser Wilhelm II had told German troops being sent to China to help repress the Boxer Rebellion to act like modern Huns—an unfortunate gaffe on his part; see Virginia Cowles, *The Kaiser* (1963), 177. Spears, *Hollywood,* 33; *Motion Picture News,* September 7, 1918, p. 1456; *The New York Times,* April 5, 1918, p. 13.

23. Charles Reed Mitchell, "New Message to America: James W. Gerard's *Beware* and World War I Propaganda," *Journal of Popular Film,* 4 (1975), 277; *Motion Picture News,* March 23, 1918, p. 1769; Brownlow, *The War,* 137.

24. Lewis Jacobs, *The Rise of American Film: A Critical History* (1939), 257-58.

25. Benjamin Hampton, *A History of the Movies* (1931), 201; "Jane Novak in an Interview with Anthony Slide," *The Silent Picture,* Spring, 1972, p. 10.

26. *The American Film Institute Catalog of Motion Pictures Produced in the United States: Feature Films, 1921-1930,* (2 vols., 1971).

27. Spears, *Hollywood,* 51; Andrew Sinclair, *John Ford* (1979), 42.

28. Bosley Crowther, *The Great Films* (1967), 79; David Zinman, *50 Classic Motion Pictures* (1970), 201.

29. Edward Wagenknecht and Anthony Slide, *The Films of D. W. Griffith* (1975), 210.

30. S. A. Diamond, *The Nazi Movement in the United States, 1924-1941* (1974), 57; Paul L. Murphy, "Sources and Nature of Intolerance in the 1920s," *Journal of American History,* 51 (1964), 71.

31. O'Connor, *The German-Americans,* 431; Arnold Offner, *American Appeasement: United States Foreign Policy and Germany, 1933-1938* (1969), 3.

32. Luebke, *Bonds of Loyalty,* 330; Ronald H. Bayor, *Neighbors in Conflict: The Irish, Germans, Jews, and Italians of New York City, 1929-41* (1978), 58.

33. Hawgood, *The Tragedy of German America,* 302; Richard Rollins, *I Find*

Treason: The Story of an American Anti-Nazi Agent (1941), 102; Diamond, *The Nazi Movement,* 337.

34. Harold Lavine and James Wechsler, *War Propaganda and the United States* (1940), 42-43.

35. *Time* magazine quoted in Joe Morella, Edward Epstein, and John Griggs, *The Films of World War II* (1973), 21; Kenneth L. Geist, *Pictures Will Talk: The Life and Times of Joseph L. Manckiewicz* (1978), 91.

36. Goldwyn quoted in Russell Shain, *An Analysis of Motion Pictures About War Released by the American Film Industry, 1939-1970* (1976), 35; Senator Gerald Nye quoted in Jowett, *Film,* 304.

37. Robert Wilson, ed., *The Film Criticism of Otis Ferguson* (1971), 254.

38. *New York Times,* December 18, 1939, p. 29.

39. *Motion Picture Herald,* June 15, 1940, p. 42.

40. Shain, *Analysis,* 291.

41. Quoted in Richard Lingeman, *Don't You Know There's A War On? The American Home Front, 1941-1945* (1970), 186; Leab, "Goethe or Attila?," 66; Hans Blumenberg, "Hollywood und Hakenkreuz," in Alice Goetz, ed., *Hollywood und die Nazis* (1977), 9.

42. Richard Polenberg, *War and Society: The United States, 1941-45* (1972), 42-43.

43. Rippley, *The German-Americans,* 214; Glazer and Moynihan, *Beyond the Melting Pot,* 311; O'Connor, *The German-Americans,* 456-57.

44. Dwight Macdonald, *The Memoirs of a Revolutionist: Essays in Political Criticism* (1957), 75.

45. Oehling, "German Americans," 60; John Mariani, "Let's Not Be Beastly to the Nazis," *Film Comment,* 15 (January-February 1979), 49.

46. Martin S. Dworkin, "Clean Germans and Dirty Politics," *Film Comment,* 3 (Winter, 1965), 3; D. A. Rayner, *The Enemy Below* (1957), 191.

47. Abby Mann, *Judgment At Nuremberg* (1961), v; Andrew Sarris, *Politics and the Cinema* (1978), 85.

48. Mariani, "Let's Not Be Beastly," 52.

9

THE YELLOW MENACE: ASIAN IMAGES IN AMERICAN FILM

Richard A. Oehling

Orientals, overwhelmingly of Chinese and Japanese extraction, comprise a relatively small ethnic minority in American society.[1] As a result of national exclusion legislation—first of the Chinese in 1884 and later, in 1924, of the Japanese—the growth of the Chinese and Japanese population was stopped at a very early point. The exclusion legislation resulted from popular anti-Asian agitation, particularly evident in California. The agitation employed various negative stereotypes of both the Chinese and Japanese, stereotypes which revealed a deep-seated and powerful prejudice against Asians.

Prejudice simply means a "pre-judgment" of something or some group before a consideration of the facts. In this context, a racial prejudice is a hostile judgment against an entire ethnic group, based not on an incident(s) nor on the actions of individuals but on an already existing hostility.[2] A stereotype is a concrete manifestation of such a prejudiced feeling; for example, hostility toward the Chinese manifested itself in several stereotyped images of the Chinese, including the characterization of the Chinese men as lusting after white women.[3]

Racial prejudice and the accompanying stereotyped images, when

widely held, are evident in the many avenues of public expression—
the press, magazines, speeches, radio, and, of course, the visual
media, "movies" and television. Films reflect existing prejudiced
stereotypes. If the audience is receptive—for whatever reasons—the
films will tend to reinforce and perhaps strengthen those stereotyped
images because the medium is so powerful in its impact.[4] Films, after
all, are made by human beings who often share society's general
climate of opinion. As a profit-center industry, Hollywood has been
particularly responsive to what it thought was public opinion at any
given moment.

That "climate" can and does change, often because of events in the
"outer" world, beyond Hollywood. In the case of the Asians, the
climate of opinion changed dramatically three times in the last century: first in the last quarter of the nineteenth century when large
numbers of Chinese and Japanese arrived in this country; second,
after 1924, when both groups were permanently excluded from
further immigration and citizenship; and third, when the end of
World War II revealed new political configurations in international
politics.

Until 1924, prejudice and stereotyping of the Japanese and Chinese
depended on domestic political and economic conditions in this
country—the same conditions which typified prejudice against most
other ethnic groups at that time. More significant, however, is the
dual focus of anti-Asian prejudice: economic competition for jobs and
the threat of "racial mongrelization," of corruption of white women
and miscegenation. Of the many ethnic groups victimized, only
blacks were feared so passionately on the sexual issue, which tradi-
tionally arouses the most violent and persistent hostility of all the
various forms of prejudice.

The second period, after 1924, is marked by a remarkable decline
of interest in the Chinese and Japanese alien residents in the United
States and an increasing concern with Japan and China as foreign
powers. The third period, since World War II, has been characterized
by shifting fortunes between our former enemies, the Japanese, and
our former allies, the Chinese. Now the rapprochement with China,
begun by President Richard M. Nixon, may signal a new era of Asian
images.

Movies are not the only cause or reflector of prejudiced attitudes,
nor are they necessarily first among the media in image formation.
For four decades, however, millions of Americans regularly attended
motion pictures, often at least once or twice a week, and that much
exposure probably had an effect. Such exposure also reveals values
already in existence, for it appears unreasonable to assume that

millions of people would continue to pay to see pictures which consistently ran against their values.[5]

Although Chinese and Japanese immigrants resided in greatest numbers on the West Coast, they also lived in some cities elsewhere in the United States.[6] The Chinese settled preponderantly in cities in California, Hawaii, New York, and Illinois.[7] The Japanese had not come with the intent of settling so heavily in cities, but Japanese occupational patterns, among other factors, led to concentrations of Japanese in the Los Angeles, San Francisco, Sacramento, Santa Clara, and Fresno areas.

The competition between Asians and unskilled American laborers stimulated negative attitudes and, therefore, negative stereotypes. Public pressure and hostility and even the passage of certain laws limiting aliens' occupations increasingly forced the Chinese and Japanese into fewer and menial occupations, often physically concentrating them in the nascent "Chinatowns" of the cities.[8] Among the Chinese, laundry work emerged quickly, as did restaurant service and personal/household service, as "Asian" occupations—all of which encouraged stereotyped images in the media. Most Japanese sought opportunities in agriculture and business and were very ambitious to advance themselves. In 1909 a commission estimated that nearly 40,000 Japanese were employed as farm laborers in the western states, but at least 1600 farms were already owned by Japanese.[9]

In America the Chinese suffered severe problems in reestablishing their traditional family structure. Chinese laboring aliens could neither bring wives with them nor afford to send for them within a reasonable period of time. Chinese males clustered together in bachelor dormitories, in circumstances which encouraged gambling, drugs, and other related vices; these practices, exaggerated, all turned up in stereotypes in the media.[10] In time, the numbers of females increased, and family life developed. The Chinese family in the United States was like that of China, for it tended to the establishment of large families with strong ties—family life as almost an entity unto itself. The Chinese-American family was—and still is somewhat—"patriarchal, patrilocal, patrilineal, and endogenous."[11] The modifications in the Chinese-American family system left untouched, however, certain liabilities—slothfulness, dependence, and even the nurturing of considerable disunity in large extended families. In addition to these troubles, the sharing of an already inadequate income among the members of a large family made the level of poverty ever greater. These aspects of Chinese family life have also been subject to stereotyping.

One very new factor in the lives of the Chinese immigrants was the appearance of "Chinatowns." These Chinese "ghettos" first arose as an attempt to encourage economic and social betterment, and even to provide some protection from the sporadic outbursts of anti-Chinese mob violence. The "Chinatowns," however, were never large enough to accomplish the economic and physical improvement of their Chinese and Japanese settlers. Eventually, the outside world saw them as tourist attractions at best, and as islands of crime and violence at worst. Caucasians visited the Chinatown section of San Francisco, for example, to see the strange and exotic sights; with increasing frequency from 1900 to 1940 visitors also came to indulge in vices less frequently tolerated in other sections of the city. Gambling, prostitution, and drug addiction grew in the Chinatown sections because of the preponderance of Chinese males living in the intolerable barracks system. Once flourishing, however, these vices and attendant gangsterism reached a peak in the period between 1910 and 1930, and found particular expression in a series of Tong wars which became nationally infamous. By 1930 the Chinese community itself had restored order to Chinatown life, curbing the Tongs as well as the earlier vices which had nurtured them. Although the Chinese themselves had begun efforts at reform as early as the 1880s, the media persisted in its emphasis on all the earlier evils of Chinatown existence.

The Japanese immigrants had to face the same male/female ratio problem as the Chinese, but the problem was less pronounced, less long-term, and much less obvious to the outside world. Virtually before the first decade of significant Japanese immigration had ended, Japanese males were contracting to bring "picture brides" to the United States for arranged marriages.

In the end, the image of both the Chinese and Japanese in the media depended more on political factors among the dominant Caucasian population of the United States than upon the characteristic behavior or attitudes of either immigrant group. Chinese immigration had been halted before the film industry even came into existence. Such was not the case with the Japanese. Thus, we have an opportunity to examine first the political, social, and economic conditions and then compare them with the manifestations of prejudice and stereotyping in the early films.

Hostility to the Japanese arose dramatically in 1900. Japanese immigration had been proceeding at a fairly low and uniform rate for about a decade before this, with approximately a thousand Japanese a year entering the United States. However, with annexation of Hawaii after the Spanish-American War, some 12,000 arrived in 1900 alone. The result was an immediate protest by many Californians. San

Francisco epitomized and dramatized the passionate issues—schooling, landowning, marriage. In March, 1900, the mayor of San Francisco, on the basis of what he knew to be an obviously false rumor, decided to quarantine the Chinese and Japanese sections of the city upon the pretext of an alleged outbreak of bubonic plague. In the same year, the labor movement began to put pressure on California Governor Henry Gage to do something about Japanese immigration. He stressed the Japanese problem in his message to the Legislature on January 8, 1901. Some of the captions of articles which appeared in the *San Francisco Chronicle* in the years after 1905 reveal much about the attitude of this influential newspaper, and perhaps public opinion in general, toward the Japanese question: "Crime and poverty go hand in hand with Asiatic labor"; "Brown men are an evil in the public schools"; "Japanese are a menace to American women"; "Brown Asiatics steal brains of whites." *The Chronicle* concluded, "Everyone of these immigrants, so far as his service is desired, is a Japanese spy."[12]

Obvious amidst the clamor was the absence of popular concern with Japan as a nation. Statesmen occasionally wrote of the strategic problems posed for the United States by the rise of Japan to great power status, but the American public seemed to be largely indifferent to these issues. They were more involved emotionally in the threat at home to the purity of the race. Film, however immature its development as of 1910, reflected that concern vividly.

In the earlier years of the motion picture industry there were dozens of films with real and imaginary settings in Japan and China, mostly or entirely dealing with the Asians in their native environment. Some of them barely had plots, being little more than fake travelogues. After 1910, however, American film producers seemed to share the same obsessions evident in the literature of the day. With very few exceptions, films about most Asians began to treat them largely as "aliens" in the United States with no attempt made to distinguish between Chinese and Japanese.

In addition to the domestic concerns, new factors heightened ill feelings after 1910. The Japanese annexation of Korea that year and the Japanese trial of Korean nationalists in 1912 brought public feeling in California to new heights. Wild rumors circulated that Japan was intending next to secure from Mexico a naval base at Magdalena Bay, in lower California. A few years later, it was rumored that the Japanese were sending spies into the Panama Canal area. All of these issues and passions became tied, in the course of time, to the question of the position of blacks in American society. Presidents Roosevelt, Taft, Wilson, and Coolidge, in succession, came to realize that Californians saw a convenient and necessary connection between their Asian problem and the South's problem of the Negro. Alliances emerged in Congress which were to succeed finally in the passage of the 1924 Immigration Act. In essence, Californians demanded the same kind of security against Asian immigration that the federal government had conceded to the South by allowing the "separate-but-equal" doctrine to become public policy.[13]

It is an altered political situation in which we need to examine the films of the "boom" period of the 1920s. Until 1924 the domestic question revolving around Japanese immigration was dominant, but emerging increasingly was the question of Japan's rise as a major and potentially threatening power.

Of the few films of the 1920s that dealt with Asians or the Asian world, the most prevalent theme was race relations between Asians and Caucasians. These films suggest that interracial love affairs and marriages cannot work out in the long run. There are no happy endings, except where whites and Asians rejoin their own.[14]

Persistent from the earliest films was the idea of *diabolical* Asians. They continually plotted and connived the destruction of America in general and white women in particular. Asians were never what they seemed to be. Ruthless and clever—one is tempted to conclude more so than white men—they serve with great subtlety and infinite patience the goal of the eventual mastery of the world by the "yellow" race. The popular serial films of the 1910 decade highlight this image of the diabolical Asian. In *The Yellow Menace* (1916)[15] the Japanese and Mexicans plot war and subversion against the United States. The audience was never certain what the villains were really hoping to accomplish overall, but in a more immediate sense each week they were committing nefarious acts such as trying to blow up a train or destroy a munitions factory.

Another common theme in films during these decades was the widespread abuse of women by Asians, that is, white slavery and the maintenance of prostitution as a major industry of the Asian subculture in the United States. In the 1927 film, *Old San Francisco,* the principal business of the Chinese appears to be prostitution.[16] And from their facial expressions, the Chinese seem to relish their "business," especially when they have a white woman to sell or buy.

Tong wars provided yet another staple in the collection of dependable themes. Between 1910-1930, the period of the Tong wars, Chinese-Americans had a high rate of arrests for prostitution, drug offenses, and violent crimes. The curbing of the Tongs led to the decline of those crime rates. Except for the period 1910-1930, Chinese-Americans had a low crime rate. They did, however, show a propensity for the nonviolent crimes of gambling and drunkenness. Japanese immigrants have always displayed a very low incidence of violent crimes; only drunkenness and gambling existed in any significant numbers. Even into the 1960s the Japanese-American crime rates were lower than comparable rates among Caucasians.[17] The film image of the Japanese did not emphasize crime until very recently with the appearance of the theme of international criminal syndicates, but such neglect did not characterize the image of the Chinese.

Two popular films, *Chinatown Nights* (1929) and *The Hatchet Man* (1932), both revolved around the subject of Tong wars and crime. Common to most of the films on Asians were the background questions of drug and alcohol consumption. Being "high" on liquor or opium was the necessary condition for any sale of female flesh, for example. Simultaneous with prostitution, opium, and alcohol went dark, heathen rites which occurred in the cellars of the Oriental ghettos of American cities. Even Long Island, without any significant Asian population, had a secret "heathen" temple where the incense was thick and the multitude of gods unknown and evil (witness Sessue Hayakawa's basement temple in *The Cheat,* 1915). The curbing of Tongs led to a significant decrease in prostitution, drug offenses, and violent crimes in fact, but the film image persisted for some time.

Several films about Asian aliens stand out above the rest in the period from 1910 to 1930: *Typhoon* (1914), *Broken Blossoms* (1919), *The Cheat* (1915), *Shadows of the West* (1921), and *Old San Francisco* (1927). In 1914, Thomas Ince, already on his way to prominence, produced *Typhoon,* starring Sessue Hayakawa, a very handsome young actor.[18] The picture has a complex story line involving elements of an interracial love affair, intrigue, and murder. The setting is contemporary Paris. Hayakawa plays a young Japanese diplomat, Dr. Tokoramo, who is busily engaged in creating a secret report on matters of French security based on stolen materials. Tokoramo has compromised his position with his own government by an affair with a French woman of the stage. The Japanese diplomatic staff gave warnings about the dangers of such a liaison, but he assured them that the girl is only a diversion and that his first loyalty is to "Nippon." Later, after a heated argument in which the courtesan calls Dr. Tokoramo a "whining yellow rat" and a "yellow blot," Tokoramo kills her. It is at this point that the most interesting aspect of the film surfaces. The other Japanese at the embassy arrive to find the evidence of the murder. They decide that Tokoramo's work is too crucial to "Nippon" to allow failure; another member of the group will take the blame for the murder in order to allow him to finish his report. The scheme works. Tokoramo is freed to finish his report, and an innocent but patriotic Japanese student willingly goes to his death for his country. Unfortunately, Tokoramo has qualms of conscience and goes insane with the

Sessue Hayakawa attempts to possess the American heroine (Fanny Ward) in The Cheat, *one of the most commercially successful films about diabolical Asians.*

feelings of his guilt over his fiancée's murder. As the police arrive now to arrest him as the true murderer, the report is burned and To-koramo dies by his own hand.

The picture had a cast of native Japanese in all of the Asian roles, but there were Caucasians in the picture and the production was by an American company. The story line and the characterizations by the actors and actresses strongly suggested deviousness and duplicity on the part of the Japanese and, at least by inference, condemned interracial love affairs as being disastrous and tragic from their very inception.

Ince produced a series of successful films, all starring Sessue Hayakawa. Increasingly, however, Hayakawa became restless with the kind of treatment which he was receiving, both in the films and, more importantly, in California society, as a Japanese. After an abortive attempt to establish an independent movie company, he decided to leave the United States and pursue his career elsewhere. He returned decades later, generally in insignificant roles, until *Bridge on the River Kwai* (1957) cast him in a leading role once again.

Broken Blossoms with Lillian Gish and Richard Barthelmess was the only really sympathetic account of the Asian in mixed-racial love stories from 1910-1930.[19] The lovers are fated to a tragic end from the beginning. The villain, the girl's father, seems to be more symbolic of an intolerant society than a true villain. Interestingly, the love between the Chinese boy and the English girl was never physical. More characteristic were *East is West* (1922) and *The Forbidden City* (1918), which revolved around the children of mixed marriages.[20] What an unhappy lot they were! The female lead in *East is West* was finally allowed a happy ending by the revelation that she was in fact white, having only been raised by a Chinese family. Norma Talmadge, on the other hand, in *The Forbidden City* first attempted to live as a Chinese, then as a white, failed at both, and in bitterness turned back to the Chinese to become the goddess figure for the Boxers. She perished with them.

The Cheat is the story of a stupid, careless, flighty American woman (Fannie Ward) who embezzles charity funds to gamble in stocks.[21]

Broken Blossoms *offered a rare sympathetic treatment of mixed racial love in early Hollywood productions. In this scene, Cheng Huan (Richard Barthelmess) meets Lucy (Lillian Gish) in his chamber.*

The stock investment fails just as the charity funds are about to be recalled, and the woman must look elsewhere than to her financially over-extended husband for help. In her plight she turns to a young and handsome Asian friend. He lends her the money, but the rest of the story revolves on his efforts to collect payment through possession of the heroine, her frantic efforts to save herself, and the eventual course of justice. The stereotypes most obvious are the duplicity and lecherousness of the villain, played by Sessue Hayakawa, his reverence for his ancestors, coupled with his cruelty and violence. In one scene, before an altar to his ancestors, he brands the fainted heroine. *The Cheat* fared very well at the box office; it may have been the real beginning of Cecil B. DeMille's fame. The shoddiness of its exaggerated melodrama was apparently more than offset by the popularity of the theme, contrasting the sweet innocence of Fannie Ward and the diabolical cunning, but handsomeness, of Hayakawa.

Between 1919 and 1922 there were a number of race riots which had a considerable effect upon securing the passage of the Immigration Act of 1924.[22] The Immigration Act represented the first *national* legislation of a discriminatory character aimed at the Japanese. Although other nationalities suffered as well, the discrimination against the Japanese was the strongest. Ironically, in time, the passage of the Act had the effect of reducing racial tension in California, and hostility against the Japanese became dormant until the late 1930s.

The pre-1924 heightened tension was reinforced and perhaps extended by the appearance of a markedly anti-Japanese film, *Shadows of the West,* produced by the Cinema Craft Motion Picture Producing Company in 1921.[23] This film, starring Pat O'Brien and Hedda Nova, is a western melodrama concerning Jim, a cow puncher, and his "buddy" and their encounter with a Japanese, Frank Akuri. This Asian, it turns out, has pledged his life to establish a Japanese colony in the United States. During one of Jim's absences, Akuri forces Jim's sweetheart, Mary, to sell her ranch to him. He then begins to set up his colony. Mary, recovering her wits, organizes her friends in an appeal to Congress. That appeal seems to be approaching success, so Akuri kidnaps Mary and plans to murder her, but Jim appears just in time. Akuri, of course, gets his just punishment. Within the framework of the melodrama one sees a scene in which a wireless operator ticks out prices which control a state-wide vegetable market. Spies dart in and out of scenes, and Japanese are shown dumping vegetables into harbors to maintain high prices. And, as always, two white girls are abducted by a group of Japanese men and are rescued only at the last moment by a squad of American Legionnaires. The American Legion in California thought so highly of the film that it exhibited it throughout the state.[24]

In both *Old San Francisco,* made in 1927, and in *The Letter,*[25] produced in 1929, sex is the critical issue. In the one, a disguised Asian, posing as an Irishman named Buckwell, tries his best to seduce or rape a young woman from the Spanish-American aristocracy of California. His intentions are eventually thwarted by the San Francisco earthquake, and the strong religious symbolism throughout the movie suggests that it is the victory of the Christian God, outraged and wrathful, against the heathen "Mongols." *The Letter,* on the other hand, is also about a love triangle but without the religious overtones. Its significance is that it includes the same emphasis on Asian deceit, prostitution, drug addiction, and corruption. In these and other anti-Asian films produced between 1910 and 1930, the most important features which display prejudice and stereotyping occur in the dramatic unfolding of the tale rather than in character development, physical casting, or script lines. Buckwell's appearance as the disguised Asian in *Old San Francisco,* for example, is not sufficiently extreme to have raised in the audience the level of prejudice or stereotyping. What he sought to do, and how his attempts were foiled, were designed to heighten the audience's emotional response to the film.

There was no sharp break in the portrayal of the Asians, but by the mid-1930s a new set of images was emerging. It had taken the decade of the twenties with its passage of highly restrictive immigration laws for American fears of Asian subversion at home to dwindle; it would not rise again until the war years brought the appearance of the serialized spy thrillers fully equipped with German and Japanese agents operating in the United States.

Another very different variety of films also appeared in this period. In the second half of the decade 1910 to 1920, several films appeared which concerned Japanese life and Japanese characters in a fashion largely devoid of stereotyping. In a few cases the films were produced by American companies and American directors, but based wholly on Japanese casts and Japanese-derived stories. In most, however, not only were the sources and the players Japanese, but the director and producer were Japanese. At the center of all of these films is Sessue Hayakawa. By 1915, with the appearance of *The Cheat* and its tremendous box office success, Hayakawa was in a position to place certain demands on movie producers. It is evident, in a film like *The Dragon Painter* (1919) that an Asian story is being presented without prejudice.[26] *The Wrath of the Gods* (1914) likewise was a story which had no animus toward the Japanese.[27] Among the other films which follow the same pattern are *Forbidden Paths* (1917), *Where Lights are Low* (1921), *The First Born* (1921), *The Vermillion Pencil* (1922), and *The Danger Line* (1924). The last four films were produced either by the

Hayakawa Feature Play Company or the R-C Picture Company, which was actually tied to Hayakawa's producing company. Most of these films starred Hayakawa and Tsuru Aoki, Hayakawa's wife.[28]

Although these films had very little or frequently no stereotyping of Western or Asian parts, there were a few aspects of the thematic treatment which tended to reinforce the more traditional and popular work of Hollywood filmmakers. *The Wrath of the Gods,* for example, is based on an actual event, an earthquake on the Japanese island of Sakura in January of 1914. An American ship is wrecked off the coast of a Japanese island, and one sailor is saved and brought back to health by a Japanese girl and her father. Inevitably, the Japanese girl and the American sailor fall in love. As her Buddhist faith has already been shaken sometime before, she abandons the last remnants of her religion and converts to Christianity. She converts her father and then goes off to marry the young man. The Japanese who live on the island are very disturbed by this perfidy, and an ugly mob murders the father. At this point, a volcano erupts and everyone on the island is killed except the young girl and her fiancé. As the couple are rescued by an American ship in the harbor, the young man says, "Your gods are powerful, but mine were more so." Apparently, even in a film about Asians involving an Asian cast, it was necessary to reaffirm the superiority of Christianity and to suggest the devastating impact of intermarriage between the races so that the film could play successfully before American audiences.

This company of Japanese actors, actresses, and production staff did not survive long and never led to other ventures of a similar nature. Such failure stands in obvious contrast to the emergence and halting success of all-black films as early as the late 1920s which survived and revived in the 1940s and again in the 1960s. The reason for the Asian failure was probably the absence of a sufficient Asian-American audience to sustain such productions.

Images of Asians in Hollywood productions were not static, however. American movies indicated America's lack of awareness of China's civil war until the late 1920s, although China had been embroiled in civil war in one form or another since the fall of the Manchus in 1911. When Americans finally did take notice, their attitudes toward the Chinese and Japanese began to change rapidly. In the 1930s, the Japanese disappeared from the screen, with the exception of an Americanized Japanese detective, Mr. Moto.[29] China and the Chinese suddenly became an object of great interest. The Chinese civil war provided both the setting and catalyst of dramatic crises in several very important and successful films. Hollywood scrutinized the phenomenon of the warlord, first in *The Bitter Tea of General Yen* (1933), then in *The General Died at Dawn* (1936) and *Oil for*

The Chinese warlord (Nils Asther) in The Bitter Tea of General Yen *reflected the Hollywood image of China as a land of contrasts. Yen was both greedy and generous, cruel and loving. The American Megan Davis (Barbara Stanwyck) found Yen's inscrutable nature both alluring and disgusting. Their eventual love match ended with Yen's suicide—Hollywood brooked no miscegenation in the 1930s.*

the Lamps of China (1935).[30] One reviewer considered *General Yen* to be a "thoughtful and sensitive confrontation between the cultures of an Oriental man and an Occidental woman"; and it is to a degree. It was also, however, a model of the new stereotypes which were developing. China is portrayed as a strange, exotic land of contrasts, and General Yen, as one of the rising warlords, exemplifies these contrasts in his person. He brutally orders the murder of numerous captives, then justifies it to his attractive American visitor, Megan Davis (Barbara Stanwyck), as being better than letting them starve to death in prison. General Yen crudely offers "sing-song" girls to an American missionary, of all people, but later recites love poetry in sweet tones and philosophizes eloquently to the heroine. The film has very odd moments. One time Barbara Stanwyck seems quite in keeping with the film's spirit in screaming at Yen that he is a "yellow swine;" another time, Western prejudice is ridiculed when in response to an American profiteer's reminder to Yen that the heroine is a white woman, Yen remarks, "I have no prejudice against her color." Of course, Yen and Megan Davis fall in love, but, equally as would be expected, that love is both platonic and fated to a tragic end; General Yen commits suicide—a practice Hollywood had long since ascribed to Asians as an almost common trait.

General Yen was something of a sympathetic character, for an attempt was made to understand him. No attempt was made to understand why the wars occurred, nor the role of imperialism in precipitating the crises which led to the downfall of the Manchu dynasty and the ensuing anarchy. The operating assumption left with the audience in *The General Died at Dawn, Oil for the Lamps of China,* and even *The Keys of the Kingdom* (1944)[31] to a degree, is that somehow Chinese society had a propensity for violence and little inclination to democracy. Picture after picture, even those with very positive images of individual Chinese, stressed the widespread corruption, vice, prostitution, and poverty of modern China; most went beyond recording China's troubles and suggested or implied an alien civilization, "brutal, windswept, empty of all but the toughest of life."

Until the 1938 release of *The Good Earth,* most films on China focused on the warlords, their troops, and the rising revolutionary movement—all in negative tones.[32] The warlords were tyrannical beasts, generally lustful, proud, greedy, cruel, and ignorant. A few, like Yen, had some redeeming virtues—perhaps a decent education, cultivated tastes, and even some ambition to improve China's position, while improving their own. If the warlords had some redeeming virtues, the common soldier had none. He was always peering around corners lustfully or indiscriminately mowing down crowds with his submachine gun. He fights for no cause save money; he abandons the warlord who is without cash, women, or plunder. The revolutionaries fared no better at the hands of Hollywood. The Communists were the villains in at least three major films of the 1930s. Generally, the characterization of them resembled the warlords; they seemed to be additional "unprincipled bandits" dominating the Chinese countryside. One reviewer described the image of communism in *Oil for the Lamps of China* as "vulturous gangsterism preying on American corporations which stand for honor and decency in their relations with China's masses."[33]

Only the peasants finally emerged from the 1930s with a positive stereotype, principally in the movie version of Pearl Buck's bestselling novel, *The Good Earth. The Good Earth* set out to make real and likable the Chinese peasants; it succeeded so well that it set the pattern for the treatment of the Chinese peasant in the war films which would flood the screen in the early 1940s. The central figures, Wang (Paul Muni) and O-Lan (Louise Rainer), are wholesome, simple people,

Chinese peasants emerged in Hollywood films of the 1930s as good people, the stuff of which democracies are made. The Good Earth *fashioned the model peasant—simple, but loving, hardworking, and trustworthy.*

warm and friendly to strangers, in love with each other, good parents to their children. Admittedly, they are uneducated and unsophisticated in the ways of the world. They love the earth with a passion perhaps unknown in the Western countries, but understandable in "primitive" China. They work very hard, and they succeed in building up the family fortune, despite several near-fatal calamities. Other films repeating the favorable image of *Good Earth* added a few minor negative elements: superstitiousness, a shallow grasp of Christianity, and petty stealing as an almost natural part of everyday life. Clearly, however, these simple people were fundamentally trustworthy and dependable and, in their fashion, the stuff of which a good democracy might be built. Why was the peasant favored over the middle class which was more likely to be comparable in lifestyle to the ordinary American? The simplest answer is that the movie capitalized upon an already successful book, but that may not be the entire explanation.

China did not have a large and influential middle class. Moreover, life in Chinese cities was commonly known to be a mixture of widely disparate opposites of almost decadent wealth and the most abject poverty and vice.

Reinforcing the new Chinese peasant image of good sense, industry, and patience was an American Chinese who triumphed over guile and evil in American cities.

Certainly one of the more popular and persistent images of the Chinese-American in the 1930s was that of Charlie Chan. In a rather large number of films, viewed from the 1930s even into the 1970s, the figure of Charlie Chan was established firmly in the minds of several generations of Americans. The stories change as little as Charlie; he is the slow-moving, methodical, intelligent detective who always unravels the mystery by careful examinations of details which contrasts so with everyone else's rash conclusions. Also part of the stereotype are Chan's pithy sayings. His large family of somewhat silly children and his almost idiotic black manservant who appeared occasionally simply heighten the impression of Chan's basic good sense and carefulness. There is always a romance in the Chan movies, but it never involves either Charlie or his children. The image is in many ways popular and positive, but one has to wonder if it is not so idiosyncratic to Charlie Chan that it had little or no carryover to Chinese-Americans generally.[34] Together, the image of the Chinese masses and the prototype of the middle-class Chinese-American, Charlie Chan, combined to lead the way to the intensely pro-Chinese images of World War II.

The attack on Pearl Harbor, then, did not catch Hollywood unprepared. The Chinese peasants, already made into sympathetic figures and likely material for allies, provided part of the stock in trade for the new war movies. The warlords and the soldiers simply had to be put into Japanese uniforms. They had never been clearly identified in the 1930s, and thus the transition was easy to accomplish. Hollywood could go back to the yellow peril films of the earlier decades for other embellishments to round off the stereotypes.

In war films such as *Dragon Seed* (1944), *God is My Co-Pilot* (1945), *Thirty Seconds Over Tokyo* (1944), and *Night Plane from Chunking* (1943) the Chinese appeared as industrious, persevering, smiling, happy allies, indomitable in the face of all kinds of adversity.[35] One American remarked in *Thirty Seconds Over Tokyo*—and he could have been speaking for all the new Chinese image films—"You're our kind of people." That was the highest compliment the filmmakers could have made to the Chinese; America said virtually the same thing about the Russians at the peak of the war in *North Star*. The negative Chinese disappeared from the face of the earth—or did they? Partly, they simply donned Japanese uniforms; but one wonders if they have not simply been shelved.

Most of us remember—from the movie showings or from the television—those sneaky, subhuman "Japs" hiding in the branches of trees on islands all across the Pacific. One Yank was always worth at least two of those "monkeys," as one film continually called them. The most persistent theme in American wartime accounts of the Japanese was their cruelty and brutality in the conduct of war. Films such as *Back to Bataan* (1945), *Guadalcanal Diary* (1943), *I Was an American Spy* (1951) (interestingly produced long after the war was over) made the

The sinister, crafty "Jap" of World War II propaganda (portrayed here by Sessue Hayakawa) loomed large in such Hollywood war films as Three Came Home *(1950). Less than a decade later, Hayakawa appeared in* The Bridge on the River Kwai *in a role which suggested the new, less hostile image of the Japanese which emerged in American films of the 1950s and 1960s.*

central lesson the barbarism of the enemy and the Americans' basic decency. In *Objective Burma* (1945) half of a group of American paratroopers is caught and butchered by a Japanese force. The audience is not shown the corpses, but there are the others' descriptions of the massacre: "cut to pieces," and "too awful to look at." One survivor, inside a house so that we cannot see him, says: "Don't touch me! Please kill me!" The paratroopers react by describing the Japanese as degenerate, immoral idiots, stinking little savages. "Let's wipe 'em out!" is the cry that goes up. And that is exactly what they do—with a gusto and a brutality not far behind the Japanese.

Another popular theme was Japanese duplicity and treachery, both before and after the war started. One favorite device for suggesting this duplicity was the use of American-speaking Japanese in night attacks; some naive American boy usually fell for that one. More interesting is the development of this theme in nonmilitary settings. In *Wake Island* (1942), for example, the Japanese envoys stop at Wake a few days before Pearl Harbor on their way to Washington. At dinner they toast the relations of the two countries and continued peace and prosperity. One might wonder how the Americans could be deceived because the Japanese look distrustful—mustached, thick glasses, very squinty-eyed, with absurdly wide grins dominating their faces. Their faces, with slight appropriate modifications, appear again when the Japanese are engaged in their barbaric customs—shooting down defenseless parachutists, strafing Red Cross ships and buildings, and bayonetting children. Add a certain frenzy, a disheveled look, and a glint in the eyes and you have the variation which conveys the lust of the Japanese soldier, a lust particularly strong for white women. Interestingly, this visual portrayal of lust resembles closely that of Chinese soldiers and bandits from the films of the 1930s and the lust of the opium dealers and owners of houses of ill repute from the films of the 1920s.

The least prejudiced and most intelligent attempt to discuss and to understand the Japanese during the war years was the 1943 film, *Behind the Rising Sun*. Unusual for wartime films about the Japanese, this one had no real combat scene between Japanese and Americans; in fact, the story takes place largely in Japan and is principally concerned with Japanese characters. It provides an explanation of sorts of how liberalism died in Japan and why the war happened. Although much more understanding than other films, *Behind the Rising Sun* also had its share of cliches and stereotypes: the ever-present thought-control police, Japanese children studying the Panama Canal to understand the world they must rule soon, the lustful, smirking Japanese soldiers about to rape Chinese women, the Japanese younger sister sold into prostitution for the family's fortune, and, of course, the "fine" Japanese art of torture ("Torture is an old art with us—slowly, quite slowly," says a Japanese interrogating officer).

The conclusion of World War II changed not only the international political structure in many critical ways, but also changed Asian images in film. Interest in war movies, the major vehicles for the negative images of the Japanese and the positive images of the Chinese, dropped off sharply. But more important was Japan's emergence first as an American satellite state and then as an ally in the new "Cold War." In that same five-year period the Chinese situation deteriorated rapidly into civil war, and then, almost before the American public could learn to accept that, the civil war was won by Communist forces whose existence was virtually unknown to the American public five years before.

By 1950 China was being viewed as a sleeping giant, an exotic mysterious land, potentially our most dangerous enemy because of its size and its preponderance in Asia. The initial success of Chinese soldiers in the Korean War, along with domestic factors, such as McCarthyism, hastened America's growing uneasiness about China and the Chinese. For the next two decades, the United States and mainland China had almost no contact. During that time they seemed to be unswervingly hostile toward each other. Then between 1970 and 1974 the Nixon administration effected a dramatic reversal in American policy toward the Chinese Communist government. Although President Nixon, who visited mainland China, may have been "ahead" of public opinion, the American people had already begun to shift their attitude toward the Chinese and to view them in a much less negative way.

How did these political developments manifest themselves in films and public opinion? In one sampling of public opinion in the 1950s certain characteristics were identified as Chinese.[36] Among the more frequently mentioned unfavorable qualities were these descriptive terms: unreliable, shrewd, dishonest, devious, opportunistic, militaristic, inscrutable, cruel, lacking in social consciousness, incompetent, inefficient, and having low intellectual capacity. Several of these had been common in the pre-1924 period. The persistence of such negative characterizations, despite the pro-Chinese World War II years, is a powerful testimonial to the survival of prejudice and stereotyping.

Since 1950, films about China and the Chinese have tended to fall into three large groups: those which deal with historical China, particularly the China of the late Empire and early Republic; films about the Communist take over of China and the actual Communist government and society born of the revolution; and movies in which

Communist China looms as a mysterious and vicious force in the near or distant future (the last films have almost nothing to do with actual events or personalities in Communist China).

Two popular films about Chinese in the last twenty years were actually about China at the turn of the century and in the 1920s: *55 Days at Peking* (1962) and *The Sand Pebbles* (1962). In both films, the Chinese are portrayed as deceitful, cruel, addicted to drugs, engaging openly and constantly in slave practices and prostitution, and harboring an intense and violent hatred of all Westerners. The Chinese appear to be ignorant and manipulated by their evil political masters. We can pass quickly over those films which concern the Communist take over and the actual functioning of the Chinese government by mentioning *Satan Never Sleeps* (1962), which was based on Pearl Buck's novel and script, and the almost countless films about the Korean War which portrayed the seemingly endless hordes of Chinese Communist soldiers pouring across the Yalu River into North Korea.

Much more interesting are a series of films which have presented the Chinese as a very mysterious society with aspirations for world domination or world destruction, either on the political or the criminal level. Consider the images of the Chinese in films ranging from *The Manchurian Candidate* (1962), *The Chairman* (1969), *Battle Beneath the Earth* (1968), *The Girl Who Knew Too Much* (1969), *Dimension 5* (1966), and the various Fu Manchu movies. Although the gain for Communist China is often very nebulous, the plot of each movie delineates the evil of these people. The means they employ have been linked with the Chinese before, particularly the traffic in drugs and prostitution. The more novel features are those which suggest techniques for world domination as varied as an enzyme to produce food in huge quantities, conditioned thought control for purposes of violence, tunnels beneath the Pacific Ocean to plant bombs under Los Angeles, and death rays which can wipe out whole cities instantaneously. These schemes for world domination closely resemble the exploits of Emperor Ming of the Flash Gordon movies of the 1930s and 1940s. Ming has been replaced physically by Fu Manchu and Dr. No and even, to a degree, by Chairman Mao, but the personalized embodiment of evil persists.

While mainland China and the United States expressed distrust of each other, Japan and the United States enjoyed a close relationship. In the 1950s and 1960s Japan successfully adopted Western democracy. Economic recovery went hand in hand with political democratization. At the same time, the American public became aware that there were disturbing social forces at work in Japan, including a radical youth movement which was both extremely anti-militaristic and pro-Communist. Likewise, Japan's physical presence on the edge of Asia made it a natural meeting point and nurturing base for certain illegal and nefarious activities of international criminals—or at least so it seemed to the American public. But both the best and the worst of political conditions eventually change with time. Japan's democracy survived the student riots, and America has come to count on Japan holding up its position in the defensive alliance of the Pacific.

The image of the Japanese over the past thirty years falls into a few broad categories. The largest, but not necessarily the most important, category includes those images of the Japanese which emerged principally in movies about World War II. Here we find a dramatic change in the stereotypes. Films about World War II which appeared in the early 1950s, such as *An American Guerrilla in the Philippines* (1950), *Three Came Home* (1950), and *Tokyo Joe* (1949), continued the image of Japanese cruelty and torture. Still present in these early retrospective accounts of World War II was the lust of the Japanese for white women, the deceit and wiliness of the Japanese generally, and their utter lack of any civilizing mores. In this same period, one film, *Go For Broke* (1951), appeared which was favorable toward the Japanese, but it was Hollywood's attempt to make amends for the American persecution of the Japanese-Americans during World War II. This film was a very positive portrayal of the Japanese-American unit of the United States Armed Forces which fought heroically in the European campaign. Otherwise, Hollywood and the nation were silent on America's injustice toward Japanese-Americans in World War II.

By the late 1950s, Hollywood's image of the Japanese enemy of World War II changed drastically. In *Battle of the Coral Sea* (1959), *Hell to Eternity* (1960), *Bridge to the Sun* (1961), and most of all, *Bridge on the River Kwai,* the Japanese appeared finally to be real human beings. They were often portrayed as stern and harsh, having possibly different moral and ethical values, but human nonetheless. In fact, even in the portrayal of different values, those differences were handled sympathetically; the audience might well have been torn between a basic orientation to American values and a strong sympathy for the Japanese opponents.

But the most clear-cut reversal of the negative stereotyping of the Japanese came with the production of *Tora! Tora! Tora!* in 1970. It is almost as if the audience is watching as neutrals in a suspenseful and monumental conflict of two great nations. Even the surprise nature of Japan's attack on Pearl Harbor is presented as Japan saw it, as an attack which would take place immediately but legitimately, after a formal declaration of war. The producers of *Tora! Tora! Tora!* created a balanced account of the contest by dividing equally the scenes between the Americans and the Japanese, and juxtaposing the careful attack preparations of the Japanese with the careless defense measures of the Americans. For perhaps the first time in decades, the Japanese were played entirely by Japanese, and the characters chosen were physical types whose visual presence would not demean the Japanese image among American viewers.

The second large group of film images concerning the Japanese comprises films about intermarriage between Japanese and Americans. From the early 1950s through the 1960s films such as *Japanese War Bride* (1952), *Cry for Happy* (1961), *A Majority of One* (1962), *My Geisha* (1962), and *Sayonara* (1957) explored this very sensitive issue. Although such films often end in tragedy or unhappiness, that is not portrayed as the inevitable result of violating some kind of natural law against the mixing of the races. In *A Majority of One,* for example, the prejudice of both Japanese and Americans appears as a natural, understandable, but regrettable phenomenon. No longer do Japanese males lecherously pursue horrified Caucasian women. In fact, more common to these films are insensitive American soldiers chasing Japanese women for momentary pleasure with little thought to the long-term results of such liaisons.

Another significant area of film imagery of the Japanese embraces those films in which Japan is the environment or setting for crime, intrigue, or international plots. As early as *Tokyo File 212* (1951), and in films such as *Call Me Mister* (1951), *House of Bamboo* (1955), and finally, *You Only Live Twice* (1967), Japan is the *scene* for stories which may or may not concern the Japanese. Frequently, there are as many Japanese working on the side of justice, law, and order as there are working for the underworld.

For the Chinese and Japanese who lived in the United States, the passage of an exclusion bill in 1924 marked a turning point in their film image. Before that date Americans were concerned with what Asians might do to American society as residents; after that date Americans began to see the Chinese and Japanese as either friendly or hostile external powers. Of course, a crisis such as the attack on Pearl Harbor revived all the old fears and created some new ones. In this most recent quarter of the century the pendulum has swung back to a degree, and now some films consider the Chinese and Japanese once again as a negative element in American life. In certain ways the negative images of the pre-1924 period have changed very little. One still finds illegal importation of women, arranged marriages, the sale into slavery of these Asian women in secret auctions, Tongs and Tong warfare, opium smoking, and large-scale traffic in drugs generally. Physical typecasting has improved somewhat, but the other aspects of image formation have remained negative.

In the early growth years of the movie industry, Asian-Americans were cast in both supporting and starring, albeit villainous, roles. That practice was short-lived and almost entirely extinct by the mid-1920s. Not until World War II did Asian-Americans return to Hollywood roles, but this time only to play Japanese villains. Hollywood reserved the heroic Chinese roles for Caucasians in make-up. In the postwar era, however, Asian characters in Hollywood movies have generally been portrayed by Asians or Asian-Americans.[37]

The rapprochement with China and the continuing friendship with Japan are likely to decrease the production of films which present either of those countries and their peoples in wholly negative ways. International criminals, such as Dr. No or the updated Fu Manchu, will still attract audiences, but it is doubtful whether there is appreciable negative transference from those images to Asians generally. Given the contradictions in America's mind about its role in Vietnam, no clear, consistent Vietnamese image has developed yet. It is only now, with the critical success of *Coming Home* (1978), *The Deer Hunter* (1978), *The Boys in Company C* (1978), and the publicity accorded *Apocalypse Now* (1979), that the subject has become fare for Hollywood.

Until the late 1920s, racial purity and the fate of white women, anxiety over jobs, and fear of subversion of our Western heritage spurred the overwhelming impulses of anti-Chinese and anti-Japanese sentiment. Since then, fear of first one enemy power and then of another fed anti-Japanese and then anti-Chinese sentiment, but these fears have abated drastically. If new villains arise, they will, in all likelihood, come from groups other than the Chinese and Japanese. With a restive Third World challenging the West, and especially the United States, perhaps Hollywood will respond by creating new villains from this world.

NOTES

1. This study deals exclusively with the Chinese and Japanese for two reasons preeminently: 1) because relatively few other Asians immigrated to the United States and were numerically insignificant when compared to the Chinese and Japanese, and 2) that the film industry, with very few exceptions, took no notice of other Asians until the war in Vietnam; even a country as large as India has rarely been used in Hollywood's stories, even as a backdrop.

2. Prejudice has been studied by some as a factor of personality, but more frequently as a phenomenon of social psychology, of group behavior; that is the perspective of this study. Similarly, one should distinguish between what might be called passive prejudice and active prejudice. It is possible only to study the *manifestations* of prejudice and to examine the possible linkage between prejudice and political, economic, and social factors around such active prejudice. See Gordon W. Allport, *The Nature of Prejudice* (1958).

3. John Appel, "The Distorted Image: Stereotype and Caricature in American Popular Graphics" (Loose-leaf binder with 35mm. slides; New York, no date).

4. Some social scientists have argued that the mass of information and the numbers of individuals to be absorbed by any human being are simply too great to manage without some form of categorizing, and that stereotyping is a form of categorizing. As such, it helps us to label, organize, and understand the world around us. Others have suggested that stereotypes cater to deep-seated psychological needs ranging from ego-inflation to the "maintenance of existing norms of group conduct." Those of a more Freudian inclination see stereotyping as a subconscious means for an individual to enjoy vicariously, through projective condemnation, a prohibited activity; for example, sexual license, dishonesty in business dealings, or laziness. And, finally, stereotyping frequently allows us laughter and the release of tension at the expense of an alien group. See Appel, "The Distorted Image," 7.

5. At their peak, movie production and circulation were impressive. In the years between 1915 and 1945 major American film producers created over 20,000 films. In one year alone, 1944, Hollywood produced 340 feature films—and this during a world-wide conflagration. Average weekly attendance for the same year was 95,000,000; and the gross receipts that year reached $1,350,000,000, making the film industry one of the largest businesses in the United States. See *Variety,* CLIII (January 5, 1944), p. 231.

6. Both groups also settled heavily in Hawaii, but the entire question of prejudice and stereotyping is very different in the Hawaiian experience.

7. In point of fact, by 1960 over fifty percent of all the Chinese in the United States actually resided in a total of twelve cities. See Shien-woo Kung, *Chinese in American Life: Some Aspects of Their History, Status, Problems and Contributions* (1962), 31, 43.

8. Kung, *Chinese in American Life,* 180.

9. Yamato Ichihashi, *Japanese in the United States* (1932), 119, 163, 190.

10. Francis L. K. Hsu, *The Challenge of the American Dream: The Chinese in the United States* (1971), 5.

11. Kung, *Chinese in American Life,* 206.

12. Carey McWilliams, *Prejudice, Japanese Americans: Symbol of Racial Intolerance* (1944), 16–19.

13. Ibid., 12 ff.

14. This analysis is based on the film descriptions in *American Film Institute Catalog of Motion Pictures Produced in the United States, 1921–1930,* Kenneth W. Munden, ed. (2 vols., 1971).

15. Although films can not be noted as one would a printed source, a consistent reference system might be of assistance to the reader. Throughout this study, therefore, in the text or in note, I will provide the name of the film, the director and/or producer, the year released, and present repository—if available: e.g., *Broken Blossoms* or *The Yellow Man and The Girl* by D. W. Griffith (1919), Museum of Modern Art, New York City.

16. *Old San Francisco* by Alan Crosland (1927), Eastman House, Rochester.

17. Kung, *Chinese,* 45–52.

18. *Typhoon* by Thomas Ince (1914), Eastman House.

19. *Broken Blossoms* by D. W. Griffith (1919), Museum of Modern Art.

20. *East is West* (1922) with Warner Oland; *The Forbidden City* (1918) with Norma Talmadge.

21. *The Cheat* by Cecil B. DeMille (1915), Eastman House.

22. "The race riots of 1919–21 had, in the opinion of Dr. Raymond Lyman

Wilbur, 'a considerable effect' in securing passage of the bill (Immigration Act of 1924), for they had made the entire nation extremely race conscious." McWilliams, *Prejudice,* 67.

23. *Shadows of the West* by Paul Hurst (1921).

24. McWilliams, *Prejudice,* 60–61.

25. *The Letter* by Jean DeLimur (1929), Museum of Modern Art.

26. *The Dragon Painter* by William Worthington (1919), Eastman House.

27. *The Wrath of the Gods* by Raymond B. West (1914).

28. Descriptions of these films can be found in *American Film Institute Catalog, 1921–1930,* I, F2.6260; II, F2.1776; III, F2.6037; IV, F2.1155.

29. Unsigned article, "Oriental Detectives on the Screen," in *Screen Facts,* II (1964), 30–39.

30. *The Bitter Tea of General Yen* by Frank Capra (1933), Museum of Modern Art; *The General Died at Dawn* by Lewis Milestone (1936); *Oil for the Lamps of China* by Mervyn LeRoy (1935).

31. *The Keys of the Kingdom* by John Stahl (1944), Library of Congress.

32. *The Good Earth* by Sidney Franklin (1938), Museum of Modern Art.

33. Andre Sennwald, "The Strand Theatre Presents . . . ," *New York Times,* June 6, 1935, p. 25.

34. Another popular stock figure of the 1930s, also a detective, was Mr. Moto; Peter Lorre played the part in several films, once the character had begun to take firm shape. Mr. Moto had the same quiet manner and care to observation of details, but he is not nearly as likable as Charlie Chan. In fact, he seems somewhat cold, calculating, perhaps even a little cruel and much more "Oriental" in his mannerisms—as Hollywood had developed the Oriental type over the years. For example, in one film, set in Peking, Mr. Moto worships at a Chinese-ancestor altar. Among the Mr. Moto films is *The Mysterious Mr. Moto* (1938).

35. The Library of Congress has copies of almost all American films made after 1941 or printed material about them. In addition the American Film Institute has published a catalog of all films released in the period 1960–69. Therefore it appears to be a waste of space to provide more than titles for commonly known films produced since World War II. See *American Film Institute Catalog of Motion Pictures Produced in the United States, 1961–1970,* Richard P. Krafsur, ed. (1976), Vols. I and II.

36. Harold Isaacs, *Scratches on Our Minds: American Images of China and India* (1958), 73.

37. There have been notable exceptions to this practice; for example, the casting of Christopher Lee, a Caucasian, as Fu Manchu.

BIBLIOGRAPHICAL ESSAY

The literature on movies is enormous. This select bibliography of books consists of important and accessible works that bear on the social history of movies in the United States. For articles on aspects of ethnicity and movies and the social history of movies, readers should consult the notes in the various chapters, the bibliographies of the works cited in this bibliography, and the following journals: *American Film, Journal of Popular Film, Film & History, Film Quarterly, Cineaste,* and *Jump Cut.*

The best treatments of the social history of America and the movies are Robert Sklar, *Movie-Made America: A Cultural History of American Movies* (1975); and Garth Jowett, *Film: The Democratic Art* (1976). Both Sklar and Jowett have useful bibliographies. Also important is Michael Wood, *America in the Movies* (1975), which offers some provocative suggestions on the relationship between American social fantasies and the movies. For some good examples of how to use American movies as social texts and historical documents see John E. O'Connor and Martin A. Jackson, eds., *American History/American Film: Interpreting the Hollywood Image* (1979), which has essays by Thomas Cripps and Daniel Leab on racial and ethnic issues in movies. There are also some interesting essays in Paul Smith, ed., *The Historian and Film* (1976); and Arthur F. McClure, ed., *The Movies: An American Idiom* (1971).

On the early history of American movies Lewis Jacobs, *The Rise of the American Film: A Critical History* (1939); and William K. Everson, *American Silent Film* (1978), are indispensable. See also Terry Ramsaye, *A Million and One Nights: A History of the Motion Picture* (1926). On the development of Old Hollywood see Philip French, *The Movie*

207

Moguls (1969); Norman Zierold, *The Moguls* (1969); and John Baxter, *Hollywood in the Thirties* (1968). An excellent sociological study of Hollywood is Hortense Powdermaker, *Hollywood: The Dream Factory* (1950), which shows Hollywood in the late 1940s. There are useful discussions of film as a reflection of contemporary problems in Andrew Bergman, *We're in the Money: Depression America and Its Films* (1971); Richard Pells, *Radical Visions and American Dreams: Culture and Social Thought in the Depression Years* (1973), chapter 6; Michael T. Isenberg, *War on Film: The American Cinema and World War I, 1914–1941* (forthcoming); Andrew Dowdy, *Movies are Better Than Ever: Wide Screen Memories of the Fifties* (1973); and Lawrence Alloway, *Violent America: The Movies, 1947–1964* (1971). On Hollywood and American movies in recent years see James Monaco, *American Film Now: The People, the Power, the Money, the Movies* (1979), which includes a "Who's Who" of American movies and some very insightful observations on the structure of the New Hollywood. For a brief overview of Hollywood in the 1960s and early 1970s see William Fadiman, *Hollywood Now: The Industry, the Agent, the Director, the Star, the Writer, the Producer, the Future* (1972). Also helpful is David Thomson, *A Biographical Dictionary of Film* (1976). Axel Madsen, *The New Hollywood: American Movies in the 70's* (1975), is worthwhile. The best history of a studio is Tino Balio, *United Artists: The Company Built by the Stars* (1976); see also Bosley Crowther, *The Lion's Share: The Story of an Entertainment Empire* (1957)

On film genres Stuart M. Kaminsky, *American Film Genres: Approaches to a Critical Theory of Popular Film* (1974), is important. More than other genres, the gangster film and the western have perpetuated certain unflattering ethnic images, and also been the vehicles for improving those images. The gangster film has evoked considerable controversy. The best books are Jack Shadoian, *Dreams and Dead Ends: The American Gangster/Crime Film* (1977); Eugene Rosow, *Born to Lose: The Gangster Film in America* (1978), which has very good annotated filmographies and some helpful suggestions about immigrants and blacks as portrayed in gangster films; and Stephen L. Karpf, *The Gangster Film: Emergence, Variation and Decay of a Genre, 1930–1940* (1973). On westerns, the other major genre with large implications for ethnic stereotyping, see George N. Fenin and William K. Everson, *The Western* (1962); and Philip French, *Westerns* (1977).

For a good bibliography on the social effects of movies consult I. C. Jarvie, *Movies and Society* (1970). On film's influence, a much debated subject, see Andrew Tudor, *Image and Influence: Studies in the Sociology of Film* (1975), for a start. On the mechanics of communicating ideas through film see Roy Paul Madsen, *The Impact of Film: How Ideas Are Communicated through Cinema and Television* (1973). There is no consensus on the power of film to manipulate, or even to influence, audiences. Studies of film and social behavior show that it is impossible to measure the exact effect films have on audiences. The most important books suggesting film's persuasive powers are Amos Vogel, *Film as a Subversive Art* (1974); the controversial study of Siegfried Kracauer, *From Caligari to Hitler: A Psychological History of the German Film* (1947); Jack Temple Kirby, *Media-Made Dixie* (1978).

There is no good study of ethnic stereotyping in American movies. For some useful essays on the subject see Randall M. Miller, ed., *Ethnic Images in American Film and Television* (1978). See also Frank Manchel's comments on stereotyping in his book, *Film Study: A Research Guide* (1973), pp. 88–122. On the state of the film industry regarding minority group participation see *Behind the Scenes: Equal Employment Opportunity in the Motion Picture Industry* (United States Commission on Civil Rights report, September, 1978). On the stereotyping and participation of particular groups in American film there are several good studies. Of the several studies of blacks and American movies the best are Thomas Cripps, *Slow Fade to Black: The Negro in American Film, 1900–1942* (1977); Cripps, *Black Film as Genre* (1978); and Daniel Leab, *From Sambo to Superspade: The Black Experience in Motion Pictures* (1975). Ralph and Natasha Friar, *The Only Good Indian: The Hollywood Gospel* (1972), which is opinionated but useful, will surely be superseded by Gretchen Bataille and Charles L. P. Silet, *The Pretend Indians: Images in the Movies* (forthcoming). Latin images are ably discussed in Allen L. Woll, *The Latin Image in American Film* (1977). Surprisingly, the filmic images of the other major ethnic groups in America have not been the subjects of book-length treatment. For the Jews, however, there is the very helpful number of the *Journal of Popular Film* (vol. 4, number 3, 1975) devoted to the image of the Jews in American movies. For some suggestions on how to approach the subject of image-making in film see Molly Haskell, *From Reverence to Rape: The Treatment of Women in the Movies* (1974); Marjorie Rosen, *Popcorn Venus: Women, Movies, and the American Dream* (1973); and Joan Mellen, *Big Bad Wolves: Masculinity in the American Film* (1977).

NOTES ON CONTRIBUTORS

Randall M. Miller is Associate Professor of History and Director of American Studies at Saint Joseph's College, Philadelphia. He is the author or editor of more than twenty articles and several books. Among his books are *"Dear Master": Letters of a Slave Family* (Cornell University Press, 1978), and with Thomas Marzik, *Immigrants and Religion in Urban America* (Temple University Press, 1977).

Gretchen Bataille teaches literature and American Indian studies at Iowa State University. She has published articles in the *Journal of Popular Film,* the *Quarterly Review of Film Studies, Women & Film,* and other journals. She co-edited the book, *The Worlds Between Two Rivers: Perspectives on American Indians* (Iowa State University Press, 1978). In 1980, Iowa State University Press will publish her book, *The Pretend Indians: Images in the Movies,* which she co-authored with Charles Silet.

Dennis Clark is the Executive Director of the Samuel S. Fels Fund in Philadelphia. He has written numerous articles and several books on American ethnicity and urban life. Among his books is the widely-acclaimed, *The Irish in Philadelphia: Ten Generations of Urban Experience* (Temple University Press, 1973).

Thomas Cripps is Professor of History at Morgan State University. He has written more than fifty articles and reviews and produced, written, or appeared in more than one hundred television programs. He wrote the script for the award-winning film, *Black Shadows on a Silver Screen* (1975). His major books include *Slow Fade to Black: The Negro in American Film* (Oxford University Press, 1977) and *Black Film as Genre* (Indiana University Press, 1978).

Patricia Erens teaches film courses at Rosary College in Illinois. She has written three books and numerous articles on film, including

210

articles on Jews and film which have appeared in *American Film, Journal of Popular Film, Jump Cut,* and *Variety.* She is completing a book on Jews in American film.

Caroline Golab is Assistant Professor of History and City Planning at the University of Pennsylvania. She has published widely on aspects of American ethnicity. She is best known for her book, *Immigrant Destinations* (Temple University Press, 1977). Her new book on ethnicity will be published shortly.

Daniel Sembroff Golden is Visiting Associate Professor of English at Northeastern University, on leave from State University College at Buffalo, where he teaches courses on film and literature. He has written several articles on Italians in American film, and he is completing a book on the same subject.

Daniel J. Leab is Associate Professor of History at Seton Hall University and Managing Editor of *Labor History.* His books include *A Union of Individuals: The Formation of the American Newspaper Guild* (Columbia University Press, 1970) and *From Sambo to Superspade: The Black Experience in Motion Pictures* (Houghton Mifflin, 1975). He has written many articles on labor history and on film.

William J. Lynch is Professor of English at Montgomery County Community College in Pennsylvania. He has written for *America* and *Best Sellers,* and he is working on a book about the literature emerging from the struggle in Northern Ireland.

Richard A. Oehling is Academic Dean and Dean of the Faculty at Assumption College in Massachusetts. He prepared the book and film capsule, *Martin Luther: The Making of a Reformer* for Indiana University Press, and he wrote several articles for *Film and History* on German and Asian images in American movies.

Charles L. P. Silet teaches in the English department at Iowa State University. He has written widely on American literature and on Indians in American film. Among his books are *The Literary Manuscripts of Upton Sinclair* (Ohio State University Press, 1972); *The Worlds Between Two Rivers: Perspectives on American Indians* (Iowa State University Press, 1978), co-edited with Gretchen Bataille; and with Gretchen Bataille, *The Pretend Indians: Images in the Movies* (Iowa State University Press, forthcoming).

Allen L. Woll is Assistant Professor of History at Rutgers University, Camden. He has written many articles on aspects of film, music, and Latin America. His books on American film include *Songs from Hollywood Musical Comedies, 1927–1976* (Garland, 1976), *The Latin Image in American Film,* (UCLA Latin American Series, 1977), and *Popular Culture in Crisis: The Hollywood Musical Goes to War* (Nelson-Hall, forthcoming).

INDEX

FILM TITLES